US-4
632

West 23
980

PERCH OF THE DEVIL

BY

GERTRUDE ATHERTON

NEW YORK
FREDERICK A. STOKES COMPANY
PUBLISHERS

August, 1914

TO

MR. FRANK J. EDWARDS AND
MR. WILTON G. BROWN

OF HELENA, MONTANA

PART I

PERCH OF THE DEVIL

PART I

I

"THE shining mountains," said Gregory Compton softly, throwing back his head, his eyes travelling along the hard bright outlines above the high valley in which his ranch lay. "The shining mountains. That is what the Indians called them before the white man came."

His wife yawned frankly. "Pity they don't shine inside as well as out—what we've got of 'em."

"Who knows? Who knows?"

"We don't. That's the trouble."

But although she spoke tartly, she nestled into his arm, for she was not unamiable, she had been married but sixteen months, and she was still fond of her husband "in a way"; moreover, although she cherished resentments open and secret, she never forgot that she had won a prize "as men go." Many girls in Butte* had wanted to marry Gregory Compton, not only because he had inherited a ranch of eleven hundred and sixty acres, but because, comprehensively, he was superior to the other young men of his class. He had graduated from the High School before he was sixteen; then after three years' work on the ranch under his unimaginative father, he had announced his intention of leaving the State unless permitted to attend the School of Mines in Butte. The old man, who by this time had taken note of the formation of his son's jaw, gave his consent rather than lose the last of his children; and for two years and a semester Gregory had been the most brilliant figure in the School of Mines.

"Old Man Compton," who had stampeded from his small farm in northern New York in the sixties to meet

* Pronounced Bute.

with little success in the mines, but more as a rancher, had been as typical a hayseed as ever punctuated politics with tobacco juice in front of a corner grocery-store, but had promised his wife on her death-bed that their son should have "schooling." Mrs. Compton, who had arrived in Montana soon after the log house was built, was a large, dark, silent woman, whom none of her distant neighbours had ever claimed to know. It was currently believed in the New York village whence she came that in the early days of the eighteenth century the sturdy Verrooy stock had been abruptly crossed by the tribe of the Oneida. Ancient history in a new country is necessarily enveloped in mist, but although the children she had lost had been fair and nondescript like their father, her youngest, and her only son, possessed certain characteristics of the higher type of Indian. He was tall and lightly built, graceful, supple, swift of foot, with the soft tread of the panther; and although his skin was no darker than that of the average brunette, it acquired significance from the intense blackness of his hair, the thin aquiline nose, the long, narrow eyes, the severe and stolid dignity of expression even in his earlier years.

He had seemed to the girls of the only class he knew in Butte an even more romantic figure than the heroes of their magazine fiction, particularly as he took no notice of them until he met Ida Hook at a picnic and surrendered his heart.

Ida, forced by her thrifty mother to accept employment with a fashionable dressmaker, and consumed with envy of the "West Siders" whose measurements she took, did not hesitate longer than feminine prudence dictated. Before she gave her hair its nightly brushing her bold unpedantic hand had covered several sheets of pink note-paper with the legend, "Mrs. Gregory Compton," the while she assured herself there was "no sweller name on West Broadway." To do her justice, she also thrilled with young passion, for more than her vanity had responded to the sombre determined attentions of the man who had been the indifferent hero of so many maiden dreams. Although she longed to be a Copper Queen, she was too young to be altogether hard; and, now that her hour was come, every soft enchantment of her sex awoke to bind and blind her mate.

Gregory Compton's indifference to women had been more pretended than real, although an occasional wild night on The Flat had interested him far more than picnics and dances where the girls used no better grammar than the "sporting women" and were far less amusing. He went to this picnic to please his old school friend, Mark Blake, and because Nine Mile Cañon had looked very green and alluring after the June rains when he had ridden through it alone the day before. The moment he stood before Ida Hook, staring into the baffling limpid eyes, about which heavy black lashes rose and fell and met and tangled and shot apart in a series of bedevilling manœuvres, he believed himself to be possessed by that intimate soul-seeking desire that nothing but marriage can satisfy. He kept persistently at her side, his man's instinct prompting the little attentions women value less than they demand. He also took more trouble to interest her verbally than was normal in one whom nature had prompted to silence, and he never would learn the rudiments of small talk; but his brain was humming in tune with his eager awakened pulses, and Ida was too excited and exultant to take note of his words. "It was probably about mines, anyway," she confided to her friends, Ruby and Pearl Miller. "Nobody talks about anything else long in this old camp."

Gregory's infatuation was by no means reduced by the fact that no less than six young men contended for the favour of Miss Hook. She was the accredited beauty of Butte, for even the ladies of the West Side had noticed and discussed her and hoped that their husbands and brothers had not. It was true that her large oval blue-grey eyes, set like Calliope's, were as shallow as her voice; but the lids were so broad and white, and the lashes so silky and oblique, that the critical faculty of man was drugged, if dimly prescient. Her cheeks were a trifle too full, her nose of a type unsung in marble; but what of that when her skin was as white as milk, the colour in cheek and lips of a clear transparent coral, that rarest and most seductive of nature's reds, her little teeth enamelled like porcelain? And had she not every captivating trick, from active eyelash to the sudden toss of her small head on its long round throat, even to the dilating nostril which made her nose for the moment look patrician and thin? Her figure, too, with its boyish hips, thin flexible waist, and full low bust, which she carried with a fine upright swing, was made the most of in a collarless blouse, closely fitting skirt, and narrow dark belt.

Miss Hook, although her expression was often wide-eyed and innocent, was quite cynically aware of her power over the passions of men. More than one man of high salary or recent fortune had tried to "annex" her, as she airily put it; her self-satisfaction and the ever-present sophistications of a mining town saving her from anything so gratuitous as outraged maidenhood.

The predatory male and his promises had never tempted her, and it was her boast that she had never set foot in the road-houses of The Flat. She had made up her mind long since to live on the West Side, the fashionable end of Butte, and was wise enough, to quote her own words, to know that the straight and narrow was the only direct route. Ambition, her sleepless desire to be a grand dame (which she pronounced without any superfluous accent), was stronger than vanity or her natural love of pleasure. By the ordinary romantic yearnings of her age and sex she was unhampered; but when she met Gregory Compton, she played the woman's game so admirably the long day through that she brushed her heavy black hair at night quite satisfied he would propose when she gave him his chance. This she withheld for several days, it being both pleasant and prudent to torment him. He walked home with her every afternoon from the dressmaking establishment on North Main Street to her mother's cottage in East Granite, to be dismissed at the gate coyly, reluctantly, indifferently, but always with a glance of startled wonder from the door.

In the course of the week she gave him to understand that she should attend the Friday Night dance at Columbia Gardens, and expected him to escort her. Gregory, who by this time was reduced to a mere prowling instinct projected with fatal instantaneity from its napping ego, was as helpless a victim as if born a fool. He thought himself the most fortunate of men to receive permission to sit beside her on the open car during the long ride to the Gardens, to pay for the greater number of her waltzes, to be, in short, her beau for the night.

The evening of Friday at Columbia Gardens is Society

Night for all respectable Butte, irrespective of class; the best floor and the airiest hall in Silver Bow County proving an irresistible incentive to democracy. Moreover, Butte is a city of few resources, and the Gardens at night look like fairyland: the immense room is hung with Chinese lanterns depending from the rafters, the music is the best in Montana; and the richer the women, the plainer their frocks. A sort of informal propriety reigns, and millionaire or clerk pays ten cents for the privilege of dancing with his lady.

Ida, who had expended five of her hard-earned dollars on a bottle of imported perfume, wore a white serge suit cut as well as any in "the grand dame bunch." After the sixth waltz she draped her head and shoulders with a coral-pink scarf and led Gregory, despite the chill of June, out to his willing fate. The park was infested by other couples, walking briskly to keep themselves warm, and so were the picnic grounds where the cottonwoods and Canadian poplars were being coaxed to grow, now that the smelters which had reduced the neighbourhood of Butte to its bones had been removed to Anaconda.

But farther up the cañon no one but themselves adventured, and here Gregory was permitted to ask this unique creature, provided with a new and maddening appeal to the senses, to renounce her kingdom and live on a ranch.

It was all very crude, even to the blatant moon, which in the thin brilliant atmosphere of that high altitude swings low with an almost impudent air of familiarity, and grins in the face of sentiment. But to Gregory, who was at heart passionate and romantic, it was a soul-quickening scene: the blazing golden disk poised on the very crest of the steep mountain before them, the murmur of water, the rustling young leaves, the deep-breasted orientally perfumed woman with the innocent wondering eyes. The moon chuckled and reminded his exacting mistress, Nature, that were he given permission to scatter some of his vast experience instead of the seductive beams that had accumulated it, this young man with his natural distinction of mind, and already educated beyond his class, would enjoy a sudden clarity of vision and perceive the defects of grammar and breeding in this elemental siren with nothing but Evian instincts to guide her.

But the dutiful old search-light merely whipped up the ancestral memories in Gregory's subconscious brain; moreover, gave him courage. He made love with such passion and tenderness that Ida, for once elemental, clung to him so long and so ardently that the grinning moon whisked off his beam in disgust and retired behind a big black cloud—which burst shortly afterwards and washed out the car tracks.

They were married in July, and Mrs. Hook, who had worked for forty years at tub and ironing-board, moved over to the dusty cemetery in September, at rest in the belief not only that her too good-looking daughter was safely "planted," but was a supremely happy woman.

Ida's passion, however, had been merely a gust of youth, fed by curiosity and gratified ambition; it quickly passed in the many disappointments of her married life. Gregory had promised her a servant, but no "hired girl" could be induced to remain more than a week on the lonely De Smet Ranch; and Mrs. Compton's temper finding its only relief in one-sided quarrels with her Chinese cooks, even the philosophical Oriental was prone to leave on a moment's notice. There were three hired men and three in the family, after John Oakley came, to cook and "clean up" for, and there were weeks at a time when Ida was obliged to rise with the dawn and occupy her large and capable but daintily manicured hands during many hours of the day.

Gregory's personality had kindled what little imagination she had into an exciting belief in his power over life and its corollary, the world's riches. Also, having in mind the old Indian legend of the great chief who had turned into shining gold after death and been entombed in what was now known prosaically as the De Smet Ranch, she had expected Gregory to "strike it rich" at once.

But although there were several prospect holes on the ranch, dug by Gregory in past years, he had learned too much, particularly of geology, during his two years at the School of Mines to waste any more time digging holes in the valley or bare portions of the hills. If a ledge existed it was beneath some tangle of shrub or tree-roots, and he had no intention of denuding his pasture until he was prepared to sell his cattle.

He told her this so conclusively a month after they were

married that she had begged him to raise sugar beets and build a factory in Butte (which he would be forced to superintend), reminding him that the only factory in the State was in the centre of another district and near the southern border, and that sugar ranged from six to seven dollars a hundredweight. He merely laughed at this suggestion, although he was surprised at her sagacity, for, barring a possible democratic victory, there was room for two beet-sugar factories in Montana. But he had other plans, although he gave her no hint of them, and had no intention of complicating his life with an uncongenial and exacting business.

By unceasing personal supervision he not only made the ranch profitable and paid a yearly dividend to his three aunts, according to the terms of his father's will, but for the last two years, after replacing or adding to his stock, he had deposited a substantial sum in the bank, occasionally permitting his astute friend, Mark Blake, to turn over a few hundreds for him on the stock-market. This was the heyday of the American farmer, and the De Smet cattle brought the highest prices in the stock-yards for beef on the hoof. He also raised three crops of alfalfa a year to insure his live stock against the lean days of a Rocky Mountain winter. He admitted to Ida that he could afford to sink a shaft or drive a tunnel in one of his hills, but added that he should contemplate nothing of the sort until he had finished his long-delayed course in the School of Mines, and had thousands to throw away on development work, miners, and machinery. At this time he saw no immediate prospect of resuming the studies interrupted by the death of his father: until John Oakley came, eight months after his marriage, he knew of no foreman to trust but himself.

Ida desired the life of the city for other reasons than its luxuries and distractions. Her fallow brain was shrewd and observing, although often crude in its deductions. She soon realised that the longer she lived with her husband the less she understood him. Like all ignorant women of any class she cherished certain general estimates of men, and in her own class it was assumed that the retiring men were weak and craven, the bold ones necessarily lacking in that refinement upon which their young lady friends prided themselves. Ida had found that Gregory, bold as his wooing had been, and arrogantly masculine as he was in most things, not only had his shynesses but was far more refined and sensitive than herself. She was a woman who prided herself upon her theories, and disliked having them upset; still more not knowing where she was at, to use her own spirited vernacular. She began to be haunted by the fear of making some fatal mistake, living, as she did, in comparative isolation with him. Not only was her womanly pride involved, as well as a certain affection born of habit and possible even to the selfish, rooted as it is in the animal function of maternity, but she had supreme faith in his future success and was determined to share it.

She was tired, however, of attempting to fathom the intense reserves and peculiarities of that silent nature, of trying to live up to him. She was obliged to resort to "play-acting"; and, fully aware of her limitations, despite her keen self-appreciation, was in constant fear that she would "make a grand mess of it." Gregory's eyes could be very penetrating, and she had discovered that although he never told funny stories, nor appeared to be particularly amused at hers, he had his own sense of humour.

II

THE young couple stood together in the dawn, the blue dawn of Montana. The sky was as cold and bright as polished silver, but the low soft masses of cloud were blue, the glittering snow on the mountain peaks was blue, the smooth snow fields on the slopes and in the valley were blue. Nor was it the blue of azure or of sapphire, but a deep lovely cool polaric blue, born in the inverted depths of Montana, and forever dissociated from art.

It was an extramundane scene, and it had drawn Gregory from his bed since childhood, but to Ida, brought up in a town, and in one whose horizons until a short while ago had always been obscured by the poisonous haze of smelters, and ores roasted in the open, it was "weird." Novels had informed her that sunrises were pink, or, at the worst, grey. There was something mysterious in this cold blue dawn up in the snow fields, and she hated mystery. But as it appeared to charm Gregory, she played up to him when he "dragged" her out to look at it; and she endeavoured to do so this morning although her own ego was rampant.

Gregory drew her closer, for she still had the power to enthrall him at times. He understood the resources within her shallows as little as she understood his depths, but although her defects in education and natural equipment had long since appalled him, he was generally too busy to think about her, and too masculine to detect that she was playing a part. This morning, although he automatically responded to her blandishments, he was merely sensible of her presence, and his eyes, the long watchful eyes of the Indian, were concentrated upon the blue light that poured from the clouds down upon the glistening peaks. Ida knew that this meant he was getting ready to make an announcement of some sort, and longed to shake it out of him. Not daring to outrage his dignity so far, she drew the fur robe that enveloped them closer and rubbed her soft hair against his chin. It was useless to ask him to deliver himself until he was "good and ready", but the less direct method sometimes prevailed.

Suddenly he came out with it.

"I've made up my mind to go back to the School."

"Back to school—are you loony?"

"The School of Mines, of course. I can enter the Junior Class where I left off; earlier in fact, as I had finished the first semester. Besides, I've been going over all the old ground since Oakley came."

"Is that what's in all them books."

"Those, dear."

"Those. Mining Engineer's a lot sweller than rancher."

"Please don't use that word."

"Lord, Greg, you're as particular as if you'd been brought up in Frisco or Chicago, instead of on a ranch."

He laughed outright and pinched her ear. "I use a good deal of slang myself—only, there are some words that irritate me—I can hardly explain. It doesn't matter."

"Greg," she asked with sudden suspicion, "why are you goin' in for a profession? Have you given up hopes of strikin' it rich on this ranch?"

"Oh, I shall never relinquish that dream." He spoke so lightly that even had she understood him better she could not have guessed that the words leapt from what he believed to be the deepest of his passions. "But what has that to do with it? If there is gold on the ranch I shall be more likely to discover it when I know a great deal more about geology than I do now, and better able to mine it cheaply after I have learned all I can of milling and metallurgy at the School. But that is not the point. There may be nothing here. I wish to graduate into a profession which not only attracts me more than any other, but in which the expert can always make a large income. Ranching doesn't interest me, and with Oakley to——"

"What woke you up so sudden?"

"I have never been asleep." But he turned away his head lest she see the light in his eyes. "Oakley gives me my chance to get out, that is all. And I am very glad for your sake——"

"Aw!" Her voice, ringing out with ecstasy, converted

the native syllable into music. "It means we are goin' to live in Butte!"

"Of course."

"And I was so took—taken by surprise it never dawned on me till this minute. Now what do you know about that?"

"We shall have to be very quiet. I cannot get my degree until a year from June—a year and seven months from now. I shall study day and night, and work in the mines during the winter and summer vacations. I cannot take you anywhere."

"Lord knows it can't be worse'n this. I'll have my friends to talk to and there's always the movin' picture shows. Lord, how I'd like to see one."

"Well, you shall," he said kindly. "I wrote to Mark some time ago and asked him to give the tenant of the cottage notice. As this is the third of the month it must be empty and ready for us."

"My goodness gracious!" cried his wife with pardonable irritation, "but you are a grand one for handin' out surprises! Most husbands tell their wives things as they go along, but you ruminate like a cow and hand over the cud when you're good and ready. I'm sick of bein' treated as if I was a child."

"Please don't look at it in that way. What is the use of talking about things until one is quite sure they can be accomplished?"

"That's half the fun of bein' married," said Ida with one of her flashes of intuition.

"Is it?" Gregory turned this over in his mind, then, out of his own experience, rejected it as a truism. He could not think of any subject he would care to discuss with his wife; or any other woman. But he kissed her with an unusual sense of compunction. "Perhaps I liked the idea of surprising you," he said untruthfully. "You will be glad to live in Butte once more?"

"You may bet your bottom dollar on that. When do we go?"

"Tomorrow."

"*Lands* sakes! Well, I'm dumb. And breakfast has to be got if I *have* had a bomb exploded under me. That Chink was doin' fine when I left, but the Lord knows——"

She walked toward the rear of the house, temper in the

swing of her hips, her head tossed high. Although rejoicing at the prospect of living in town, she was both angry and vaguely alarmed, as she so often had been before, at the unimaginable reserves, the unsuspected mental activities, and the sudden strikings of this life-partner who should have done his thinking out loud.

"Lord knows," thought Mrs. Compton, as she approached her kitchen, with secret intent to relieve her feelings by "lambasting" the Mongolian and leaving Oakley to shift for himself, "it's like livin' with that there Sphinx. I don't s'pose I'll ever get used to him, and maybe the time'll come when I won't want to."

III

G REGORY stood for some time longer, leaning on the gate and waiting for the red fire to rise above the crystal mountains. He was eager for the morrow, not only because he longed to be at the foundation stones of his real life but because his mind craved the precise training, the logical development, the intoxicating sense of expansion which he had missed and craved incessantly during the six years that had elapsed since he had been torn from the School of Mines. Moreover, his heart was light; at last he was able to shift the great responsibilities of his ranch to other shoulders.

Some six months since, his friend, Mark Blake, had recommended to him a young man who not only had graduated at the head of his class in the State College of Agriculture, but had served for two years on one of the State Experimental Farms. "What he don't know about scientific farming, dry, intensive, and all the rest, isn't worth shucks, old man," Blake had written. "He's as honest as they come, and hasn't a red to do the trick himself, but wants to go on a ranch as foreman, and farm wherever there's soil of a reasonable depth. Of course he wants a share of the profits, but he's worth it to you, for the Lord never cut you out for a rancher or farmer, well as you have done. What you want is to finish your course and take your degree. Try Oakley out for six months. There'll be only one result. You're a free man."

The contract had been signed the day before. But Oakley had been a welcome guest in the small household for more than practical reasons. Until the night of his advent, when the two men sat talking until daylight, Gregory had not realised the mental isolation of his married life. Like all young men he had idealised the girl who made the first assault on his preferential passion; but his brain was too shrewd, keen, practical, in spite of its imaginative area, to harbor illusions beyond the brief period of novelty.

13

It had taken him but a few weeks to discover that although his wife had every charm of youth and sex, and was by no means a fool, their minds moved on different planes, far apart. He had dreamed of the complete understanding, the instinctive response, the identity of tastes, in short of companionship, of the final routing of a sense of hopeless isolation he had never lost consciousness of save when immersed in study.

Ida subscribed for several of the "cheapest" of the cheap magazines, and, when her Mongolians were indulgent, rocked herself in the sitting-room, devouring the factory sweets and crude mental drugs with much the same spirit that revelled above bargain counters no matter what the wares. She "lived" for the serials, and attempted to discuss the "characters" with her husband and John Oakley. But the foreman was politely intolerant of cheap fiction, Gregory open in his disgust.

He admitted unequivocally that he had made a mistake, but assuming that most men did, philosophically concluded to make the best of it; women, after all, played but a small part in a man's life. He purposed, however, that she should improve her mind, and would have been glad to move to Butte for no other reason. He had had a sudden vision one night, when his own mind, wearied with study, drifted on the verge of sleep, of a lifetime on a lonely ranch with a woman whose brain deteriorated from year to year, her face faded and vacuous, save when animated with temper. If the De Smet Ranch proved to be mineralised, Oakley, his deliverer, would not be forgotten.

He moved his head restlessly, his glance darting over as much of his fine estate as it could focus, wondering when it would give up its secrets, in other words, its gold. He had never doubted that it winked and gleamed, and waited for him below the baffling surfaces of his land. Not for millions down would he have sold his ranch, renounced the personal fulfilment of that old passionate romance.

Gregory Compton was a dreamer, not in the drifting and aimless fashion of the visionary, but as all men born with creative powers, practical or artistic, must be. Indeed, it is doubtful if the artistic brain—save possibly where the abnormal tracts are musical in the highest sense —ever need, much less develop, that leaping vision, that power of visualising abstract ideas, of the men whose gifts for bold and original enterprise enable them to drive the elusive wealth of the world first into a corner, then into their own pockets.

When one contemplates the small army of men of great wealth in the world today, and, just behind, that auxiliary regiment endowed with the talent, the imagination, and the grim assurance necessary to magnetise the circulating riches of our planet; contemptuous of those hostile millions, whose brains so often are of unleavened dough, always devoid of talent, envious, hating, but sustained by the conceit which nature stores in the largest of her reservoirs to pour into the vacancies of the minds of men; seldom hopeless, fooling themselves with dreams of a day when mere brute numbers shall prevail, and (human nature having been revolutionised by a miracle) all men shall be equal and content to remain equal;—when one stands off and contemplates these two camps, the numerically weak composed of the forces of mind, the other of the unelectrified yet formidable millions, it is impossible to deny not only the high courage and supernormal gifts of the little army of pirates, but that, barring the rapidly decreasing numbers of explorers in the waste places of the earth, in them alone is the last stronghold of the old adventurous spirit that has given the world its romance.

The discontented, the inefficient, the moderately successful, the failures, see only remorseless greed in the great money makers. Their temper is too personal to permit them to recognise that here are the legitimate inheritors of the dashing heroes they enjoy in history, the bold and ruthless egos that throughout the ages have transformed savagery into civilisation, torpor into progress, in their pursuit of gold. That these "doing" buccaneers of our time are the current heroes of the masses, envious or generous in tribute, the most welcome "copy" of the daily or monthly press, is proof enough that the spirit of adventure still flourishes in the universal heart, seldom as modern conditions permit its expansion. For aught we know it may be this old spirit of adventure that inspires the midnight burglar and the gentlemen of the road, not merely the desire for "easy money." But these are the flotsam. The boldest imaginations and the most romantic hearts are sequestered in the American "big business" men of today.

Gregory Compton had grown to maturity in the most romantic subdivision of the United States since California retired to the position of a classic. Montana, her long winter surface a reflection of the beautiful dead face of the moon, bore within her arid body illimitable treasure, yielding it from time to time to the more ardent and adventurous of her lovers. Gold and silver, iron, copper, lead, tungsten, precious and semi-precious stones—she might have been some vast heathen idol buried aeons ago when Babylon was but a thought in the Creator's brain, and the minor gods travelled the heaving spaces to immure their treasure, stolen from rival stars.

Gregory had always individualised as well as idealised his state, finding more companionship in her cold mysteries than in the unfruitful minds of his little world. His youthful dreams, when sawing wood or riding after cattle, had been alternately of desperate encounters with Indians and of descending abruptly into vast and glittering corridors. The creek on the ranch had given up small quantities of placer gold, enough to encourage "Old Compton," least imaginative of men, to use his pick up the side of the gulch, and even to sink a shaft or two. But he had wasted his money, and he had little faith in the mineral value of the De Smet Ranch or in his own luck. He was a thrifty, pessimistic, hardworking, down-east Presbyterian, whose faith in predestination had killed such roots of belief in luck as he may have inherited with other attributes of man. He sternly discouraged his son's hopes, which the silent intense boy expressed one day in a sudden mood of fervour and desire for sympathy, bidding him hang on to the live stock, which were a certain sure source of income, and go out and feed hogs when he felt onsettled like.

He died when Gregory was in the midst of his Junior year in the School of Mines, and the eager student was obliged to renounce his hope of a congenial career, for the present, and assume control of the ranch. It was heavily mortgaged; his father's foreman, who had worked on the ranch since he was a lad, had taken advantage of the old man's failing mind to raise the money, as well as to obtain his signature to the sale of more than half the cattle. He had disappeared with the concrete result a few days before Mr. Compton's death.

It was in no serene spirit that Gregory entered upon the

struggle for survival at the age of twenty-one. Bitterly resenting his abrupt divorce from the School of Mines, which he knew to be the gateway to his future, and his faith in mankind dislocated by the cruel defection of one whom he had liked and trusted from childhood, he seethed under his stolid exterior while working for sixteen hours a day to rid the ranch of its encumbrance and replace the precious cattle. But as the greater part of this time was spent out of doors he outgrew the delicacy of his youth and earlier manhood, and, with red blood and bounding pulses, his bitterness left him.

He began to visit Butte whenever he could spare a few days from the ranch, to "look up" as his one chum, Mark Blake, expressed it; so that by the time he married he knew the life of a Western mining town—an education in itself—almost as well as he knew the white and silent spaces of Montana. With the passing of brooding and revolt his old dreams revived, and he spent, until he married, many long days prospecting. He had found nothing until a few weeks ago, early in October, and then the discovery, such as it was, had been accidental.

There had been a terrific wind storm, beginning shortly after sundown, reaching at midnight a velocity of seventy-two miles an hour, and lasting until morning; it had been impossible to sleep or to go out of doors and see to the well-being of the cattle.

The wind was not the Chinook, although it came out of the west, for it was bitterly cold. Two of the house windows facing the storm were blown in and the roof of a recent addition went off. As such storms are uncommon in Montana, even Gregory was uneasy, fearing the house might go, although it had been his father's boast that not even an earthquake could uproot it. After daybreak the steady fury of the storm ceased. There was much damage done to the outbuildings, but, leaving Oakley to superintend repairs, Gregory mounted his horse and rode over the ranch to examine the fences and brush sheds. The former were intact, and the cattle were huddled in their shelters, which were built against the side of a steep hill. A few, no doubt, had drifted before the storm, but would return in the course of the day. Here and there a pine tree had been blown over, but the winter wheat and alfalfa were too young to be injured.

He rode towards the hill where the wind had done its most conspicuous damage. It was a long steep hill of granite near the base and grey limestone above topped with red shales, and stood near the northeast corner of the ranch. Its rigid sides had been relieved by a small grove of pines; but although in spring it was gay with anemones and primrose moss, and green until late in July, there was nothing on its ugly flanks at this time of the year but sunburnt grass.

The old pines had clung tenaciously to the inhospitable soil for centuries, but some time during the night, still clutching a mass of earth and rock in their great roots, they had gone down before the storm.

Gregory felt a pang of distress; in his boyhood that grove of pines had been his retreat; there he had dreamed his dreams, visualised the ascending metals, forced upward from the earth's magma by one of those old titanic convulsions that make a joke of the modern earthquake, to find a refuge in the long fissures of the cooler crust, or in the great shattered zones. He knew something of geology and chemistry when he was twelve, and he "saw" the great primary deposits change their character as they were forced closer to the surface, acted upon by the acids of air and water in the oxide zone.

There he had lived down his disappointments, taken his dumb trouble when his mother died; and he had found his way blindly to the dark little grove after his father's funeral and he had learned the wrong that had been done him.

He had not gone there since. He had been busy always, and lost the habit. But now he remembered, and with some wonder, for it was the one ugly spot on the ranch, save in its brief springtime, that once it had drawn his feet like a magnet. Hardly conscious of the act, he rode to the foot of the hill, dismounted and climbed towards the grove which had stood about fifty feet from the crest.

The ruin was complete. The grove, which once may have witnessed ancient rites, was lying with its points in the brown grass. Its gaunt roots, packed close with red earth and pieces of rock, seemed to strain upward in agonised protest. Men deserted on the battlefield at night look hardly more stricken than a tree just fallen.

As Gregory approached his old friends his eyes grew

narrower and narrower; his mind concentrated to a point as sharp and penetrating as a needle. If the storm, now fitful, had suddenly returned to its highest velocity he would not have known it. He walked rapidly behind the vanquished roots and picked out several bits of rock that were embedded in the earth. Then he knelt down and examined other pieces of rock in the excavation where the trees had stood. Some were of a brownish-yellow colour, others a shaded green of rich and mellow tints. There was no doubt whatever that they were float.

He sat down suddenly and leaned against the roots of the trees. Had he found his "mine"? Float indicates an ore body somewhere, and as these particles had been prevented from escaping by the roots of trees incalculably old, it was reasonable to assume that the ores were beneath his feet.

His brain resumed its normal processes, and he deliberately gave his imagination the liberty of its youth. The copper did not interest him, but he stared at the piece of quartz in his hand as if it had been a seer's crystal. He saw great chambers of quartz flecked with free gold, connected by pipes or shoots equally rich. Once he frowned, the ruthlessly practical side of his intelligence reminding him that his labours and hopes might be rewarded by a shallow pocket. But he brushed the wagging finger aside. He could have sworn that he felt the pull of the metals within the hill.

He was tired and hungry, but his immediate impulse, as soon as he had concluded that he had dreamed long enough, was to go for his tools and run a cut. He sprang to his feet; but he had taken only a few steps when he turned and stared at the gashed earth, his head a little on one side in an attitude that always indicated he was thinking hard and with intense concentration. Then he set his lips grimly, walked down the steep hillside, mounted his horse, and rode home. In the course of the afternoon he returned to the hill, picked all the pieces of float from the soil between the tree-roots, and buried them, stamping down the earth. A few days later there was a light fall of snow. He returned once more to the hill, this time with two of his labourers, who cut up the trees and hauled them away. For the present his possible treasure vault was restored to the seclusion of its centuries.

He had made up his mind that the ores should stay where they were until he had finished his education in the School of Mines. He had planned to finish that course, and what he planned he was in the habit of executing. This was not the time for dreams, nor for prospecting, but to learn all that the School could teach him. Then, if there were valuable ore bodies in his hill he could be his own manager and engineer. He knew that he had something like genius for geology, also that many veins were lost through an imperfect knowledge (or sense) of that science in mining engineers; on the other hand, that the prospector, in spite of his much vaunted sixth sense, often failed, where the hidden ores were concerned, through lack of scientific training. He determined to train his own faculties as far as possible before beginning development work on his hill. Let the prospector's fever get possession of him now and that would be the end of study. The hill would keep. It was his. The ranch was patented.

When he had finished the interment of the float he had taken a small notebook from his pocket and inscribed a date: June the third, eighteen months later. Not until that date would he even ride past his hill.

Born with a strong will and a character endowed with force, determination and a grimly passive endurance, it was his pleasure to test and develop both. The process was satisfactory to himself but sometimes trying to his friends.

Until this morning he had not permitted his mind to revert to the subject. But although the hill—Limestone Hill it was called in the commonplace nomenclature of the country—was far away and out of the range of his vision, he could conjure it up in its minutest external detail, and he permitted himself this luxury for a few moments after his wife had left him to a welcome solitude. On this hill were centred all his silent hopes.

If he had been greedy for riches alone he would have promoted a company at once, if a cut opened up a chamber that assayed well, and reaped the harvest with little or no trouble to himself. But nothing was farther from his mind. He wanted the supreme adventure. He wanted to find the ores with his own pick. After the adventure, then the practical use of wealth. There was much he could do for his state. He knew also that in one group of brain-cells, as yet unexplored, was the ambition to enter the lists of "doing" men, and pit his wits against the best of them. But he was young, he would have his adventure, live his dream first. Not yet, however.

The swift passing of his marital illusions had convinced him that the real passion of his life was for Montana and the golden blood in her veins. Placer mining never had interested him. He wanted to find his treasure deep in the jealous earth. He assured himself as he stood there in the blue dawn that it was well to be rid of love so early in the game, free to devote himself, with no let from wandering mind and mere human pulses, to preparation for the greatest of all romances, the romance of mining. That he might ever crave the companionship of one woman was as remote from his mind as the possibility of failure. To learn all that man and experience could teach him of the science that has been so great a factor in the world's progress; to magnetise a vast share of Earth's riches, first for the hot work of the battle, then for the power it would give him; to conquer life; these were a few of the flitting dreams that possessed him as he watched the red flame lick the white crests of the mountains, and the blue clouds turn to crimson; his long sensitive lips folded closely, his narrow eyes penetrating the mists of the future, neither seeing nor considering its obstacles, its barriers, its disenchantments. Thrice happy are the dreamers of the world, when their imaginations are creative, not a mere maggot wandering through the brain hatching formless eggs of desire and discontent. They are the true inheritors of the centuries, whether they succeed or fail in the eyes of men; for they live in vivid silent intense drama as even they have no power to live and enjoy in mortal conditions.

IV

THE Comptons were quickly settled in the little cottage in East Granite Street, for as Mrs. Hook's furniture was solid Ida had not sold it. There was little to do, therefore, but repaper the walls, build a bathroom, furnish a dining-room, send the parlour furniture to the upholsterers —Ida had had enough of horsehair—and chattel the kitchen.

Ida had several virtues in which she took a vocal pride, and not the least of these was housekeeping in all its variety. The luxurious side of her nature might revel in front parlours, trashy magazines, rocking-chairs and chewing-gum, but she never indulged in these orgies unless her house were in order. After her arrival in Butte it was quite a month before she gave a thought to leisure. They spent most of this time at a hotel, but Ida was out before the stores opened, and divided her day between the workmen at the cottage, the upholsterer, and the bargain counter. She was "on the job" every minute until the cottage was "on wheels." Her taste was neither original nor artistic, but she had a rude sense of effect, and a passion for what she called colour schemes. She boasted to Gregory at night, when she had him at her mercy at the hotel dinner table, that although everything had to be cheap except the kitchen furnishings, colours did not cost any more than black or drab. When the cottage was in order, and they moved in, he saw its transfigured interior for the first time. The bedroom was done in a pink that set his teeth on edge, and the little parlour was papered, upholstered, carpeted, cushioned in every known shade of red.

"All you want is a chromo or two of Indian battle-grounds—just after," he remarked.

Ida interrupted tartly:

"Well, I should think you'd be grateful for the contrast

22

to them everlasting white or brown mountains. We don't get away from them even in town, now the smoke's gone."

"One would think Montana had no springtime."

"Precious little. That's the reason I've got a green dining-room."

Gregory, who had suffered himself to be pushed into an armchair, looked at his wife speculatively, as she rocked herself luxuriously, her eyes dwelling fondly on the magenta paper, the crimson curtains, the turkey red and crushed strawberry cushions of the divan, the blood-red carpet with its still more sanguinary pattern. What blind struggle was going on in that uninstructed brain against the commonplace, what seed of originality, perhaps, striving to shoot forth a green tip from the hard crust of ignorance and conceit?

He had made up his mind to suggest the tillage of that brain without delay, but, knowing her sensitive vanity, cast about for a tactful opening.

"Do you really intend to do your own work?" he asked. "I am more than willing to pay for a servant."

"Not much. I'm goin' to begin to save up for the future right now. I'll put out the wash, but it's a pity if a great husky girl like me can't cook for two and keep this little shack clean. You ain't never goin' to be able to say I didn't help you all I could."

Gregory glowed with gratitude as he looked at the beautiful face of his wife, flushed with the ardour of the true mate.

"You are all right," he murmured.

"The less we spend the quicker we'll get rich," pursued Mrs. Compton. "I don't mind this triflin' work, but it would have made me sick to stay much longer on that ranch workin' away my youth and looks and nothin' to show for it. Now that you've really begun on somethin' high-toned and that's bound to be a go, I just like the idea of havin' a hand in the job."

"Ah!— Well— If you have this faith in my power to make a fortune—if you are looking forward to being a rich man's wife, to put it crudely—don't you think you should begin to prepare yourself for the position——"

"Now what are you drivin' at?" She sprang to her feet. Her eyes blazed. Her hands went to her hips. "D'you mean to say I ain't good enough? I suppose you'd be throwin' me over for a grand dame when you get up in the world like some other millionaires we know of, let alone politicians what get to thinkin' themselves statesmen, and whose worn-out old wives ain't good enough for 'em. Well, take this from me and take it straight—I don't propose to wear out, and I don't propose——''

"Sit down. I shall be a rich man long before you lose your beauty. Nor have I any social ambitions. The world of men is all that interests me. But with you it will be different——''

"You may betcherlife it'll be different—some! When I have a cream-coloured pressed brick house with white trimmings over there in Millionaire Gulch nobody'll be too good for me."

"You shall live your life to suit yourself, in the biggest house in Butte, if that is what you want. But there is more in it than that."

"Clothes, of course. *Gowns!* And jewels, and New York—Lord! wouldn't I like to swell up and down Peacock Ally! And Southern California, and Europe, and givin' balls, and bein' a member of the Country Club."

"All that, as a matter of course! But you would not be content with the mere externals. Whether you know it or not, Ida, you are an ambitious woman." This was a mere gambler's throw on Gregory's part. He knew nothing of her ambitions, and would have called them by another name if he had.

"Not know it? Well, you may just betcherlife I know it!"

"But hardly where ambition leads. No sooner would you be settled in a fine house, accustomed to your new toys, than you would want society. I don't mean that you would have any difficulty gaining admittance to Butte society, for it is said that none in the world is more hospitable and less particular. But whether you make *friends* of the best people here, much less become a leader, depends—well, upon several things——''

"Fire away," said Ida sulkily. "You must be considerable in earnest to talk a blue streak!"

"Business may take me to New York from time to time, but my home shall remain here. I never intend to abandon my state and make a fool of myself on New York's doorstep as so many Montanans have done. Nail up that fact and never forget it. Now, you would like to win an unassailable position in your community, would you not?''

"Yep."

Gregory abandoned tact. "Then begin at once to prepare yourself. You must have a teacher and study—English, above all things."

"My Goo-r-rd!" She flushed almost purple. For the moment she hated him. "I've always suspicioned you thought I wasn't good enough for you, with your graduatin' from the High School almost while you was in short pants, and them two years and over at that highbrow School of Mines; and now you're tellin' me you'll be ashamed of me the minute you're on top!"

Gregory made another attempt at diplomacy. What his wife achieved socially was a matter of profound indifference to him, but she must reform her speech if his home life was to be endurable.

"I am forcing my imagination to keep pace with your future triumphs," he said with the charming smile that disarmed even Ida when irate. "If you are going to be a prominent figure in society——"

"My land, you oughter heard the grammar and slang of some of the newest West Siders when they were makin' up their minds at Madame O'Reilley's, or havin' their measures took. They don't frighten me one little bit."

"There is a point. To lead them you must be their superior—and the equal of those that have made the most of their advantages."

"That's not such a bad idea."

"Think it over." He rose, for he was tired of the conversation. "These western civilisations are said to be crude, but I fancy they are the world in little. Subtlety, a brain developed beyond the common, should go far——"

"Greg, you are dead right!" She had suddenly remembered that she must play up to this man who held her ambitions in his hand, and she had the wit to acknowledge his prospicience, little as were the higher walks of learning to her taste. She sprang to her feet with a supple undulating movement and flung herself into his arms.

"I'll begin the minute you find me a teacher," she exclaimed. Then she kissed him. "I'm goin' to keep right along with you and make you proud of me," she murmured. "I'm crazy about you and always will be. Swear right here you'll never throw me over, or run round with a P'rox.''

Gregory laughed, but held her off for a moment and stared into her eyes. After all, might not study and travel and experience give depth to those classic eyes which now seemed a mere joke of Nature? Was she merely the natural victim of her humble conditions? Her father had been a miner of a very superior sort, conservative and contemptuous of agitators, but a powerful voice in his union and respected alike by men and managers. Mrs. Hook had been a shrewd, hard-working, tight-fisted little woman from Concord, who had never owed a penny, nor turned out a careless piece of work. Both parents with education or better luck might have taken a high position in any western community. He knew also the preternatural quickness and adaptability of the American woman. But could a common mind achieve distinction?

Ida, wondering ''what the devil he was thinking about,'' nestled closer and gave him a long kiss, her woman's wisdom, properly attributed to the serpent, keeping her otherwise mute. Gregory snatched her suddenly to him and returned her kiss. The new hope revived a passion by no means dead for this beautiful young creature, and for the hour he was as happy as during his rosy honeymoon.

V

WHEN the cottage was quite in order Mrs. Compton invited two of her old friends to lunch. As the School of Mines was at the opposite end of the city, Gregory took his midday meal with him.

Miss Ruby Miller and her twin-sister Pearl were fine examples of the self-supporting young womanhood of the West. Neither had struggled in the extreme economic sense, although when launched they had taken a man's chances and asked no quarter. Born in a small town in Illinois, their father, a provident grocer, had permitted each of his daughters to attend school until her fifteenth year, then sent her to Chicago to learn a trade. Ruby had studied the mysteries of the hair, complexion, and hands; Pearl the science that must supplement the knack for trimming hats. Both worked faithfully as apprentice and clerk, saving the greater part of their earnings: they purposed to set up for themselves in some town of the Northwest where money was easier, opportunities abundant and expertness rare. What they heard of Montana appealed to their enterprising minds, and, beginning with cautious modesty, some four years before Ida's marriage, Ruby was now the leading hair-dresser and manicure of Butte, her pleasant address and natural diplomacy assisting her competent hands to monopolise the West Side custom; Pearl, although less candid and engaging, more frank in reminding her customers of their natural deficiencies, was equally capable; if not the leading milliner in that town of many milliners, where even the miners' wives bought three hats a season, she was rapidly making a reputation among the feathered tribe. She now ranked as one of the most successful of the young business women in a region where success is ever the prize of the efficient. Both she and her sister were as little concerned for their future as the metal hill of Butte itself.

"Well, what do you know about that?" they cried

simultaneously, as Ida ushered them into the parlour.
"Say, it's grand!" continued Miss Ruby with fervour.
"Downright artistic. Ide, you're a wonder!"

Miss Pearl, attuned to a subtler manipulation of colour,
felt too happy in this intimate reunion and the prospect
of "home-cooking," to permit even her spirit to grin.
"Me for red, kiddo," she said. "It's the colour a hard
workin' man or woman wants at the end of the day—
warm, and comfortin', and sensuous-like, and contrastin'
fine with dirty streets and them hills. Glory be, but this
chair's comfortable! I suppose it's Greg's."

"Of course. Luckily a woman don't have the least
trouble findin' out a man's weak points, and Greg has a
few, thank the goodness godness. But come on to the
dining-room. I've got fried chicken and creamed potatoes
and raised biscuit."

The guests shrieked with an abandon that proclaimed
them the helpless victims of the Butte restaurant or the
kitchenette. The fried chicken in its rich gravy, and the
other delicacies, including fruit salad, disappeared so rapidly that there was little chance for the play of intellect
until the two girls fled laughing to the parlour.

"It's all very well for Pearl," cried Miss Ruby, disposing her plump figure in Gregory's arm-chair, and taking the pins from a mass of red hair that had brought her
many a customer; "for she's the kind that'll never have
to diet if she gets rich quick. I ought to be shas-
saying round with my hands on my hips right now, but I
won't."

Miss Pearl extended herself on the divan, and Ida rocked
herself with a complacent smile. One of her vanities was
slaked, and she experienced a sense of immense relief in
the society of these two old friends of her own sort.

"Say!" exclaimed Miss Miller, "if we was real swell,
now, we'd be smokin' cigarettes."

"What!" cried Ida, scandalised. "No lady'd do such
a thing. Say, I forgot the gum."

She opened a drawer and flirted an oblong section of
chewing-gum at each of her guests, voluptuously inserting
a morsel in the back of her own mouth. "Where on earth
have you seen ladies smokin' cigarettes?"

"You forget I'm in and out of some of our best families. In other words them that's too swell—or too lazy—

to come to me, has me up to them. And they're just as nice—most of 'em—as they can be; no more airs than their men, and often ask me to stay to lunch. I ain't mentionin' no names, as I was asked not to, for you know what an old-fashioned bunch there is in every Western town—well, they out with their gold tips after lunch, and maybe you think they don't know how. I have my doubts as to their enjoyin' it, for tobacco is nasty tastin' stuff, and I notice they blow the smoke out quicker'n they take it in. No inhalin' for them. But they like *doin'* it; that's the point. And I guess they do it a lot at the Country Club and at some of the dinners where the Old Guard ain't asked. They smoke, and think it's vulgar to chew gum! We know it's the other way round.''

''Well, I guess!'' exclaimed the young matron, who had listened to this chronicle of high life with her mouth open. ''What their husbands thinkin' about to permit such a thing! I can see Greg's face if I lit up.''

''Oh, their husbands don't care,'' said Pearl, the cynic. ''Not in that bunch. They're trained, and they don't care, anyhow. Make the most of Greg now, kiddo. When he strikes it rich, he'll be just like the rest of 'em, annexin' right and left. Matter of principle.''

''Principle nothing!'' exclaimed Ruby, who, highly sophisticated as any young woman earning her living in a mining town must be, was always amiable in her cynicism. ''It's too much good food and champagne, to say nothin' of cocktails and highballs and swell club life after the lean and hungry years. They're just like kids turned loose in a candy store, helpin' themselves right and left with both hands. Dear old boys, they're so happy and so jolly you can't help feelin' real maternal over 'em, and spoilin' 'em some more. I often feel like it, even when they lay for me—they look so innocent and hungry-like; but others I could crack over the ear, and I don't say I haven't. Lord, how a girl alone does get to know men! I wouldn't marry one of them if he'd give me the next level of the Anaconda mine. Me for the lonesome!''

''Well, I'm glad I'm married,'' said Ida complacently. ''The kind of life I want you can only get through a husband. Greg's goin' to make money, all right.''

''Greg won't be as bad as some,'' said the wise Miss Ruby. ''He's got big ideas, and as he don't say much

about 'em, he's likely thinkin' about nothin' else. At
least that's the way I figure him out. The Lord knows
I've seen enough of men. But you watch out just the
same. Them long thin ones that looks like they was all
brains and jaw is often the worst. They've got more
nerves. The minute the grind lets up they begin to look
out for an adventure, wonderin' what's round the next
corner. Wives ain't much at supplyin' adventure——''

"Well, let's quit worryin' about what ain't happened,"
said Miss Pearl abruptly. Men did not interest her.
"Will he take you to any of the dances? That's what I
want to know. You've been put up and elected to our
new and exclusive Club. No more Coliseum Saturday
Nights for us—Race Track is a good name for it. We've
taken a new little hall over Murphy's store for Saturday
nights till the Gardens open up, and we have real fun.
No rowdyism. We leave that to the cut below. This Club
is composed of real nice girls and young men of Butte who
are workin' hard at something high-toned and respectable,
and frown hard on the fast lot."

"Sounds fine. Perhaps Greg'll go, though he studies
half the night. Do you meet at any other time? Is it
one of them mind improvers, too?"

"Nixie. We work all week and want fun when we get
a few hours off. I improve my mind readin' myself to
sleep every night——''

"What do you read?" interrupted Ida, eagerly.

"Oh, the mags, of course, and a novel now and then.
But you don't need novels any more. The mags are wonders! They teach you all the life you don't know—all
the way from lords to burglars. Then there's the movin'
pictures. Lord, but we have advantages our poor mothers
never dreamed of!"

"Greg wants me to study with a teacher." Ida frowned
reminiscently and fatidically. "He seems to think I didn't
get nothin' at school."

"Well, what do you know about that?" gasped Miss
Miller. Pearl removed her gum with a dry laugh.

"If a man insinuated I wasn't good enough for him—"
she began; Ruby, whose quick mind was weather-wise, interrupted her.

"Greg's right. He's got education himself and's proved
he don't mean to be a rancher all his life. What's more,

I've heard men say that Gregory Compton is bound one way or another to be one of the big men of Montana. He's got the brains, he's got the jaw, and he can outwork any miner that ever struck, and no bad habits. Ide, you go ahead and polish up.''

''Why should I? I never could see that those bonanzerines were so much better'n us, barring clothes.''

''You don't know the best of 'em, Ide. Madame O'Reilley was too gaudy to catch any but the newest bunch. The old pioneer guard is fine, and their girls have been educated all over this country and the next. Lord! Look at Ora Blake! Where'd you beat her? In these new Western towns it's generally the sudden rich that move to New York to die of lonesomeness, and nowhere to show their clothes but Peacock Alley in the Waldorf-Astoria. The *real* people keep their homes here, if they are awful restless; and I guess the Society they make, with their imported gowns and all, ain't so very different from top Society anywheres. Of course, human nature is human nature, and some of the younger married women are sporty and take too much when a bunch goes over to Boulder Springs for a lark, or get a crush on some other woman's husband—for want mostly of something to do; but their grammar's all right. I hope you'll teach them a lesson when you're on top, Ide. Good American morals for me, like good American stories. I always skip the Europe stories in the mags. Don't seem modern and human, somehow, after Butte.''

''Now I like Europe stories,'' said Ida, ''just because they are so different. The people in 'em ain't walkin' round over gold and copper when they're dishwashin' or makin' love, but their mines have been turned centuries ago into castles and pictures and grand old parks. There's a kind of halo——''

''Halo nothin'!'' exclaimed Miss Pearl, who was even more aggressively American than her sister. ''It's them ridiculous titles. And kings and queens and all that antique lot. I despise 'em, and I'm dead set against importin' foreign notions into God's own country. We're dyed-in-the-wool Americans—out West here, anyhow—including every last one of them fools that's buyin' new notions with their new money. All their Paris clothes *and* hats, *and* smokin' cigarettes, *and* loose talk can't

make 'em anything else. Apin' Europe and its antiquated
morals makes me sick to my stomach. Cut it out, kid,
before you go any further. Stand by your own country
and it'll stand by you.''

"Well, I've got an answer to that. In the first place
I'd like to know where you'll find more girls on the loose
than right here in Butte—and I don't mean the sporting
women, either. Why, I meet bunches of schoolgirls every
day so painted up they look as if they was fixin' right
now to be bad; and as for these Eastern workin' girls who
come out here after jobs, pretendin' it's less pressure and
bigger pay they're after, when it's really to turn loose and
give human nature a chance with free spenders—well, the
way they hold down their jobs and racket about all night
beats me. None of *them's* been to Europe, I notice, and
I'd like to bet that the schoolgirls that don't make mon-
keys of themselves is the daughters of them that has.''

"Oh, the schoolgirls is just plain little fools and no
doubt has their faces held under the spout for 'em when
they get home. But as for the Eastern girls, you hit it
when you said they come out here to give human nature a
chance. Some girls is born bad, thousands and thousands
of them; and reformers might just as well try to grow
strawberries in a copper smelter as to make a girl run
straight when she is lyin' awake nights thinkin' up new
ways of bein' crooked. But the rotten girls in this town
are not the whole show. And lots of women that would
never think of goin' wrong—don't naturally care for that
sort of thing a bit—just get their minds so mixed up by
too much sudden money, and liberty, and too much high
livin' and too much Europe and too much nothin' to do,
that they just don't know where they're at; and it isn't
long either before they get to thinkin' they're not the
dead swell thing unless they do what the nobility of Europe
seems to be doin' all the time——''

"Shucks!" interrupted Ruby, indignantly. "It's just
them stories in the shady mags, and the way our women
talk for the sake of effect. There's bad in America and
good in poor old Europe. I'll bet my new hat on it. Only,
over there the good is out of sight under all that sportin'
high life everybody seems to write about. Over here
we've got a layer of good on top as thick as cream, and
every kind of germ swimmin' round underneath. Lord

knows there are plenty of just females in this town, of all towns, but the U. S. is all right because it has such high standards. All sorts of new-fangled notions come and go but them standards never budge. No other country has anything like 'em. Sooner or later we'll catch up. I'm great on settin' the right example and I'm dead set on uplift. That's one reason we're so strict about our Club membership. Not one of them girls can get in, no matter how good her job or how swell a dresser she is. And they feel it, too, you bet. The line's drawn like a barbed-wire fence.''

"I guess you're dead right," admitted Ida. "And my morals ain't in any danger, believe me. I've got other fish to fry. I've had love's young dream and got over it. I'm just about dead sick of that side of life. I'd cut it out and put it down to profit and loss, but you've got to manage men every way nature's kindly provided, and that's all there is to it.''

"My land!" exclaimed Ruby. "If I felt that way about my husband I'd leave him too quick.''

"Oh, no, you wouldn't. You can make up your mind to any old thing. That's life. And I guess life never holds out both hands full at once. Either, one's got a knife in it or it's out of sight altogether.''

Ruby snorted with disgust. "Once more I vow I'll marry none of them. Me for self-respect.''

"Now as to Europe," pursued Ida. "You're just noth-in' till you've been, both as to what you get, and sayin' you've been there——''

"Ida," said Ruby, shaking her wise red head, "don't you go leavin' your husband summers, like the rest. Men don't get much chance to go to Europe. They prefer little old New York, anyhow—when they can get on there alone. I wonder what ten thousand wives that go to Europe every summer think their husbands are doin'? I haven't mani-cured men for nine years without knowin' they need watchin' every minute. Why, my lord! they're so tickled to death when summer comes round they can hardly wait to kiss their wives good-by and try to look lonesome on the platform. They'd like to lie down and kick up their heels right there at the station. And I didn't have to come to Butte to find that out.''

"Greg'll never run with that fast lot.''

"No, but he might meet an affinity; and there's one of *them* lyin' in wait for every man."

Ida's brow darkened. "Well, just let her look out for herself, that's all. I'll hang on to Greg. But it ain't time to worry yet. Let's have a game of poker."

VI

GREGORY, through the offices of his friend, Mark Blake, found a teacher for Ida before the end of the week, Mr. William Cullen Whalen, Professor of English in the Butte High School.

Mr. Whalen's present status was what he was in the habit of designating as an ignominious anti-climax, considering his antecedents and attainments; but he always dismissed the subject with a vague, "Health—health—this altitude—this wonderful air—climate—not for me are the terrible extremes of our Atlantic seaboard. Here a man may be permitted to live, if not in the deeper sense—well, at least, there are always one's thoughts—and books."

He was a delicate little man as a matter of fact, but had East winds and summer humidities been negligible he would have jumped at the position found for him by a college friend who had gone West and prospered in Montana. This friend's letter had much to say about the dry tonic air of winter, the cool light air of summer, the many hours he would be able to pass in the open, thus deepening the colour of his corpuscles, at present a depressing shade of pink; but even more about a salary far in excess of anything lying round loose in the East. Mr. Whalen, who, since his graduation from the college in his native town, had knocked upon several historic portals of learning in vain, finding himself invariably outclassed, had shuddered, but accepted his fate by the outgoing mail. Of course he despised the West; and the mere thought of a mining camp like Butte, which was probably in a drunken uproar all the time, almost nauseated him. However, in such an outpost the graduate of an Eastern college who knew how to wear his clothes must rank high above his colleagues. It might be years before he could play a similar rôle at home. So he packed his wardrobe, which included spats and a silk hat, and went.

Nature compensates even her comparative failures by

endowing them with a deathless self-conceit. Whalen was a man of small abilities, itching ambition, all the education his brains could stand, and almost happy in being himself and a Whalen. It was true that Fortune had grafted him on a well-nigh sapless branch in a small provincial town, while the family trunk flourished, green, pruned, and portly, in Boston, but no such trifle could alter the fact that he was a Whalen, and destined by a discriminating heredity to add to the small but precious bulk of America's literature. Although he found Butte a city of some sixty thousand inhabitants, and far better behaved than he had believed could be possible in a community employing some fifteen thousand miners, he was still able to reassure himself that she outraged every sensibility. He assured himself further that its lurid contrasts to the higher civilisation would play like a search-light upon the theme for a novel he long had had in mind: the subtle actions and reactions of the Boston temperament.

But that was three years ago, and meanwhile several things had happened to him. He had ceased to wear his spats and silk hat in public after their first appearance on Broadway; the newsboys, who were on strike, had seen to that. He wrote his novel, and the *Atlantic Monthly*, honored by the first place on his list, declined to give space to his innocent plagiarisms of certain anæmic if literary authors now passing into history. An agent sent the manuscript the rounds without avail, but one of the younger editors had suggested that he try his hand at Montana. He was more shocked and mortified at this proposition than at the failure of his novel. Time, however, as well as the high cost of living in Butte, lent him a grudging philosophy, and he digested the advice. But his were not the eyes that see. The printed page was his world, his immediate environment but a caricature of the subtle realities. Nevertheless, he had what so often appears in the most unlikely brains, the story-telling kink. Given an incident he could work it up with an abundance of detail and "psychology," easily blue-pencilled, and a certain illusion. Condescend to translate his present surroundings into the sacred realm of American fiction he would not, but he picked the brains of old-timers for thrilling incidents of the days when gold was found at the roots of grass, and the pioneers either were terrorized by the lawless element or executed upon it a summary and awful justice. Some of his tales were so blood-curdling, so steeped in gore and horror, that he felt almost alive when writing them. It was true that their market was the Sunday Supplement and the more sensational magazines, whose paper and type made his soul turn green; but the pay was excellent, and they had begun to attract some attention, owing to the contrast between the fierceness of theme and the neat precise English in which it was served. Butte valued him as a counter-irritant to Mary McLane, and he became a professional diner-out.

"Do you think he'll condescend to tutor?" Gregory had asked of Blake. Whalen was by no means unknown to him, but heretofore had been regarded as a mere worm.

"Sure thing. Nobody keener on the dollar than Whalen. He'll stick you, but he knows his business. He's got all the words there are, puts 'em in the right place, and tones 'em up so you'd hardly know them."

VII

IDA was out when her prospective tutor called, and she was deeply impressed by the card she found under the door: "Mr. William Cullen Whalen," it was inscribed.

It was the custom of the gentlemen of her acquaintance to express their sense of good fellowship even upon the formal pasteboard. "Mr. Matt Dance," "Mr. Phil Mott," "Mr. Bill Jarvis," the legends read. Ida felt as if she were reciting a line from the Eastern creed as her lips formed again and again the suave and labial syllables on her visitor's card. She promptly determined to order cards for her husband on the morrow—he was so remiss as to have none—and they should be engraved, in small Roman letters: "Mr. Gregory Verrooy Compton."

"And believe me," she announced to her green dining-room, as she sat down before her husband's desk, "that is some name."

Her note to Professor Whalen, asking him to call on the following afternoon at two o'clock, was commendably brief, so impatient was she to arrive at the signature, "Mrs. Gregory Verrooy Compton;" little conceiving the effect it would have upon Mr. Whalen's fastidious spine.

He called at the hour named, and Ida invited him into the dining-room. It was here that Gregory read far into the night, and she vaguely associated a large table with much erudition. Moreover, she prided herself upon her economy in fuel.

Mr. Whalen sat in one of the hard upright chairs, his stick across his knee, his gloves laid smartly in the rolling brim of his hat, studying this new specimen and wondering if she could be made to do him credit. He was surprised to find her so beautiful, and not unrefined in style—if only she possessed the acumen to keep her ripe mouth shut. In fact he found her quite the prettiest woman he had seen in Butte, famous for pretty women; and—and—he searched conscientiously for the right word, and blushed as he found it—the most seductive. Ida was vain of the fact that she wore no corset, and that not the least of her attractions was a waist as flexible as an acrobat's. What flesh she had was very firm, her carriage was easy and graceful, the muscles of her back were strong, her lines long and flowing; she walked and moved at all times with an undulating movement usually associated with a warmer temperament. But nature often amuses herself bestowing the semblance and withholding the essence; Ida, calculating and contemptuous of the facile passions of men, amused herself with them, confident of her own immunity.

It was now some time since she had enjoyed the admiration of any man but her husband, and his grew more and more sporadic, was long since dry of novelty. Like most Western husbands, he would not have permitted her to make a friend of any other man, nor even to receive the casual admirer when he was not at home. Ida was full of vanity, although she would have expressed her sudden determination to captivate "little Whalen" merely as a desire to keep her hand in. He was the only man upon whom she was likely to practise at present (for Gregory would have none of the Club dances), and vanity can thirst like a galled palate. She had "sized him up" as a "squirt" (poor Ida! little she recked how soon she was to be stripped of her picturesque vocabulary), but he was "a long sight better than nothing."

After they had exhausted the nipping weather, and the possibility of a Chinook arriving before night—there was a humming roar high overheard at the moment—she lowered her black eyelashes, lifted herself against the stiff back of her chair with the motion of a snake uncoiling, raised her thick white lids suddenly, and murmured:

"Well, so you're goin' to polish me off? Tell me all my faults! Fire away. I know you'll make a grand success of it. Lord knows (her voice became as sweet as honey), you're different enough from the other men in this jay town."

Mr. Whalen felt as if he were being drenched with honey dew, for he was the type of man whom women take no trouble to educate. But as that sweet unmodulated voice stole about his ear porches he drew himself up stiffly, conscious of a thrill of fear. To become enamoured of the wife of one of these forthright Westerners, who took the law into their own hands, was no part of his gentle programme; but he stared at her fascinated, never having felt anything resembling a thrill before. Moreover, like all people of weak passions, more particularly that type of American that hasn't any, he took pride in his powers of self-control. In a moment he threw off the baleful influence and replied drily.

"I think the lessons would better be oral for a time. Do—do I understand that I am to correct your individual method of expression?"

"That's it, I guess."

"And you won't be offended?" Mr. Whalen's upper teeth were hemispheric, but he had cultivated a paternal and not unpleasing smile. Even the pale blue orbs, fixed defiantly upon the siren, warmed a trifle.

"Well, I don't s'pose I'll like bein' corrected better'n the next, but that's what I'm payin' for. Now that my husband's studyin' for a profession, I guess I'll be in the top set before so very long. There's Mrs. Blake, for instance—her husband told Mr. Compton she'd call this week. Is she all that she's cracked up to be?"

"Mrs. Blake has had great advantages. She might almost be one of our own products, were it not for the fact that she—well—seems deliberately to wish to be Western." He found himself growing more and more confused under the steady regard of those limpid shadowy eyes—set like the eyes of a goddess in marble, and so disconcertingly shallow. He pulled himself up sharply. "Now, if I may begin—you must not sign your notes, 'Mrs. Gregory Verrooy Compton'——"

Ida's eyes flashed wide open. "Why not, I'd like to know? Isn't it as good a name as yours?"

"What has that to do with it? Ah—yes—you don't quite understand. It is not the custom—in what we call society—to sign in that manner—it is a regrettable American provincialism. If you really wish to learn——"

"Fire away," said Ida sullenly.

"Sign your own name—may I ask what it is?"

"My name was Ida Maria Hook before I married."

"Ida is a beautiful and classic name. We will eliminate the rest. Sign yourself Ida Compton—or if you wish to be more swagger, Ida Verrooy Compton——"

"Land's sake! We'd be laughed clean out of Montana."

"Yes, there is a fine primitive simplicity about many things in this region," replied Mr. Whalen, thinking of his spats and silk hat. "But you get my point?"

"I get you."

"Oh!—We'll have a little talk later about slang. And you mustn't begin your letters, particularly to an acquaintance, 'Dear friend.' This is an idealistic and—ah—bucolic custom, but hardly good form."

He was deeply annoyed at his lack of fluency, but Ida once more was deliberately "upsetting" him. She smiled indulgently.

"I guess I like your new-fangled notions. I'll write all that down while you're thinkin' up what to say next."

She leaned over the table and wrote slowly that he might have leisure to admire her figure in profile. But he gazed sternly out of the window until she swayed back to the perpendicular and demanded,

"What next? Do you want me to say băth and căn't?"

"Oh, no, I really shouldn't advise it, not in Butte. I don't wish to teach you anything that will add to the discomforts of life—so long as your lines are cast here. Just modify the lamentably short American *a* a bit." And he rehearsed her for a few moments.

"Fine. I'll try it on Greg—Mr. Compton. If he laughs I'll know I'm too good, but if he only puckers his eyebrows and looks as if somethin' queer was floatin' round just out of sight, then I'll know I've struck the happy medium. I'll be a real high-brow in less than no time."

"You certainly are surprisingly quick," said Professor Whalen handsomely. "In a year I could equip you for our centres of culture, but as I remarked just now it would not be kind to transform you into an exotic. Now, suppose we read a few pages of this grammar——"

"I studied grammar at school," interrupted Ida haughtily. "What do you take Butte for, anyhow. It may be a mining-camp, and jay enough compared with your old Boston, but I guess we learn something mor'n the alphabet at all these big red brick schoolhouses we've got—Montana's famous for its grand schoolhouses——"

"Yes, yes, my dear Mrs. Compton. But, you know, one forgets so quickly. And then so many of you don't stay in school long enough. How old were you when you left?''

"Fifteen. Ma wouldn't let me go to the High."

"Precisely. Well, I will adhere to my original purpose, and defer books until our next lesson. Perhaps you would like me to tell you something more of our Eastern methods of speech—not only words, but—er—syntax——"

"Oh, hang your old East! You make me feel downright patriotic.''

Professor Whalen was conscious that it was a distinct pleasure to make those fine eyes flash. "One would think we were not all Americans," he said with a smile.

"Well, I guess you look upon America as East and West too. Loads of young surveyors and mining men come out here to make their pile, and at first Montana ain't good enough to black their boots, but it soon takes the starch out of 'em. No use puttin' on dog here. It don't work.''

"Oh, I assure you it's merely a difference of manner—of—er tradition. We—and I in particular—find your West most interesting—and significant. I—ah—regard it as the great furnace under our civilization.''

"And we are the stokers! I like your impudence!''

He had no desire to lose this remunerative pupil, whose crude mind worked more quickly than his own. She was now really angry and he made a mild dive in search of his admitted tact.

"My dear lady, you put words into my mouth that emanate from your own clever brain, not from my merely pedantic one. Not only have I the highest respect for the West, and for Montana in particular, but please remember that the contempt of the East for the West is merely passive, negative, when compared with the lurid scorn of the West for the East. 'Effete' is its mildest term of opprobrium. I doubt if your 'virile' Westerner believes us to be really alive, in a condition to inhabit aught but a museum. Your men when they 'make their pile', or take a vacation, never dream of going to Boston, seldom, indeed, to Europe. They take the fastest train for New York—and by no means with a view to exploring that wilderness for its oases of culture——''

"Well, I guess not!" cried Ida, her easy good nature restored. "All-night restaurants, something new in the way of girls—'chickens' and 'squabs'—musical shows, watchin' the sun rise—that's their little old New York. They always come home shakin' themselves like a New-foundland puppy, or purrin' like a cat full of cream, but talkin' about the Great Free West, God's Own Country, and the Big Western Heart. I've a friend who does mani-curin', and she knows 'em like old shoes.''

Whalen, who had a slight cultivated sense of humor, laughed. "You are indeed most apt and picturesque, dear Mrs. Compton. But—while I think of it—you mustn't drop your final *gs*. That, I am told, is one of the fashion-able divagations of the British aristocracy. But with us it is the hallmark of the uneducated. Now, I really have told you all you can remember for one day, and will take my leave. It is to be every other day, I understand. On Wednesday, then, at two?''

VIII

IDA walked to the gate with him. She was quite a head taller than he, but subtly made him feel that the advantage was his, as it enabled her to pour the light of her eyes downward. He picked his way up the uneven surface of East Granite Street, slippery with a recent fall of snow, not only disturbed, but filled with a new conceit; in other words thrilling with his first full sense of manhood.

Ida looked after him, smiling broadly. But the smile fled abruptly, her lips trembled, then contracted. Advancing down the street was Mrs. Mark Blake. Ida had known her enterprising young husband before he changed his name from Mike to Mark, but she knew his lady wife by sight only; Mrs. Blake had not patronized Madame O'Reilley. Ruby and Pearl pronounced her "all right", although a trifle "proud to look at." Ida assumed that she was to receive the promised call, and wished she could "get out of it." Not only did she long for her rocker, gum and magazine, after the intellectual strain of the past hour, but she had no desire to meet Mrs. Blake or any of "that crowd" until she could take her place as their equal. She had her full share of what is known as class-consciousness, and its peculiar form of snobbery. To be patronized by "swells", even to be asked to their parties, would give her none of that subtle joy peculiar to the climbing snob. When the inevitable moment came she would burst upon them, dazzle them, bulldoze and lead them, but she wanted none of their crumbs.

But she was "in for it." She hastily felt the back of her shirtwaist to ascertain if it still were properly adjusted, and sauntered towards the cottage humming a tune, pretending not to have seen the lady who stopped to have a word with Professor Whalen. "Anyhow, she's not a bonanzerine," thought Ida. "I guess she did considerable scrapin' at one time; and Mark, for all he could make shoe-blackin' look like molasses, ain't a millionaire yet."

44

She might indeed, further reflected Ida, watching the smartly tailored figure out of the corner of her eye, be pitied, for she had been "brought up rich, expecting to marry a duke, and then come down kaplunk before she'd much more'n a chance to grow up." Her father, Judge Stratton, a graduate of Columbia University, had been one of the most brilliant and unscrupulous lawyers of the Northwest. He had drawn enormous fees from railroads and corporations, and in the historic Clark-Daily duels for supremacy in the State of Montana, and in the more picturesque battle between F. Augustus Heinze and "Amalgamated" (that lusty offspring of the great Standard Oil Trust), when the number of estimable citizens bought and sold demonstrated the faint impress of time on original sin, his legal acumen and persuasive tongue, his vitriolic pen, ever had been at the disposal of the highest bidder.

He had been a distinguished resident of Butte but a few years when he built himself a spacious if hideous residence on the West Side. But this must have been out of pure loyalty to his adopted state, for it was seldom occupied, although furnished in the worst style of the late seventies and early eighties. Mrs. Stratton and her daughter spent the greater part of their time in Europe. As Judge Stratton disliked his wife, was intensely ambitious for his only child, and preferred the comforts of his smaller home on The Flat, he rarely recalled his legitimate family, and made them a lavish allowance. He died abruptly of apoplexy, and left nothing but a life insurance of five thousand dollars; he had neglected to take out any until his blood vessels were too brittle for a higher risk.

Mrs. Stratton promptly became an invalid, and Ora brought her home to Butte, hoping to save something from the wreck. There was nothing to save. As she had not known of the life insurance when they received the curt cablegram in Paris, she had sold all of her mother's jewels save a string of pearls, and, when what was left of this irrelative sum after the luxurious journey over sea and land, was added to the policy, the capital of these two still bewildered women represented little more than they had been accustomed to spend in six months. When Mark Blake, who had studied law in Judge Stratton's office after graduating from the High School, and now seemed to be in a fair way to inherit the business, besides being County Attorney at the moment, implored Ora to marry him, and manifested an almost equal devotion to her mother, whom he had ranked with the queens of history books since boyhood, she accepted him as the obvious solution of her problem.

She was lonely, disappointed, mortified, a bit frightened. She had lived the life of the average American princess, and although accomplished had specialised in nothing; nor given a thought to the future. As she had cared little for the society for which her mother lived, and much for books, music, and other arts, and had talked eagerly with the few highly specialised men she was fortunate enough to meet, she had assumed that she was clever. She also believed that when she had assuaged somewhat her appetite for the intellectual and artistic banquet the gifted of the ages had provided, she might develop a character and personality, possibly a gift of her own. But she was only twenty when her indulgent father died, and, still gorging herself, was barely interested in her capacities other than receptive, less still in the young men that sought her, unterrified by her reputation for brains. She fancied that she should marry when she was about twenty-eight, and have a salon somewhere; and the fact that love had played so little a part in her dreams made it easier to contemplate marriage with this old friend of her childhood. His mother had been Mrs. Stratton's seamstress, to be sure, but as he was a good boy,—he called for the frail little woman every evening to protect her from roughs on her long walk east to the cottage her husband had built shortly before he was blown to pieces somewhere inside of Butte—he had been permitted to hold the dainty Ora on his knee, or toss her, gurgling with delight, into the air until he puffed.

Mark had been a fat boy, and was now a fat young man with a round rosy face and a rolling lazy gait. He possessed an eye of remarkable shrewdness, however, was making money rapidly, never lost sight of the main chance, and was not in the least surprised when his marriage lifted him to the pinnacle of Butte society. In spite of his amiable weaknesses, he was honest if sharp, an inalienable friend, and he made a good husband according to his lights. Being a man's man, and naturally elated at his election to the exclusive Silver Bow Club soon after his marriage to the snow maiden of his youthful dreams, he formed the habit of dropping in for a game of billiards every afternoon on his way home, and returning for another after dinner. But within three years he was able to present the wife of whom he was inordinately proud with a comfortable home on the West Side, and he made her an allowance of ever increasing proportions.

Ora, who had her own idea of a bargain, had never complained of neglect nor intimated that she found anything in him that savoured of imperfection. She had accepted him as a provider, and as he filled this part of the contract brilliantly, she felt that to treat him to scenes whose only excuse was outraged love or jealousy, would be both unjust and absurd. Moreover, his growing passion for his club was an immense relief after his somewhat prolonged term of marital uxoriousness, and as her mother died almost coincidentally with the abridgment of Mr. Blake's home life, Ora returned to her studies, rode or walked for hours, and, after her double period of mourning was over, danced two or three times a week in the season, or sat out dances when she met a man that had cultivated his intellect. For women she cared little.

It never occurred to Mark to be jealous of his passionless wife, although he would have asserted his authority if she had received men alone in the afternoon. But Ora paid a scrupulous deference to his wishes in all respects. She even taught herself to keep house, and her servants manners as well as the elements of edible cooking. This she regarded as her proudest feat, for she frankly hated the domestic details of life; although after three years in a "Block",—a sublimated lodging house, peculiar to the Northwest—she enjoyed the space and privacy of her home. Mark told his friends that his wife was the most remarkable woman in Montana, rarely found fault, save in the purely mechanical fashion of the married male, and paid the bills without a murmur. Altogether it was a reasonably happy marriage.

Ora Blake's attitude to life at this time was expressed in the buoyancy of her step, the haughty carriage of her head, the cool bright casual glance she bestowed upon the world in general. Her code of morals, ethics, manners, as well as her acceptance of the last set of conditions she would have picked from the hands of Fate, was summed up in two words: *noblesse oblige*. Of her depths she knew as little as Gregory Compton of his.

"This is Mrs. Compton, I am sure," she said in her cool even voice, as she came up behind the elaborately unconscious and humming Ida. "I am Mrs. Blake."

"Pleased to meet you," said Ida formally, extending a limp hand. "Come on inside."

Mrs. Blake closed her eyes as she entered the parlour, but opened them before Ida had adjusted the blower to the grate, and exclaimed brightly:

"How clever of you to settle so quickly. I shouldn't have dared to call for another fortnight, but Mr. Compton told my husband yesterday that you were quite in order. It was three months before I dared open my doors."

"Well," drawled Ida, rocking herself, "I guess your friends are more critical than mine. And I guess you didn't rely wholly on Butte for your furniture. I had Ma's old junk, and the rest cost me just two hundred dollars."

"How very clever of you!" But although Mrs. Blake was doing her best to be spontaneous and impressed, Ida knew instantly that she had committed a solecism, and felt both angry and apprehensive. She was more afraid of this young woman than of her professor. Once more she wished that Mrs. Blake and the whole caboodle would leave her alone till she was good and ready.

Ora hastened on to a safer topic, local politics. Butte, tired of grafting politicians, was considering the experiment of permitting a Socialist of good standing to be elected mayor. Ida, like all women of the smaller Western towns, was interested in local politics, and, glad of the impersonal topic, gave her visitor intelligent encouragement, the while she examined her critically. She finally summed her up in the word "pasty", and at that stage of Ora Blake's development the description was not inapt. She took little or no interest in her looks, although she dressed well by instinct; and nature, supplemented by her mother, had given her style. But her hair was almost colourless and worn in a tight knot just above her neck, her complexion was weatherbeaten, her lips rather pale, and her body very thin. But when men whose first glance had been casual turned suddenly, wondering at themselves, to examine that face so lacking in the potencies of colouring, they discovered that the eyes, deeply set and far apart, were of a deep dark blazing grey, that the nose was straight and fine, the ears small, the mouth mobile, with a slight downward droop at the corners; also that her hands and feet were very slender, with delicate wrists and ankles. Ida, too, noted these points, but wondered where her "charm" came from. She knew that Mrs. Blake possessed this vague but desirable quality, in spite of her dread reputation as a "high-brow", and her impersonal attitude toward men.

Ruby had informed her that the men agreed she had charm if she would only condescend to exert it. "And I can feel it too," she had added, "every time I do her nails—she never lets anyone do that hair of hers or give her a massage, which she needs, the Lord knows. But she's got fascination, magnetism, whatever you like to call it, for all she's so washed out. Somehow, I always feel that if she'd wake up, get on to herself, she'd play the devil with men, maybe with herself."

Ida recalled the comments of the wise Miss Miller and frowned. This important feminine equipment she knew to be her very own, and although she would have been proud to admit the rivalry of a beautiful woman, she felt a sense of mortification in sharing that most subtle and fateful of all gifts, sex-magnetism, with one so colourless and plain. That the gifts possessed by this woman talking with such well-bred indifference of local affairs must be far more subtle than her own irritated her still more. It also filled her with a vague sense of menace, almost of helplessness. Later, when her brain was more accustomed to analysis, she knew that she had divined—her consciousness at that time too thick to formulate the promptings of instinct—that when man is taken unawares he is held more firmly captive.

Ida, staring into those brilliant powerful eyes, felt a sudden desperate need to dive through their depths into this woman's secret mind, to know her better at once, get rid of the sense of mystery that baffled and oppressed her. In short she must know where she was at and know it quick. It did not strike her until afterward as odd that she should have felt so intensely personal in regard to a woman whose sphere was not hers and whose orbit had but just crossed her own.

For a time she floundered, but feminine instinct prompted the intimate note.

"I saw you talkin'—talking to the professor," she said casually. "I suppose you know your husband got him for me."

"I arranged it myself—" began Mrs. Blake, smiling, but Ida interrupted her sharply:

"Greg—Mr. Compton didn't tell me he had talked to you about it."

"Nor did he. I have had the pleasure of meeting Mr. Compton but once—the day I married; he was my husband's best man. Mark never can get him to come to the house, hardly to the club. But my husband naturally would turn over such a commission to me. I hope you found the little professor satisfactory."

"He'll do, I guess. He knows an awful lot, and I have a pretty good memory. But to get—and practice—it all —well, I guess that takes years." She imbued her tones with a pathetic wistfulness, and gazed upon her visitor with ingenuous eyes, brimming with admiration. "It must be just grand to have got all that education, and to have lived in Europe while you were growing up. Nothing later on that you can get is the same, I guess. You look just about as polished off as I look raw."

"Oh! No! No!" cried Ora deprecatingly, her cheeks flooding with a delicate pink that made her look very young and feminine. She had begun by disliking this dreadfully common person, but not only was she by no means as innocent of vanity as she had been trying for years to believe, but she was almost emotionally swift to respond to the genuine appeal. And, clever as she was, it was not difficult to delude her.

"Of course I had advantages that I am grateful for, but I have a theory that it is never too late to begin. And you are so young—a few months of our professor— are you really ambitious?"

"You bet." Ida committed herself no further at the moment.

"Then you will enjoy study—expanding and furnishing your mind. It is a wonderful sensation!" Mrs. Blake's eyes were flashing now, her mouth was soft, her strong little chin with that cleft which always suggests a whirlpool, was lifted as if she were drinking. "The mo-

ment you are conscious that you are using the magic keys
to the great storehouses of the world, its arts, its sciences,
its records of the past—when you begin to help yourself
with both hands and pack it away in your memory—always
something new—when you realise that the store is inexhaustible—that in study at least there is no ennui—Oh,
I can give you no idea of what it all means—you will find
it out for yourself!''

"Jimminy!" thought Ida. "I guess not! But that ain't
where her charm for men comes from, you bet!" Aloud
she said, with awe in her voice:

"No wonder you know so much when you like it like
that. But don't it make you—well—kinder lonesome?"

"Sometimes—lately——" Mrs. Blake pulled herself up
with a deep blush. "It has meant everything to me, that
mental life, and it always shall!"

The astute Ida noted the defiant ring in her voice, and
plunged in. "I wonder now? Say, you're a pretty woman
and a young one, and they say men would go head over
ears about you if you'd give 'em a show. You've got a
busy husband and so have I. Husbands don't companion
much and you can't make me believe learning's all. Don't
you wish these American Turks of husbands would let us
have a man friend occasionally? They say that in high
society in the East and in Europe, the women have all
the men come to call on them afternoons they like, but the
ordinary American husband, and particularly out West—
Lord! When a woman has a man call on her, she's about
ready to split with her husband—belongs to the fast set—
and he's quail hunting somewheres else. Of course I've
known Mark all my life—and you who was—were brought
up in the real world—it must be awful hard on you.
Wouldn't you like to try your power once in a while, see
how far you could go—just for fun? I guess you're not
shocked?"

"No, I'm not shocked," said Ora, laughing. "But I
don't believe men interest me very much in that way—
although, heaven knows, there are few more delightful
sensations than talking to a man who makes you feel as
if your brain were on fire. I don't think I care to have
American men, at least, become interested in me in any
other way. In Europe——" She hesitated, and Ida
leaned forward eagerly.

"Oh, do tell me, Mrs. Blake! I don't know a blamed thing. I've never been outside of Montana."

"Well—I mean—the American man takes love too seriously. I suppose it is because he is so busy—he has to take life so seriously. He specialises intensely. It is all or nothing with him. Of course I am talking about love. When they play about, it is generally with a class of women of which we have no personal knowledge. The European, with his larger leisure, and generations of leisure in his brain, his interest in everything, and knowledge of many things,—above all of the world,—has reduced gallantry to a fine art. He may give his fancy, his sentiment, his passion, even his leisure, to one woman at a time, but his heart—well, unless he is very young—that remains quite intact. Love is the game of his life with a change of partner at reasonable intervals. In other words he is far too accomplished and sophisticated to be romantic. Now, your American man, although he looks the reverse of romantic, and is always afraid of making a fool of himself, when he does fall in love with a woman—say, across a legal barrier—must annihilate the barrier at once; in other words, elope or rush to the divorce court. It isn't that he is more averse from a liaison than the European, but more thorough. It is all or nothing. In many respects he is far finer than the European, but he makes for turmoil, and, less subtle, he fails to hold our interest."

"You mean he don't keep us guessing? Well, you're right about most of them. I never saw a boy I couldn't read like a page ad., until I met my husband. I thought I knew him, too, till I'd been married to him awhile. But, my land, he gets deeper every minute. I guess if I hadn't married him he'd have kidnapped me, he was that gone, and forgetting anything else existed. Of course, I didn't expect that to last, but I did think he'd go on being transparent. But, believe me, the Sphinx ain't a patch on him. I sometimes think I don't know him at all, and that keeps me interested."

"I should think it might!" exclaimed Mrs. Blake, thinking of her own standard possession. "But then Mr. Compton is a hard student, and is said to have a voracious as well as a brilliant mind. No doubt that is the secret of what appears on the surface as complexity and secretiveness. I know the symptoms!"

"P'raps. But—well, I live with him, and I suspicion otherwise. I suspect him of having as many kind of leads, and cross-cuts, and 'pockets', and veins full of different kinds of ore in him as we've got right under our feet in Butte Hill. Do you think"—she spoke with a charming wistfulness—'that when I know more, have opened up and let out my top story, as it were, I shall understand him better?"

And again Ora responded warmly, "Indeed, yes, dear Mrs. Compton. It isn't so much what you put into your mind—it's more the reflex action of that personal collection in developing not only the mental faculties, but one's intuitions, one's power to understand others—even one whose interests are different, or whose knowledge is infinitely greater than our own."

"I believe you could even understand Greg!" Ida spoke involuntarily and stared with real admiration at the quickened face with its pink cheeks and flashing eyes, its childish mobile mouth. Ora at the moment looked beautiful. Suddenly Ida felt as if half-drowned in a wave of ambiguous terror. She sat up very straight.

"I guess you're right," she said slowly. "You've made me see it as the others haven't. I'll work at all that measly little professor gives me, but—I don't know—somehow, I can't think he'll do much more than make me talk decent. There's nothing *to* him."

Ora's heart beat more quickly. Her indifference had vanished in this intimate hour, also her first subtle dislike of Ida, who's commonness now seemed picturesque, and whose wistful almost complete ignorance had made a strong appeal to her sympathies. For the first time in her lonely life she felt that she had something to give. And here was raw and promising material ready and eager to be woven, if not into cloth of silver, at least into a quality of merchandise vastly superior to that which the rude loom of youth had so far produced. All she knew of Gregory Compton, moreover, made her believe in and admire him; the loneliness of his mental life with this woman appalled her. This was not the first time she had been forced to admit of late that under the cool bright surface of her nature were more womanly impulses than formerly, a spontaneous warmth that was almost like the quickening of a child; but she had turned from the consciousness with an impatient: "What nonsense! What on earth should I do with it?" The sense that she was of no vital use to anyone had discouraged her, dimmed her interest in her studies. Her husband could hire a better housekeeper, find a hundred girls who would companion him better, And what if she were *instruite?* So were thousands of women. Nothing was easier.

But this clever girl of the people, who might before many years had passed be one of the rich and conspicuous women of the United States, above all, the wife of one of the nation's "big men," working himself beyond human capacity, harassed, needing not only physical comfort at home, but counsel, companionship, perfect understanding,—might it not be her destiny to equip Ida Compton for her double part? Ora's imagination, the most precious and the most dangerous of her gifts, was at white heat. To her everlasting credit would be the fashioning of a helpmate for one of her country's great men. It would be enough to do as much for the state which her imperfect father had loved so passionately; but her imagination would not confine Gregory Compton within the limitations of a state. It was more than likely that his destiny would prove to be national; and she had seen the wives of certain men eminent in political Washington, but of obscure origin. They were Ida's mannered, grooved, crystallised; women to flee from.

She leaned forward and took Ida's hand in both of hers. "Dear Mrs. Compton!" she exclaimed. "Do let me teach you what little I know. I mean of art—history —the past—the present—I have portfolios of beautiful photographs of great pictures and scenes that I collected for years in Europe. It will do me so much good to go over them. I haven't had the courage to look at them for years. And the significant movements, social, political, religious,—all this theft under so many different names,— Christian Science, the 'Uplift' Movement, Occultism— from the ancient Hindu philosophy—it would be delightful to go into it with some one. I am sure I could make it all most interesting to you."

"My Gorrd!" thought Ida. "Two of 'em! What am I let in for?" But the undefined sharp sense of terror lingered, and she answered when she got her breath,

"I'd like it first rate. The work in this shack is nothing. Mr. Compton leaves first thing in the morning, and don't show up till nearly six. The professor's coming for an hour every other afternoon. But if I go to your house I want it understood that I don't meet anyone else. I've got my reasons.''

"You shall not meet a soul. Can't you imagine how sick I am of Butte? We'll have heavenly times. I was wondering only the other day of what use was all this heterogeneous mass of stuff I'd put into my head. But,'' she added gaily, "I know now it was for you to select from. I am so glad. And—and——'' Her keen perceptions suggested a more purely feminine bait. "You were with Madame O'Reilley, were you not? I get my things from a very good dressmaker in New York. Perhaps you would like to copy some of them?''

"Aw! Would I?'' Ida gasped and almost strangled. For the first time during this the most trying day of her life she felt wholly herself. "You may just bet your life I would. I need new duds the worst way, even if I'm not a West Sider. I've been on a ranch for nearly a year and a half, and although Mr. Compton won't take me to any balls, there are the movin' pictures and the mats— matinées; *and* the street, where I have to show up once in a while! I used to think an awful lot of my looks and style, and I guess it's time to begin again. I can sew first rate, make any old thing. Do you mean it?''

"Indeed I do! I *want* to be of help to you in every way.'' She rose and held Ida's hand once more in hers, although she did not kiss her as another woman might have done. "Will you come to-morrow—about two?''

"You may bet your bottom dollar I'll come. I haven't thanked you, but maybe I'll do that some other way.''

"Oh, I shouldn't wonder,'' said Mrs. Blake lightly.

IX

BUTTE, "the richest hill in the world" (known at a period when less famous for metals and morals as "Perch of the Devil"), is a long scraggy ridge of granite and red and grey dirt rising abruptly out of a stony uneven plain high in the Rocky Mountains. The city is scooped out of its south slope, and overflows upon The Flat. Big Butte, an equally abrupt protuberance, but higher, steeper, more symmetrical, stands close beside the treasure vault, but with the aloof and somewhat cynical air of even the apocryphal volcano. On all sides the sterile valley heaves away as if abruptly arrested in a throe of the monstrous convulsion that begat it; but pressing close, cutting the thin brilliant air with its icy peaks, is an irregular and nearly circular chain of mountains, unbroken white in winter, white on the blue enamelled slopes in summer.

For nearly half the year the whole scene is white, with not a tree, nor, beyond the straggling town itself, a house to break its frozen beauty. It is only when the warm Chinook wind roars in from the west and melts the snow much as lightning strikes, or when Summer herself has come, that you realize the appalling surface barrenness of this region devastated for many years by the sulphur and arsenic fumes of ore roasted in the open or belching from the smelters. They ate up the vegetation, and the melting snows and heavy June rains washed the weakened earth from the bones of valley and mountain, leaving both as stark as they must have been when the earth ceased to rock and began to cool. Since the smelters have gone to Anaconda, patches of green, of a sad and timid tenderness, like the smile of a child too long neglected, have appeared between the sickly grey boulders of the foothills, and, in Butte, lawns as large as a tablecloth have been cultivated. Anaconda Hill at the precipitous eastern end of the city, with its tangled mass of smokestacks, gallows-

frames, shabby grey buildings, trestles, looks like a gigan-
tic shipwreck, but is merely the portal to the precious ore
bodies of the mines whose shafts, levels, and cross-cuts to
the depth of three thousand feet and more, pierce and
ramify under city and valley. These hideous buildings
through which so many hundreds of millions have passed,
irrupt into the very back yards of some of the homes, built
too far east (and before mere gold and silver gave place to
copper) ; but the town improves as it leaps westward.
The big severe solid buildings to be found in every modern city sure of its stability crowd the tumble-down wood
structures of a day when no man looked upon Butte as
aught but a camp. And although the streets are vocifer-
ously cobbled, the pavements are civilised here and there.

Farther west the houses of the residence section grow
more and more imposing, coinciding with the sense of
Butte's inevitableness. On the high western rim of the
city (which exteriorly has as many ups and downs as
the story of its vitals) stands the red School of Mines.
It has a permanent expression of surprise, natural to a
bit of Italian renaissance looking down upon Butte.

Some of the homes, particularly those of light pressed
brick, and one that looks like the northeast corner of the
upper story of a robber stronghold of the middle ages, are
models of taste and not too modest symbols of wealth; but
north and south and east and west are the snow wastes
in winter and the red or grey untidy desert of sand and
rock in summer.

But if Butte is the ugliest city in the United States, she
knows how to make amends. She is alive to her finger tips.
Her streets, her fine shops, her hotels, her great office
buildings, are always swarming and animated. At no time,
not even in the devitalised hours that precede the dawn,
does she sink into that peace which even a metropolis wel-
comes. She has the jubilant expression of one who coins
the very air, the thin, sparkling, nervous air, into shining
dollars, and, confident in the inexhaustible riches beneath
her feet, knows that she shall go on coining them for ever.
Even the squads of miners, always, owing to the three
shifts, to be seen on the street corners, look satisfied and
are invariably well-dressed. Not only do these mines with
their high wages and reasonable hours draw the best class
of workingmen, but there are many college men in them,

many more graduates from the High Schools of Montana. The "Bohunks," or "dark men," an inferior class of Southern Europeans, who live like pigs and send their wages home, rarely if ever are seen in these groups.

And if Butte be ugly, hopelessly, uncompromisingly ugly, her compensation is akin to that of many an heiress: she never forgets that she is the richest hill in the world. Even the hard grip of the most unassailable trust in America, which has absorbed almost as much of Montana's surface as of its hidden treasure, does not interfere with her prosperity or supreme complacency. And although she has her pestilential politicians, her grafters and crooks, and is so tyrannically unionized that the workingman groans under the yoke of his brother and forgets to curse the trust, yet ability and talent make good as always; and in that electrified city of permanent prosperity there is a peculiar condition that offsets its evils: it is a city of sudden and frequent vacancies. New York, Europe, above all, California, swarm with former Montanans, particularly of Butte, who have coppered their nests, and transplanted them with a still higher sense of achievement.

Ora was thinking of Butte and the world beyond Butte, as she splashed along through the suddenly melted snow toward her home on the West Side. The Chinook, loud herald from Japan, had swept down like an army in the night and turned the crisp white streets to rivers of mud. But Ora wore stout walking boots, and her short skirt, cut by a master hand, was wide enough to permit the impatient stride she never had been able to modify in spite of her philosophy and the altitude. She walked several miles a day and in all weathers short of a blizzard; but not until the past few weeks with the admission that her increasing restlessness, her longing for Europe, was growing out of bonds. She wondered to-day if it were Europe she wanted, or merely a change.

She had, of course, no money of her own, and never had ceased to be grateful that her husband's prompt and generous allowance made it unnecessary to ask alms of him. Three times since her marriage he had suddenly presented her with a checque for several hundred dollars and told her to "give her nerves a chance" either down "on the coast," or in New York. She had always fled to New York, remained a month or six weeks, gone day and night to opera, theatre, concerts, art exhibitions, not forgetting her tailor and dressmaker; returning to Butte as refreshed as if she had taken her heart and nerves, overworked by the altitude, down to the poppy fields of Southern California.

Her vacations and her husband's never coincided. Mark always departed at a moment's notice for Chicago or New York, alleging pressing business. He returned, after equally pressing delays, well, complacent, slightly apologetic.

Ora knew that she had but to ask permission to spend the rest of the winter in New York, for not only was Mark the most indulgent of husbands, but he was proud of his wife's connections in the American Mecca, not unwilling to read references in the Butte newspapers to her sojourn among them. The "best people" of these Western towns rarely have either friends or relatives in the great cities of the East. The hardy pioneer is not recruited from the aristocracies of the world, and the dynamic men and women that have made the West what it is have the blood of the old pioneers in them.

Ora was one of the few exceptions. Her father had been the last of a distinguished line of jurists unbroken since Jonathan Stratton went down with Alexander Hamilton in the death struggle between the Federal and the new Republican party. Ora's mother, one of New York's imported beauties for a season, who had languished theretofore on the remnants of a Louisiana plantation, impecunious and ambitious, but inexperienced and superficially imaginative, married the handsome and brilliant lawyer for love, conceiving that it would be romantic to spend a few years in a mining camp, where she, indubitably, would be its dominant lady. Butte did not come up to her ideas of romance. Nor had she found it possible to dislodge the passively determined women with the pioneer blood in their veins. The fumes afflicted her delicate lungs, the altitude her far more delicate nerves. Judge Stratton deposited her in the drawing-room of an eastern bound train with increasing relish. Had it not been for his little girl he would have bade her upon the second or third of these migrations to establish herself in Paris and return no more.

During these long pilgrimages Ora, even while attending school in New York, Paris, Berlin, Rome, Vevey, had

seen something of society, for Mrs. Stratton was ever surrounded by it, and did not approve of the effect of boarding school diet on the complexion.   But the ardours of her
mind, encouraged always by her father, who never was too
busy to write to her, had made her indifferent to the advantages prized by Mrs. Stratton.

To-day she was conscious of a keen rebellious desire for
something more frivolous, light, exciting, than had entered her life for many a year.   There can be little variety
and no surprises in the social life of a small community—
for even scandal and divorce grow monotonous—and although she could always enjoy an hour's intellectual companionship with the professors of the School of Mines,
whenever it pleased her to summon them, Ora, for the first
time in her twenty-six years, had drifted into a condition
of mind where intellectual revels made no appeal to her
whatever.

She had wondered before this if her life would have
been purely mental had her obligations been different,
but had dismissed the thought as not only dangerous but
ungrateful.   She had reason to go on her knees to her
intellect, its ambitions and its furniture, for without it
life would have been insupportable.   She ordered her
quickening ego back to the rear, or the depths, or wherever
it bided its time, none too amenable; she was only beginning to guess the proportions it might assume if encouraged; the vague phantoms floating across her mind,
will-o'-the-wisps in a fog bank, frightened her.   Several
months since she had set her lips, and her mind the task
of acquiring the Russian language.   It had always been
her experience that nothing compared with a new language
as a mental usurper.

She had entered into a deliberate partnership with a
man who protected and supported her, and she would keep
the letter, far as its spirit might be beyond the reach of
her will.   Even were she to become financially independent,
it was doubtful if she would leave him for a long period;
and for New York and its social diversions she cared not
at all.   What she wanted was adventure—she stumbled on
the word, and stopped with a gasp.   Adventure.   For the
first time she wished she were a man.   She would pack two
mules with a prospector's outfit and disappear into the
mountains.

She swung her mind to the Russian grammar, enough
to impale it in the death agony; but when she had entered
her home, and, after a visit to her leisurely cook, who was
a unionized socialist, ascended to her bedroom and stood
before her mirror, she decided that it was her singular
interview with the wife of Gregory Compton that had
thrown her mind off its delicate balance. She recalled
that Mrs. Compton—certainly an interesting creature in
spite of her appalling commonness—had told her fla-
grantly that she was young, pretty, and attractive to men,
even as are young and pretty women without too much
brains. The compliment—or was it the suggestion?—
had thrilled her, and it thrilled her again. Men sometimes
had tried to make love to her, but she had ascribed such
charm as she appeared to possess to the automatically
vibrating magnet of youth; and although she had never
been above a passing flirtation, either in her mother's salon
or in Butte, she merely had been bored if the party of
the other part had taken his courage in his hands on the
morrow. Scruples did not trouble her. The American
woman, she would have reasoned, is traditionally "cold."
American men, brought up on her code of ethics, are able
to take care of themselves.

Had she been superficial in her conclusions? Could she
attract men more potently than by a merely girlish charm
and a vivacious mind? Her memory ran rapidly over
the functions of the winter, particularly the dinners and
dances. She could not recall a passing conquest. She was
angry to feel herself shiver, but she jerked off her hat, and
the pins out of her fine abundant hair. She was twenty-six.
Had she gone off? Faded? She never had been called a
beauty, never had had the vanity to think herself a beauty,
but she remembered that sometimes in an animated company she had glanced into the passing mirror and thought
herself quite pretty, with her pink cheeks and sparkling
eyes. But normally she was too washed-out for beauty,
however good her features might be, and of course she had
no figure at all. She dressed well from force of habit, and
she had the carriage at least to set off smartly cut gar-
ments, but as much might be said of a dressmaker's
"form."

And her skin was sallow and sunburned and weatherbeaten and dry, as any neglected skin in a high altitude **is**

sure to be. Once it had been as white as her native snows. Her hair, also the victim of the high dry air, and exposed to the elements for hours together, was more colourless than Nature had made it—dull—dead. She held out a strand in dismay, remembering how her *cendré* hair had been admired in Paris; then with a sudden sense of relief (it escaped from the cellar where her ego was immured on bread and water) she informed herself that it was her duty to invoke the services of Miss Ruby Miller. No woman with proper pride—or self-respect—would let her skin go to pot, no, not at any age; certainly not at twenty-six. She recalled an impulsive remark of Miss Miller's a few months since when arranging her hair for a fancy-dress ball, and gave another sigh—of hope.

So does Nature avenge herself.

X

SHE heard her husband's voice as he entered the house, and hastily changed her walking suit for one of the soft tea gowns she wore when they were alone. This was a simple thing of a Copenhagen-blue silk, with a guimpe of fine white net, and trimmed about the neck and half sleeves with the newest and softest of the year's laces. She noticed with some satisfaction that her neck, below the collar line, was very white; and she suddenly covered the rest of it with powder, then rubbed the puff over her face. It was ordinary "baby powder" for the bath, for she never had indulged in toilet accessories, but it answered its purpose, if only to demonstrate what she might have been had she safeguarded the gifts of nature. And the dull blue gown was suddenly becoming.

Her husband, who had spent the intervening time in the library, ran upstairs whistling in spite of his girth—he was the lightest dancer in Butte—and knocked on her door before going to his own room.

"Say," he said, as he chucked her under the chin, and kissed her maritally, "but you look all right. Run down stairs and hold your breath until I've made myself beautiful. I've got big news for you."

She rustled softly down the stair, wondering what the news might be, but not unduly interested. Mark was always excited over his new cases. Perhaps he had been retained by Amalgamated. She hoped so. He deserved it, for he worked harder than anyone knew. And she liked him sincerely, quite without mitigation now that the years had taught him the folly of being in love with her.

And he certainly had given her a pretty home. The house was not large enough to be pointed out by the conductor of the "Seeing Butte Car," but it had been designed by a first rate architect, and had a certain air of spaciousness within. Mrs. Stratton had furnished a flat in Paris two years before her husband's death, her excuse

63

being that the interior of the Butte house got on her nerves, and there was no other way to take in household goods free of duty. Ora had shipped them when the news of her father's death and their own poverty came, knowing that she would get a better price for the furniture in Butte, where some one always was building, than in Paris.

Before it arrived she had made up her mind to marry Mark Blake, and although it was several years before they had a house she kept it in storage. In consequence her little drawing-room with its gay light formal French furniture was unique in Butte, city of substantial and tasteful (sometimes) but quite unindividual homes. Mark was thankful that he was light of foot, less the bull in the china shop than he looked, and would have preferred red walls, an oriental divan and Persian rugs. He felt more at home in the library, a really large room lined from floor to ceiling not only with Ora's but Judge Stratton's books, which Mark had bought for a song at the auction; and further embellished with deep leather chairs and several superb pieces of carved Italian furniture. Ora spent the greater part of her allowance on books, and many hours of her day in this room. But to-night she deliberately went into the frivolous French parlour, turned on all the lights, and sat down to await her husband's reappearance.

Mark, who had taken kindly to the idea of dressing for dinner, came running down stairs in a few moments.

"In the doll's house?" he called out, as he saw the illumination in the drawing-room. "Oh, come on into a real room and mix me a cocktail."

"It isn't good for you to drink cocktails so long before eating; Huldah, who receives 'The People's War Cry' on Monday, informed me that dinner would be half an hour late."

"I wish you'd chuck that wooden-faced leaden-footed apology for a servant. This is the third time——"

"And get a worse? Butte rains efficient servants! Please sit down. I—*feel* like this room to-night. You may smoke."

"Thanks. I believe this is the first time you have given me permission. But I'm bound to say the room suits you."

Ora sat in a *chaise-longue* of the XVme Siècle, a piece of furniture whose awkward grace gives a woman's arts full scope. Much exercise had preserved the natural supple- ness of Ora's body and she had ancestral memories of all arts and wiles. Mark seated himself on the edge of a stiff little sofa covered with faded Aubusson tapestry, and hunched his shoulders.

"If the French women furnish their rooms like this I don't believe all that's said about them," he commented wisely. "Men like to be comfortable even when they're looking at a pretty woman."

"Mama let me choose the furniture for this room, and I wasn't thinking much about your sex at the time. I—I think it expressed a side of me that I wasn't con- scious of then."

"It's a pretty room all right." Mark lit the consolatory cigarette. "But not to sit in. What struck you to-night?"

"Oh, I'd been thinking of Paris."

Mark's face was large and round and bland; it was only when he drew his brows together that one saw how small and sharp his eyes were.

"H'm. I've wondered sometimes if you weren't hanker- ing after Europe. I suppose it gets into the blood."

"Oh, yes, it gets into the blood!" Ora spoke lightly, but she was astonished at his insight.

"I've never been able to send you—not as you were used to going—I don't see you doing anything on the cheap——"

"Oh, my dear Mark, you are goodness itself. I've thought very little about it, really."

"Suppose you found yourself suddenly rich, would you light out and leave me?"

"We'd go together. It would be great fun being your cicerone."

"No chance! I'm going to be a rich man inside the next ten years, and here I stick. And I don't see myself travelling on a woman's money, either. But I suppose you'd be like all the rest if you could afford it?"

"Oh, I don't know. Of course I look forward to spend- ing a year in Europe once more—I'd hardly be human if I didn't. But I can wait for you."

"I've always admired your philosophy," he said grimly. "And now I've got a chance to put it to a real test. I believe you are in a way, if not to be rich, at least to make a pretty good haul.''

"What do you mean?" Ora sat up straight.

"Your father made a good many wild-cat investments when he first came out here, and the one he apparently thought the worst, for I found no mention of it among his papers, was the Oro Fino Primo mine, which he bought from a couple of sharks in the year you were born— that's where you got your name, I guess. One of the men was a well known prospector and the Judge thought he was safe. The ore assayed about eighty dollars a ton, so he took over the claim, paid the Lord knows how much to the prospector, who promptly lit out, had it patented, and set a small crew to work under a manager. They found nothing but low grade ore, which in those days roused about as much enthusiasm as country rock. The mine had been salted, of course. It was some time before your father would give up, and he spent more than the necessary amount of money to perfect the patent; always hoping. When he was finally convinced there was nothing in it he quit. And it was characteristic of your father that when he quit he quit for good. He simply dismissed the thing from his mind. Well, times have changed since then. New processes and more railroads have caused fortunes to be made out of low grade ore when there is enough of it. Some people would rather have a big lode of low grade ore than a pockety vein of rich quartz. As you know, abandoned mines are being leased all over the state, and abandoned prospect holes investigated. Well, there you are. This morning two mining engineers from New York came into my office with a tale of woe. They came out here to look about, and after considerable travel within a reasonable distance of railroads found an old prospect hole with a shaft sunk about fifty feet. It looked abandoned all right, but as the dump was still there and they liked the looks of it they went to the De Smet ranch house —the hole is just over the border of Greg's ranch—and made inquiries. Oakley, who is a monomaniac on the subject of intensive farming and doesn't know a mine from a gopher hole, told them that the adjacent land belonged to no one but the government. So they staked their claim, recorded it in Virginia City, retimbered the shaft and sank it twenty feet deeper. They began to take out ore that looked good for fifteen dollars a ton. Then along comes an old prospector and tells them the story of the mine. They leave their two miners on the job and post up to Helena to have the records examined in the Land Office. There, sure enough, they find that the mine was duly patented by Judge Stratton, and all of the government requirements complied with. So they come to me. They want a bond and lease for three years—which means they may have the privilege of buying at the end of the lease—and offer you ten per cent. on the net proceeds. I haven't given them my answer yet, for I'm going to take Greg out there next Sunday and have a look at it. There was a sort of suppressed get-rich-quickishness in their manner, and their offer was not what you would call munificent. Greg is a born geologist, to say nothing of his training. I don't mean so much in the School of Mines, but he was always gophering about with old prospectors, and ran away into the mountains several times when his father was alive. Never showed up all summer. He's at ore now every spare moment he gets, and is as good an assayer as there is in the state. If there's mineral on his own ranch he'll find it, and if there isn't he'll find it elsewhere. So, I do nothing till he's looked the property over. But in any case I think I can promise you a good lump of money."

Ora's breath was short. Her face had been scarlet for a few moments but now showed quite pale under the tan and powder. When her husband finished, however, and she replied, "How jolly," her voice was quite steady.

"And shall you fly off and leave me if it pans out?"

"Of course not. What do you take me for?"

"To tell you the truth it will mean a good deal to me if you stay until the fall. I've a client coming out here from New York whom I am trying to persuade to buy the old Iron Hat mine. There's a fortune in it for anyone with money enough to spend rebuilding the old works and putting in new machinery and timbers; and a big rake-off for me, if I put the deal through. Well, this client figures to bring his wife and daughter, and you could help me a lot—persuade them they'd have the time of their lives if they spent several months of every year out here for a while—he's a domestic sort of man. After that take a flyer if you like. You deserve it."

"How nice of you! Here is dinner at last." Ora felt almost physically sick, so dazzling had been the sudden prospect of deliverance, followed by the certainty, even before her husband asked for the diplomatic assistance she so often had given him, that she could not take advantage of it. Noblesse oblige! For the moment she hated her watchword.

She mixed a cocktail with steady hand. "I'll indulge in a perfect orgie of clothes!" she said gaily. "And import a chef. By the way," she added, as she seated herself at the table and straightened the knives and forks beside her plate, "what do you think I let myself in for to-day?"

"Not been speculating? There's a quart of Worcestershire in this soup."

"I'll certainly treat you to a chef. No, not speculating —I wonder if it mightn't be that? I called on your friend's wife——"

"Good girl! She's not your sort, but she's Greg's wife——"

"I thought she was quite terrible at first, but I soon became interested. She's clever in her way, ignorant as she is, and has individuality. Before I knew it I had offered to take a hand in her education——"

"Good lord! What sort of a hand?"

"Oh, just showing her my portfolios, giving her some idea of art. It sounds very elemental, but one must begin somewhere. She knows so little that it will be like teaching a child a b c."

"I'm afraid it will bore you."

"No, I like the idea. It is something new, and change is good for the soul. I have an idea that I shall continue to find her as interesting as I intend she shall find the 'lessons'."

"She'll get more than lessons on art. She'll get a good tone down, and she needs that all right. Poor old Greg! He deserved the best and he got Ida Hook. I tried to head him off but I might as well have tried to head off a stampede to a new gold diggings. He ought to have married a lady, that's what."

Ora glanced up quickly, then, thankful that her husband was intent upon his carving, dropped her eyes. It was the first time he had ever hinted at the differences of class. In his boyhood there had been a mighty gulf between his

mother and the haughty Mrs. Stratton who employed her
in what was then the finest house in Butte. But he was
too thoroughly imbued with the spirit of the West, in
which he had spent his life, to recognise any difference in
class save that which was determined by income. As soon
as his own abilities, industry, and the turn of Fortune's
wheel, placed him in a position to offer support to the two
dainty women that had been his ideals from boyhood,
he knew himself to be their equal, without exhausting himself in analysis.

As for Ora, the West was quick in her blood, in spite
of her heritage and education. Her father had assumed
the virtue of democracy when he settled in Montana. In
the course of a few years a genuine liking and enthusiasm
for his adopted state, as well as daily associations, transformed him into as typical a Westerner as the West ever
turned out of her ruthless crucible. He even wore a Stet-
son hat when he visited New York. His wife's "airs" had
inspired him with an increasing disgust which was one of
the most honest emotions of his life, and the text of his repeated warnings to his daughter, whom he was forced to
leave to the daily guidance of his legal wife (Ora's continued presence in Butte, would, in truth, have caused
him much embarrassment), had been to cherish her Western birthright as the most precious of her possessions.

"Remember this is the twentieth century," he had written to her not long before his death. "There is no society
in the world to-day that cannot be invaded by a combination of money, brains, and a certain social talent—common enough. The modern man, particularly in the United
States, makes himself. His ancestors count for nothing,
if he doesn't. If he does they may be a good asset, for
they (possibly) have given him breeding ready made,
moral fibre, and a brain of better composition than the
average man of the people can expect. But that is only
by the way. The two most potent factors in the world
today are money and the waxing, rising, imperishable democratic spirit. That was reborn out here in the West, and
the West is invading and absorbing the East. The old un-
American social standards of the East are expiring in the
present generation, which resort to every absurdity to main-
tain them; its self-consciousness betraying its recognition
of the inevitable. Twenty years hence this class will be, if

still clinging to its spar, as much of a national joke as the Western women were when they first flashed their diamonds in Peacock Alley. That phase, you may notice, is so dead that the comic papers have forgotten it. The phase was inevitable, but our women are now so accustomed to their money that they are not to be distinguished from wealthy women anywhere except that their natural hospitality and independence make them seem more sure of themselves. Of course the innately vulgar are to be found everywhere, and nowhere more abundantly than in New York.

"Twenty years from now, the West will have overrun the East; it will have helped itself with both hands to all the older civilisation has to give, and it will have made New York as democratic as Butte—or London! So don't let yourself grow up with any old-fashioned nonsense in your head. I want you to start out in life modern to the core, unhampered by any of the obsolete notions that make your mother and most of our relations a sort of premature has-beens. When your time comes to marry, select a Western man who either has made his own fortune or has the ability to make it. Don't give a thought to his origin if his education is good, and his manners good enough. You can supply the frills. I wouldn't have you marry a man that lacked the fundamentals of education at least, but better that than one whose brain is so full of old-fashioned ideas that it has no room for those that are born every minute. And I hope you will settle here in this state and do something for it, either through the abilities of the man you marry or with your own. It isn't only the men that build up a new state. And if you marry a foreigner never let me see nor hear from you again. They are all very well in their way, but it is not our way."

Ora, who had worshipped her father and admired him above all men, never forgot a word he uttered, and knew his letters by heart. Possibly it was the memory of this last of his admonitions which had enabled her to sustain the shock of a proposal from the son of her mother's old seamstress and of a miner who had died in his overalls underground. It is doubtful if she would have been conscious of the shock had it not been for Mrs. Stratton's lamentations. That lady from her sofa in one of the humbler Blocks, had sent wail after wail in the direction of the impertinent aspirant. Ora, during the brief period in which she made her decision, heard so much about the "bluest blood of the South," and the titled foreigners whom she apparently could have had for the accepting when she was supposed to belong to the Millionaire Sisterhood, that she began to ponder upon the violent contrasts embodied in Mark with something like rapture. After the marriage was accomplished, Mrs. Stratton had the grace to wail in solitude, and shortly after moved on to a world where only the archangels are titled and never have been known to marry. Ora had not given the matter another thought. Mark had been carefully brought up by a refined little woman, his vicious tendencies had been negligible, and he was too keen to graduate from the High School and make his start in life to waste time in even the milder forms of dissipation. When he married he adapted himself imperceptibly to the new social world he entered; if not a Beau Brummel, nor an Admirable Crichton, he never would disgrace his aristocratic wife; and, unlike Judge Stratton, he wore a silk hat in New York.

His last remark apparently had been a mere vapour from his subconscious mind, for he went on as soon as he had taken the edge from his appetite, "Perhaps Ida Hook can be made into one. I've seen waitresses and chambermaids metamorphosed by a million or two so that their own husbands wouldn't recognise them if they stayed away too long. But it takes time, and Ida has an opinion of herself that would make an English duchess feel like a slag dump. Say—do you know it was through me Greg met her? It was that week you were out on the Kelley ranch. I met two or three of the old crowd on the street and nothing would do but that I should go to their picnic for the sake of old times. Greg was in town and I persuaded him to come along. Didn't want to, but I talked him over. Guess there's no escaping our fate. Possibly I couldn't have corralled him if it hadn't been for reaction—he'd been whooping it up on The Flat. Well, I wished afterward that I'd left him to play the wheel and all the rest of it for a while longer. Greg never loses his head—that is to say he never did till he met Ida Hook. The sporting life never took a hold on him, for while he went in for it with the deep deliberation that was born in him, it's just that deliberation that saves him from going too far. He cuts loose the minute he figured out beforehand to cut loose, and all the king's horses—or all the other attractions—couldn't make him put in another second. A girl shot herself one night out at the Five Mile House because he suddenly said good-bye and turned on his heel. She knew he meant it. He never even turned round when he heard her drop——"

"What a brute!"

"Greg? Not he. I've known him to sit up all night with a sick dog——"

"I hate people that are kind to animals and cruel to one another."

"Greg isn't cruel. He said he was going and he went; that's all. It's his way. Girls of that kind are trash, anyhow, and when a woman goes into the sporting life she knows enough to take sporting chances."

"You are as bad as he."

Mark stared at her in open-eyed amazement. He never had seen her really roused before. "Don't you bother your dear little head," he said soothingly. "Angels like you don't know anything about that sort of life—and don't need to."

Ora's anger vanished in laughter. "Well, suppose you give me a hint about his wife. I really am interested, and delighted at the prospect of being of some use in the world."

"You're all right! Ida—well, I guess you'll do a lot for her, by just having her round. She's no fool—and she certainly is a looker. If you tone her down and polish her up I'll feel it's a sort of favour to myself. Greg'll be one of the richest men in this country some day,—if he has to walk over a few thousand fellow citizens to get there—and I don't want to see him queered by a woman. Seen that before."

"I intend to do my best, but for her sake, not his——"

"Say!" It was patent that Mark had an inspiration. "Why not take Ida with you to Europe? I don't like the idea of a dainty little thing like you" (Ora was five feet six) "travelling alone, and a husky girl like Ida could take care of you while putting on a few coats of European polish. Greg can afford it; he must have cleared a good many thousands on his ranch during the last two years, besides what I've turned over for him; and he can live here with me and get all the comforts of home. I'll let you off for six months. What do you say?''

Ora was looking at him with pink cheeks and bright eyes. "You are sure you won't mind?''

"I'll miss you like fun, of course; especially when you look as pretty as you do this minute, but I think it would be a good thing for you and better for Ida—and I'll fire this cook.''

"Will Mr. Compton give his consent?''

"No one on God's earth would take chances on what Gregory Compton would do until he had done it, but I don't mind throwing a guess that he could live without Ida for six months and not ask me to dry his tears. And there isn't a mean bone in his body.''

"It would interest me immensely to take Mrs. Compton abroad. Now hurry if you expect to get a seat at one of the bridge tables. It is late——''

"I rather thought I'd like to stay and talk to you——''

"How polite of you! But I'm tired out and going straight to bed. So toddle along.''

XI

"TAILORED suits have to be made by a tailor, but I'd like first rate to copy this one you call a little afternoon frock. It's got the style all right, and I could get some cheap nice-looking stuff."

Ida was gloating over Ora's limited but fashionable wardrobe, and while she held the smart afternoon frock out at arm's length, her eye wandered to an evening gown of blue satin and chiffon that lay over the back of a chair.

"Glory!" she sighed. "But I'd like to wear a real gown like that. Low neck, short sleeves! I've got the neck and arms too, you bet——"

"Why not copy it?" Ora was full of enthusiasm once more. "You can do it here, and I have an excellent seamstress——"

"Where'd I wear a rig like that? Even if I made it in China silk and Greg took me anywheres, I couldn't. We don't go in for real low necks in our bunch."

"But surely you'll go to the Junior Prom?"

Ida opened her mouth as well as her eyes. "The Junior Prom? I never thought of it. Of course I'd be asked, Greg being in the Junior Class and all——"

"Naturally."

Ida frowned. "Well, I ain't going. I said I wouldn't go anywheres—to any swell blowouts, until I'm as big as anybody there."

"But the School of Mines is composed of young men of all classes. Each asks his friends. The Prom is anything but an exclusive affair. You go out to the Garden dances on Friday nights in summer?"

"Oh, in that jam—and everybody wearing their suits, or any old thing——"

"Well, I think you should go to the Prom. Mr. Compton is the star pupil in the School of Mines. The professors talk of no one else. I rather think your absence would cause comment."

"Well—maybe I'll go. I'd like to all right. But I can't wear low-neck. I guess you know it wouldn't do."

"No doubt you are right." Ora made no attempt at conversion; it was encouraging that Ida had certain inclinations toward good taste, even if they were prompted by expediency.

"Jimminy, but your room's pretty!" exclaimed Ida. "Mine's pink—but lawsy!"

She gazed about the room, which, although she never had seen the sea, recalled descriptions of its shells washed by its foam. She knit her brows. "I guess it takes experience, and seein' things," she muttered. Her eyes travelled to the little bed in one corner. It would have looked like a nun's, so narrow and inconspicuous was it, had it not been for its cover of pale pink satin under the same filmy lace.

"Sakes alive!" she exclaimed. "Don't you sleep with your husband?"

Ora was angry to feel herself coloring. She answered haughtily, "We have separate rooms. It is the custom— I mean—I have always seen——"

"I've heard it was the stunt among swells, but I don't hold to it. It's only at night that you've really got a chance to know where a man is; and the more rope you give him the more he'll take. What's to prevent Mark slippin' out when he thinks you're asleep? Or coming home any old time? Besides, some men talk in their sleep. That gives you another hold. I'm always hoping Greg will, as he talks so little when he's awake. You bet your life he never gets a room to himself."

"Poor Mr. Compton!" thought Ora. "I fancy he'll expiate." "Shall we go down stairs?" she asked. "I got my portfolios out this morning."

She tactfully had shown Ida her wardrobe first, and the guest descended to the library in high good humour. For an hour they hung over the contents of the Italian portfolios. Ida was enchanted with the castles and ruins, listened eagerly to the legends, and was proud of her own knowledge of the horrors enacted in the Coliseum. But over the photographs of the masterpieces in the Pitti and the Uffizi she frankly yawned.

"No more cross-eyed saints, and fat babies and shameless sporting women in mine," she announced. "Them virgins sitting on thrones, holding four-year-olds trying to look like six months, make me tired."

"Oh, well, I fancy you must see the old masters for the first time in their proper setting—and wonderful colouring——" Ora wondered if the masterpieces would appear somewhat overrated to herself if seen for the first time in Butte. It certainly was interesting to watch the effect of fixed standards—or superstitions—upon an untrained but remarkably sharp mind.

"That Last Supper looks like they'd been eating the paint," pursued Ida.

Ora laughed. "I shan't show you any more pictures to-day. This furniture is Italian—Florentine and Venetian. Let me tell you something about it."

"I'd like to see all your rooms." Ida rose and stretched herself luxuriously. Ora thought she looked like a beautiful Persian cat. "Houses interest me mor'n pictures, although I'll buy them too some day. Not old masters, though. They'd give me the willys. This carved oak with faded gilt panels is a dream!" she exclaimed with instant appreciation. "I'd learn wood-carving if there was anyone in this God-forsaken camp to teach it."

Ora clapped her hands, and once more to Ida's startled eyes she looked like a very young girl. "I studied several of the crafts when I was in Germany," she cried, "wood-carving, brass-hammering, enamelling. I'll set up a work-shop—let me see, the attic would be the best place, and the furnace warms it—and teach you, and work myself. It's just what I need. I wonder I never thought of it——"

"Need what?" interrupted Ida sharply.

"Oh, a relief from too much study. There's nothing like a craft for mental workers—I should have thought of it before," she repeated. "What do you say?"

"I'd like it first rate, and I guess you'll find me quick enough with my hands, whatever you think of my cocoa-nut."

"I think very highly of your cocoanut. This is my little drawing-room."

Ida stood on the threshold for a few moments without comment. She had never cast a thought to her Puritan inheritance, but anger, disapproval, possessed her. She hated the room, but had no reason to give.

"You don't like my favourite room?" asked Ora, who was watching her curiously.

"Is it your favourite room?" She turned this over.
"No, I guess I like the heavy, solid, durable things best."
She struggled for her reasons. "You get your money's
worth in them. This looks like the first Chinook would
blow it clear over into North Dakota, or as if you might
come in some morning and find a heap of dust where it
had been the night before—like a corpse when the air's
let in. I didn't mind your bedroom being dainty and
looking like some sea shells I saw once in a picture frame,—
it looks all of a piece, too, you might say; but this—with
them queer thin faded out chairs and sofas—the colours on
the wood even, and in them pictures over the doors and
mantel, look like they would do the final disappearing act
while you wait—well, there's something kinder mysterious
—ghostly—it looks so stiff—and—at the same time—so
kinder immoral——"

"I wonder if what you are groping for is the atmosphere of the past, which all old furniture must have, particularly if rearranged in something like its original setting." Ora was regarding her with a new interest. "This
furniture came out of a *hôtel*—what we would call a residence—with a history—several histories, I should think—
and I fancy it was all frivolous, and wicked, and exciting——"

"I ain't no spiritualist!" said Ida tartly. "Is that what
you're driving at?"

"I don't know that I was thinking of occultism, even,"
said Ora lightly. "But it is interesting to find these old
things have atmosphere for you as well as for me——"

"Why is it your favourite room? Because it has 'atmosphere'?"

"I don't know. I doubt if I have ever given the matter a thought."

'So this is your favourite room." Ida turned her back
on it. "H'm. Well, maybe I'll understand some things
better one of these days than I do now. Perhaps," with
one of her uncanny flashes of intuition, "I'll understand it
when I do you."

"Let us go up to the attic and look it over. I'll have
the table and benches made to-morrow." Something was
moving toward expression in her own mind, but she flung it
aside and ran up the stair followed by Ida, who dismissed
the subject as promptly.

XII

THERE had been a good deal of haggling over the lease of the Oro Fino Primo mine, the engineers demanding a three years' lease and bond, proposing to purchase it at the end of that period for fifty thousand dollars. Nor were they willing to pay more than ten per cent. in royalty, displaying the assay report on the ore and arguing that after the necessary outlay on development work, the ore body might be too small to repay them.

Mark, however, was determined not to close with them until he had visited the claim with Gregory Compton, and this proved to be impossible for several weeks. The engineers, unable to proceed, had dismissed their men. They threatened to withdraw their offer and look for another abandoned property. Mark told them to go ahead, and they remained in Butte.

In the course of a month Mark and Gregory were both free on a Sunday. They took a train for Pony, hired a rig and drove over to the Stratton claim, dignified by the name of mine.

The claim was on a small table-land between Gregory's own hill, which terminated just beyond the borders of his ranch, and another slope covered with pines and firs. The engineers had put up a windlass, retimbered the shaft, sunk it twenty feet lower, and added a pile of dirty looking ore to the original half-obliterated heap about the collar of the shaft.

Gregory picked up half a dozen pieces of various sizes and examined them. "Their assay was about right, I should think," he said. "Looks like good low grade ore, but not too good. It will do no harm to assay it myself, however," and he dropped the sample into the pocket of his coat. Suddenly he gave a startled exclamation, and Mark saw his nostrils dilate, his nose almost point, as he darted forward and kicked aside a heap of loosely piled quartz.

78

Then he knelt down and lifted out several lumps of greyish-black ore.

"What is it?" asked Mark curiously, and feeling something of the excitement of the hunter whose gun is trained on a bear. "D'you mean they've found copper glance?"

"At a depth of sixty feet? Not exactly. This is a basic igneous rock called pyroxenite, that may not be rich in gold but is more than likely to be—particularly as our friends have hidden it so carefully and said nothing about it. It may assay anywhere from ten dollars a ton to five hundred. I'm going down."

The shaft was inclined, four by eight, and timbered with lagging. Gregory lit the candle he had brought and descended the ladder. He remained below about ten minutes; when he returned to the surface he was excited and triumphant.

"They've begun to drift on the vein," he announced. "They've gone about three feet—it must have been then they learned the history of the claim. It's pyroxenite all right, every inch of it."

"Well, damn them!" said Mark.

"They can't plead that they didn't recognise the ore, uncommon as it is, because they began to drift the moment they struck the vein. It dips toward the ranch," he added abruptly.

Mark whistled. "It's pretty close. That would be a kettle of fish—if it apexed on your land! Lawsuit. Friendship of a life-time broken. The beautiful Mrs. Mark Blake brings suit against the now famous Gregory Compton——"

"Oh, nonsense!" said Gregory shortly. But he was disturbed nevertheless.

"But there's no nonsense in the idea that your own ore bodies may be just over the border. Why don't you sink a shaft, just for nuts."

Gregory, who was still excited, felt an impulse to confide his discovery to his friend. But his natural secretiveness overcame him and he turned abruptly away. "When I have finished at the School," he said, "no doubt I'll begin gophering again, but not before. What are you going to do about this? Let them have it?"

"I'll let them have a piece of my mind first. What do

you advise?—that I work the mine, myself? I could easily form a company if the ore is as rich as you think."

"I wouldn't take the chances. Lease the claim to them for a year. They'll take it for that time with all this ore in sight. If they've hit a large chamber they'll soon be netting several thousand dollars a day. If it's only a pocket, let them find it out. At the end of a year you'll know a good deal more about the mine than you do now. But keep an eye on them so that they don't gouge, and make them pay you twenty per cent. royalty."

'They'll pay it through the nose," said Mark emphatically.

Gregory laughed. "You feel as virtuously indignant as if you had never tried to do anybody yourself. It's do or be done out West as well as back East, and precious few mines have a clean history. Marcus Daly never would have got the best part of Butte Hill if he hadn't kept his mouth shut."

"It isn't that I'm so virtuous," said Mark ingenuously, "but I don't like the idea that anybody so nearly got the best of me. And just look at the way they covered it up."

Gregory had kicked aside the greater part of a pile of grey ore, and revealed quite a hillock of the pyroxenite. He put several pieces in his pocket, discarding the first specimens. "I'll get to work on this to-night," he said, "and let you know first thing in the morning. But I'm willing to wager that it runs from sixty to a hundred dollars a ton."

"And not a fleck of gold to be seen!" Mark, who, like all intelligent men of mining localities, had some knowledge of ores, examined the dark rock attentively. "They're some geologists," he added with unwilling admiration. "This would fool any ordinary mining engineer. Say!" he cried, "I'll not tell Ora until she's ready to leave—she's figuring on going to Europe in the fall. It will be the surprise of her life, for I led her to think she'd get only a hundred or so a month. Don't say a word about it to Ida."

Gregory turned away to hide a curl of his lip. "I suppose we'd better go over and see Oakley, as we're so close," he said. "He'll probably talk for an hour on his hobby, but any knowledge comes in useful to a lawyer."

"What's he done."

"He figured out that Iowa and the Dakotas and Kansas were likely to have a drought next year, so he will sow about five hundred acres with flax in May. He has already put in about three hundred acres of winter wheat. The bottoms are reserved for alfalfa. He raises the capital and gets half profits. If it turns out as he expects he'll have something at the end of a year to live on besides enthusiasm for intensive farming."

They were driving toward Pony two hours later when Gregory said abruptly, "I'm glad that your wife and mine have taken to each other. It is a great thing for Ida. The improvement is wonderful." He forebore to add, even to the man who had known his wife since childhood, "I don't see what Mrs. Blake gets out it," but possibly the irrepressible thought flew into Mark's mind, for he replied promptly:

"It's great for Ora. She's tired of everybody else here; tired of so much reading too. I've seen that for some time, though I haven't let on. A new interest was just what she wanted. Every clever woman has a touch of the school ma'am in her, and no one can deny that Ida's refreshing. To Ora she's almost a novelty. I think she rather hates to make her over, but she's working on her as hard as I work on a case. Ora's the thorough sort. What she does is done with all her might and main. Otherwise she don't do it at all. She's equally accomplished at that!"

He decided that this was the propitious moment; Gregory was in an uncommonly melting mood, for him. "Say!" he continued, "Ora and I have put up a little job on you. I've told her to take her new money and go to Europe for six months or so—By James, she shall go, even if this thing hangs fire and I have to sell some stock. It's over six years since she's seen Europe, and I guess she pines for it all right. Well, she wants to take Ida."

Gregory demanded with unexpected promptness, "How much would it cost?"

"Oh, about a hundred to New York and a hundred and fifty over," said Mark vaguely. "Of course when two are together it costs less. And in Europe distances are short. Ora says she shall go to *pensions* instead of hotels, if only because they would be two young women alone; and they cost much less. They can also travel second-class, and third in Germany and Switzerland. Ora says she and her friends always did it in summer because it was cooler and more interesting. She's sent for a lot of Baedekers, is going to make a close estimate, then double it."

"One of my aunts died the other day and left me a thousand dollars; she had no family. Ida can have it. Of course I could send her more if she needed it, but she's clever with money."

"That will do it." (He knew that if it did not Ora, who would pay the bills, would manage to hoodwink Ida.) "And you must live with me. It'll be fine. Bachelor's Hall. We'll do as we damn please."

Gregory shook hands with him, his strong hard face illuminated with the infrequent smile that gave it something of a sweet woman's charm. "Thanks, old man," he said fervently. "Sounds good!"

XIII

SEVERAL weeks passed before Ora sent for Miss Ruby Miller. She was busier during those weeks than she had been for many months. Ida came every other day at one o'clock and remained until five. They carved wood in the attic, and looked at pictures or read in the library during the hour and a half that included tea. Ida confessed that during the latter interval she was so bored sometimes she could scream, but added that she would stick it out if she yawned every tooth in her head loose. One thing that never bored her was the picture of Ora—her working blouse changed for a dainty house gown—presiding at the tea-table. She studied every detail, every gesture; she even cultivated a taste for tea, which heretofore she had regarded· as fit for invalids only, like jellies and cup-custard.

Ora's alternate days and many of her evenings were filled with social duties. Butte was indulging in one of its hurricanes of festivity. Mrs. O'Hagan, who lived in the largest and finest house on the West Side, gave a series of dinner dances. Mrs. Burke, who owned the big ugly red house of appalling architecture built by Judge Stratton in the eighties, gave several entertainments in honour of two young visitors from Denver. Mrs. Maginnis, who lived in another palatial residence far west and far from the old Stratton house—which in its day had expressed the extreme limit of the city, as of fashion—gave a ball as brilliant as anything Ora had seen in a distant hemisphere. Flowers may be scarce in Butte, but flowers and palms may be imported by the carload from Helena, and the large rooms looked like an oasis in the grey desert of Butte. Every woman wore a ball gown made by some one of the great reiterative masters, and there were no wall flowers; for, although the tango had not yet set the whole world dancing, the women of Montana never had interpreted grey hairs as a signal to retire.

It was on the day after this ball that Ora had telephoned to Miss Miller. "Can you give me an hour or two to-morrow?" she asked.

"Sure. Can I come early? I've got fourteen heads to dress for the Cameron ball, and most of them want a facial too?"

"A what?"

"Face massage, and touchin' up generally."

"Oh."

"It's fine. Makes you feel as good as you look. What did you want me to do?"

"Oh, shampoo my hair. I want to consult you about it, too—and manicure."

"Well, I'll bring the creams along, and if you want a massage I'll be ready."

Ora had succeeded in making Miss Miller propose what she had quite made up her mind to try, and she rang off with a smile. The evening before she had thought herself the plainest woman at the party, and the effect of this discouraging conclusion had been to kill her animation and sag her shoulders until she knew she must look as dowdy as she felt. For the first time she realised how a blighted vanity may demoralise the proudest intellect. It was time to get a move on, as her new but rapidly developing friend would put it.

Ora was very proud of her work. She gave Professor Whalen due credit, and knew that Ida toiled at her exercises, but doubted if the uninspiring pedant would have been retained had it not been for the sense of emulation, slightly tinctured by jealousy, she managed to rouse in her new boon companion when they were together. But Ida was now exercising something of her latent force of character, determined to make the most of advantages for which she knew many a sudden-rich woman would "give her eye teeth." She would polish up "good and plenty" before her husband made his strike; and waste no precious time on the inside of her skull when she had the cash to spend on its outside.

After the first week she dropped no more g's, her grammar rapidly improved, and although she never would be a stylist, nor altogether forswear slang, not only because the ready-made phrase appealed to her unliterary mind, but because its use was ingrained, she reserved it more and more for those that best could appreciate it. As it annoyed Professor Whalen excessively, she went afield for new phrases "for the fun of seeing him wriggle."

On the other hand, whenever she felt in the mood, she gazed at him with penitent languid eyes, promised never to use slang again, and amused herself racking other nerves. She knew just how far to go and "turned him off," or "switched him back on to the track" before any real harm was done. Some day she might let him make a scene just for the fun of the thing, but not until she was "good and ready."

Her feeling for Ora was more difficult to define. Sometimes she almost loved her, not only inspired by gratitude, but because Ora's personal magnetism was intensified by every charm of refinement, vivacity, mental development, as well as by a broad outlook on life and a sweetness of manner which never infuriated her by becoming consciously gracious. At other times she hated her, for she knew that no such combination ever could be hers. Ora was a patrician born of patricians. She might go to the devil, preside over one of the resorts down on The Flat, take to drink and every evil way, and still would she be patrician. Herself might step into millions and carry her unsullied virtue to her grave and she never would be the "real thing." For the first time she understood that being "a lady" had little to do with morals or behaviour. Nothing irritates the complacent American more than the sudden appreciation of this fact.

"But I guess I'll be as good as some others," Ida consoled herself. "After all, I don't see so many Ora Blakes lying round loose. People don't bother much these days if your clothes make their mouth water and your grammar don't queer you."

Gregory, when he had time to think about it—he read even at the breakfast and dinner-table, and had an assay plant in the cellar—was charmed with her improvement, and told her abruptly one day that if she kept faithfully to her tasks until November he would give her the thousand dollars he had received under the will of his aunt. "And you can do what you like with it," he added. "I shan't ask you. That's the way I enjoyed money when I was a kid, and I guess women are much the same."

"A thousand dollars!" Ida was rigid, her mouth open.

"Geewhil—I beg pardon—My! But you are good!" She paused to rearrange her thoughts, which were in danger of flying off into language her husband was paying to remodel. "Can I really do anything with it I like?"

"You can." He smiled at her bright wide-open eyes and flaming cheeks.

"I ain't—haven't said anything about it as I didn't think it would be any sort of use, but Ora is going to Europe in the fall, and she told me Mark was going to try to persuade you to let me go with her. Now I can go on my thousand dollars, if you don't mind. Mark wants you to stay with him."

"He spoke to me about it—I had forgotten. There couldn't be a better arrangement. This is the time for you to go to Europe—while your mind is still plastic."

"You don't seem to mind my going a little bit." Rapture gave place to suspicion. Ida was not born with faith in man.

"My dear child! What good am I to you now? You might be keeping house for a deaf mute. All I need is the right kind of food and a comfortable bed. I'll get both at Mark's. Next year you would see even less of me than you do now. We get our last and most practical drilling in ore-dressing, metallurgy, power-utilisation, and geology. We shall be off half the time on geological expeditions, visits to mines in other parts of the state, smelters, the most up-to-date of the cyanide mills. So you see how much I shall be at home. Go to Europe and enjoy yourself."

"All right. I'll go. You bet. And I'll not miss a trick. There'll never be a thousand dollars better spent."

XIV

"NOW I've got you where I want you, and I'm goin' to talk—goin' to say something I've been dyin' to say for two or three years."

Ora's head was in the wash-basin. Miss Miller was leisurely spraying out the lime juice with which she had drenched her hair. Ora gasped, then gurgled something unintelligible, which Miss Ruby interpreted as encouragement to proceed. Mrs. Blake's manner ever since the hairdresser's arrival had been uncommonly winning, with something half-appealing, half-confiding that flew straight not only to that experienced young woman's sympathies but to her professional instinct.

"It's this," she continued. "You need a thorough overhauling. In these days, particularly in this altitude, women take care of themselves as they go along, but you don't. You've lost your complexion ridin' and walkin' for hours without a veil, sometimes without a hat, and you with a delicate skin like a baby's and not even using creams. I heard a man say only last Sunday—I was givin' his wife a facial and he was sittin' round—that it was an awful pity you had gone off so, as you were the prettiest thing he ever laid eyes on when you came back after your pa's death, and if Mark—Mr. Blake—hadn't snapped you up before any other young man got a look at you you'd have had a dozen chances, for all you've got such a reputation for brains. 'A man can stand brains in a white lily of a girl,' says he, 'but when she gets older she's either got to keep her complexion or cut out the brains, and Ora Blake's done neither'—Say if you squirm like that you'll get your mouth and eyes full of lemon. His wife said she didn't believe men cared for them thin white women anyway—she's bustin' with health herself— and he gave a grunt that means a lot to a girl who knows men like I do. You never did make anything of yourself and you've let yourself go these last two or three years

87

something shameful. If you'd take yourself in hand, get on to yourself once for all, you'd have people twistin' their necks off to look at you and callin' you a Mariposa lily, or a Princess Pine, or a White Gladiolus and other poetry names like that. And you could get the reputation of a beauty all right. It makes me sick."

"Could you make me into a beauty?" Ora's voice was remarkably languid considering the flaming hue of her face, which, however, may have been due to its prolonged sojourn in the wash-basin. Miss Miller had wrung her hair out and was rubbing it vigorously.

"Couldn't I *just?*"

As Mrs. Blake maintained a dignified silence, Miss Ruby proceeded to develop her theme. "Now, your hair, for instance. That's the reason I used lemon today. You've been usin' soap, and, what with this dry climate, and no care, it's as harsh and broken as if you'd been usin' soda on it every day. It's lemon and hot water for you, first, last and always, and eggs after a journey. It needs a couple of months of hand-massage every other day right now; after that it will be up to you. Brush it night and morning and use a tonic twice a year."

She paused and Ora waited with eyes closed to conceal her impatience. Finally she opened them irresistibly and met Miss Ruby's in the mirror. They, too, looked embarrassed. Ora's smile was spontaneous and sweet and not too frequent. It seldom failed to melt reserve and inspire confidence. She played this card without delay.

"Why don't you go on?" she asked. "All that is most interesting and valuable. I shall remember every word of it."

"Well—I was afraid that what I want to say most might sound as if I was drummin' up trade, and the Lord knows I've got more to do than I could manage if there was ten days in every week. I turned down two ladies today to come here. I never shampoo the day of a ball."

"My dear Miss Miller! You are an artist, and like all artists, you not only aim at perfection yourself but your eyes and fingers ache at imperfection. I suppose an author rewrites sentences as he reads them, and painters must long to repaint every picture they see. As for you—we are your page and canvas, and naturally we have the good fortune to interest you."

"That's it!" cried Miss Ruby, glowing. "That's the size of it, only I couldn't ever say it like that. Well, now, if you want this skin to look like a complexion and not like a hide, I've got to give you a massage every third day for quite a while. It not only needs creams and cold applications—hot only once in a while—but an awful lot of hand massage. It's all run down and needs stimulating the worst way. Another year and you'd be havin' lines. You can't leave yourself to nature up here. She's in too great a hurry to take back what she gave. And you must cut out hot breads and trash and wear a veil when you go out in the sun and wind. And you go to Boulder Springs once a week and take a vapour bath."

"But I'll always look washed-out."

"Not if you look fresh, and wear colours that suit you."

"And I never was called a beauty. That man, whoever he was, merely remembered the usual prettiness of youth. Every young girl is pretty unless she is ugly."

"Well, I guess you didn't take enough pains to make people think you were a beauty. Some—Ida Compton, for instance—don't need to do anything but just show themselves. Any fool—particularly a man—can see black hair and red and white skin, and meltin' eyes, and lashes a yard long, and a dashin' figure. But odd and refined types like you—well, you've got to help it out."

"How very interesting! Do you mean I must go about telling people that I am really beautiful, if they will only look at me long enough? Or—possibly—do you mean that I should make up?"

"I don't mean either, 'though in a way I mean both. In the first place you've got to make the most of your points. You're not a red blonde or a gold blonde, but what the French call sendray; in plain English, you've got ash-coloured hair. Now, that makes the blondest kind of blonde, but at the same time it's not so common, and nature has to give it to you. Art can't. What you want to do is to let people see that your colouring is so rare that you can't get enough of it yourself, and by and by people will think they can't either. You've been wearin' all this hair twisted into a hard knot down on your neck. That don't show off the hair and don't suit your face, which is kinder square. I'm goin' to pull it soft about your face and ears and then coil it softly on top of your head. That'll give length to your face, and look as if you was proud of your hair—which you will be in a month or two. You mustn't pay too much attention to the style of the moment. You're the sort to have a style of your own and stick to it.''

"I'm in your hands," murmured Ora. "What next?"

"Did you really lose interest in yourself?" asked Miss Miller curiously, and with the fine freedom of the West from class restraint. "Or didn't you ever have any?"

"A little of both. When I was a girl I was a frightful pedant—and—Oh, well—Butte is not Europe, and I took refuge more than ever in books, particularly as I could have nothing of the other arts. You know the resources of Butte!"

"I'm glad you're goin' to Europe again, where I guess all kinds of variety are on tap.—Say, perhaps you'll find out all the new kinks for the complexion in Paris, and tell me when you come back."

"I will indeed!"

"I don't hold to rippin' the skin off, or hoistin' it up," said Miss Miller firmly. "All any skin needs is steady treatment, and constant care—constant, mind you, and never forget it. Now there's your profile. It's grand. The way I'm goin' to fix your hair'll show it off, and don't you let it get scooped round the eyes, like so many women do. Massage'll prevent that. I wish your eyebrows and lashes was black, like so many heroines in novels has. The contrast would be fine. But brown'll do, and I guess the natural is your lay. Luckily them black grey eyes is a high note, and when you get your lips real red, you'll have all the colour your style can carry. The gleamin' white skin'll do the rest.''

"How am I to get red lips, and what's to make my skin gleam?"

"You're anæmic. You go to a doctor and get a tonic right off. When I get through with your complexion it'll gleam all right. No powder for you. It improves most women, but you want high lights. I don't mean shine when I say gleam, either. I mean that you've got the kind of skin that when the tan's off and it's toned up and is in perfect condition (you've got to be that inside, too), sheds a sort of white light. It's the rarest kind, and I guess it does the most damage.''

"And what good is all this beautifying to do me? And why make me dangerous? Surely you are not counselling that I begin a predatory raid on other women's husbands, or even on the 'brownies'?"

"Well, I guess not. I don't approve of married women lettin' men make love to them, but I do believe in a woman makin' the most of herself and gettin' all the admiration that's comin' to her. If you can be a beauty, for the Lord Almighty's sake be one. Believe me, it'll make life seem as if it had a lot more to it."

"I shouldn't wonder!"

"And you go in right off for deep breathin' and Swedish exercises night and mornin'. It's the style to be thin, but you want to develop yourself more. And they keep you limber—don't forget that. When a woman stiffens up she's done for. Might as well get fat round her waist. Now shut your eyes, I'm goin' to massage."

XV

"**I** WONDER!" thought Ora, "I wonder!"

It was some four months after her first séance with Miss Ruby Miller. There was no question of the improvement in her looks, owing, perhaps, as much to a new self-confidence as to the becoming arrangement of her hair and the improved tint and texture of her skin. The tonic and a less reckless diet had also done their work; her eyes were even brighter, her lips pink. Moreover, it was patent that the sudden reformation was as obvious to Butte as to herself. Women confessed to a previous fear that the "altitude had got on her nerves or something"; as for the men, they may or may not have observed the more direct results of Miss Miller's manipulations, but it was not open to doubt that her new interest in herself had revived her magnetism and possibly doubled it.

Ora turned from the mirror in her bedroom, where she had been regarding her convalescing beauty with a puzzled frown, and stared down at the rough red dirt of her half-finished street—she lived far to the west. Her eyes travelled up to the rough elevation upon which stood the School of Mines in its lonely splendour, then down to the rough and dreary Flat. It stretched far to the south, a hideous expanse, with its dusty cemetery, its uninviting but not neglected road houses, its wide section given over to humble dwellings, with here and there a house of more pretensions, but little more beauty. It was in one of these last, no doubt, that her father had kept his mistress, whose children, she was vaguely aware, attended the public schools under his name. These houses, large and small, were crowded together as if pathetically conscious that the human element must be their all, in that sandy, tree-less, greenless waste.

There was something pathetic, altogether, thought Ora, in the bright eagerness with which even the wealthy class made the most of their little all. They were so proud of

Columbia Gardens, a happy-go-lucky jumble of architectures and a few young trees, a fine conservatory and obese pansies on green checkers of lawn; they patronised its Casino so conscientiously on Friday nights when the weather would permit. During the winter, they skated on their shingled puddle down on The Flat as merrily and thankfully as though it were the West End of London or one of the beautiful lakes in one of the beautiful German "gartens." They motored about the hideous environs, and hung out of the car to emphasise their rapture at the lonely tree or patch of timid verdure; they entertained royally in their little Club House, out in another desolate waste, or played golf without envy or malice. In short they resolutely made the most of Butte when they were in it; they patted Butte and themselves on the back daily; they loved it and they were loyal to it and they got out of it as often as they possibly could.

"And I!" thought Ora, with a sense of panic. "I, who will probably get away every five years or so—what am I waking up for—to what end? I wonder!"

She walked slowly downstairs and, avoiding the little French drawing-room, went into the library and sat down among her books. Sash curtains of a pale canary colour shut out the rough vacant lots and ugly dwellings above her home, and cast a mellow glow over the brown walls and rows of calf-bound books. Judge Stratton had read in four modern languages and two dead ones. The love of reading, of long evenings alone in his deserted "mansion," had been as striking a characteristic of his many-sided ego as his contempt for moral standards. Ora, who had grown into a slow but fairly thorough knowledge of her father's life and character, permitted her thoughts to flow freely this afternoon and to speculate upon what her life might have been had Judge Stratton been as upright as he was intellectually gifted; if her mother had possessed the brains or charm to keep him ensnared; if she herself had been left, an orphan at twenty, with the fortune she inevitably would have inherited had her father behaved himself—instead of finding herself penniless, ignorant of all practical knowledge, a querulous invalid on her hands, her only suitor the "hustling" son of her mother's old seamstress.

Ora admitted no disloyalty to Mark as she put these

questions for the first time squarely to herself. She intended to continue to treat him with unswerving friendship, to give him all the assistance in her power, as long as she lived. And, as husbands went, she made no doubt that he was one to thank her grudging providence for. But that she would have considered him for a moment had she inherited the fortune her father had made and dissipated was as likely as that she would have elected to live her life in Butte.

She knew Mark's ambitions. Washington was his goal, and he was by no means averse from being governor of his state meanwhile. Nor would he have been a genuine American boy, born in the traditional log cabin—it had been a log cabin as a matter of fact—if he had not cherished secret designs on the White House. In all this, did it prove to be more or less, she could be of incalculable assistance to him. And she was the more determined to render this assistance because she had accepted his bounty and was unable to love him.

She concluded with some cynicism that the account would be squared, being by no means blind to what she had done for him already in the way of social position and prestige; still, it was not only his right, but a penance demanded by her self-respect. She was living the most unidealistic life possible to a woman of her pride and temperament, but she would redeem it as far as lay in her power.

She moved impatiently, her brows puzzled again, and something like fear in her heart. What did this slow awakening portend? Why had she instinctively held it back with all her strength, quite successfully until her newborn vanity, with its infinite suggestions, had quickened it suddenly into imperious expression?

Certainly she was conscious of no desire for a more idealistic union with another man. If she had inherited a fortune, she would have married no one; not then, at all events; nothing had been further from her desire. She would have lived in Europe and travelled in many lands. Beyond a doubt her hunger for the knowledge that lies in books would have been satiated long since, never would have assumed a discrepant importance. She would be uniformly developed, and she would have met many men. With the double passport of birth and wealth, added to the fine manner she owed to her Southern mother, her natural vivacity and magnetism, and a physical endowment that she now knew could have been trained into positive beauty, she would have had her pick of men. And when a woman may choose of the best, with ample time at her disposal, it was incredible that the true mate, the essential companion, should not be found before it was too late. Most marriages are makeshifts; but for the fortunate few, with the intelligence to wait, and the developed instinct to respond, there was always the possibility of the perfect union.

Ora made a wry face at this last collocation. She had no yearning for the "perfect union." Matrimony had been too unutterably distasteful. She turned hastily from the subject and recalled her father's impassioned desire that she should make the West her home, her career, marry a Western man, give him and her state the benefit of her endowments and accomplishments. Possibly, surfeited with Europe, she would have returned to Montana to identify herself with its progress, whether she married or not. She was artistic by temperament and training, and correspondingly fastidious; she cordially detested all careers pursued by women outside those that were the natural evolution of an artistic gift. But she could have built herself an immense and splendid house, filled it with the most exquisite treasures American money could coax from the needy aristocracy of Europe, and have a famous salon; invite the pick of the artistic, literary, musical, and political world to visit her for weeks or months at a time, house parties of a hundred or more, and so make her state famous for something besides metals, intensive farming, and political corruption. No one could deny that the state would benefit exceedingly.

Conceivably, in time she would take a husband, assuredly one of high ambitions and abilities, one whose fortunes probably would take him to Washington.

This brought her back to Mark, and she laughed aloud. She had been romancing wildly; of late she had grudgingly admitted that nature may have composed her to be romantic after she had recovered from the intellectual obsession; and the circle had brought her round to her husband! He was "forging ahead" with extraordinary rapidity. She made no doubt that he would be a million-

aire within the ten years' limit he had set himself. Nor
would he rely alone upon his legal equipment and the many
opportunities to exercise it when a man was "on the job
all the time"; he watched the development of Montana's
every industry, new and established. He "bought in on
the ground floor," gambled discreetly in copper, owned
shares in several new and promising mines, and property
on the most picturesquely situated of the new lakes con-
structed for power supply. He invested what he could
afford, and with the precision of the man on the spot.
Yes, he would be one of the Western millionaires, even if
not one of the inordinate ones, and before his ten years had
passed, if no untoward event occurred.

And it was on the cards that she would have her own
fortune before long. She knew that Mark (who had her
power of attorney) had made better terms with the engineers than he had anticipated, and he dropped mysterious
hints which, knowing his level head, made her indulge in
ornate dreams now and again. But he only smiled teasingly when she demanded a full explanation, and told her
that she would realise how good or how bad her mine was
when she went to the bank to sign her letter of credit.

For one thing she felt suddenly grateful. She knew
that the mine had been leased for a year only and without
bond. If, during that time it "panned out," she would
stipulate to mine it herself when the contract expired.

She sat up very straight and smiled. That was what
she would have liked! If her father had but willed her
this mine and capital enough to work it alone! Her fingers
fluttered as they always did when handling ore; she had
wondered before if the prospector's fever were in her
blood. How she should have enjoyed watching the rock
come up in the buckets as the shaft sank foot by foot, until
they struck the vein; always expecting chambers of incredible richness, gold, copper, silver. She would even
learn to do the pleasant part of her own assaying; and
she suddenly experienced an intense secretive jealous love
for this mine that was hers and in which might be hidden
shining blocks of those mysterious primary deposits deep
in the sulphide zone; forced up through the veins of earth,
but born how or where man could only guess. It was a
mystery that she wanted to feel close to and alone with,
far in the winding depths of her mine.

She got up and moved about impatiently. Her propensity to dream extravagantly was beginning to alarm her, and she wished uneasily that she could discover the gift to write and work it off. Where would it lead her? But she would not admit for a moment that her released imagination, pulsing with vitality, and working on whatever she fed it, only awaited the inevitable moment when it could concentrate on the one object for which the imagination of woman was created.

The pendulum swung back and more evenly. She told herself it was both possible and probable that she had a good property, however short it might fall of Butte Hill. She renewed her determination to mine it herself, and work, work, work. Therein lay safety. The future seemed suddenly full of alarms.

And there was Mark, his career, his demands, dictated not so insistently by him as by herself.

Ora's soul rose in a sudden and desperate revolt beside which her rising aversion from unmitigated intellect was a mere megrim. She felt herself to be her father's daughter in all her newly-opened aching brain cells. He had lived his life to please himself, and if his temptations and weaknesses might never be hers—how could she tell?—his intense vitality survived in her veins, his imperious spirit, his scornful independence. She glanced at the rows of calf-bound books he had handled so often. Something of his sinister powerful personality seemed to steal forth and encompass her, sweep through the quickened corridors of her brain. Mark Blake was not the man he would have chosen for his daughter. Western, Mark might be to the core, but he was second-rate, and second-rate he would remain no matter what his successes.

And, she wondered, what would this proud ambitious parent, whose deepest feeling had been for his one legitimate child, say to her plan to play second fiddle for life to a man of the Mark Blake calibre? He had wanted her to marry in the West, but he had been equally insistent that she should develop a personality and position of her own. No devoted suffragist could have been a more ardent advocate of woman's personal development than Judge Stratton had been where his daughter was concerned. To the rights of other women he had never cast a thought.

This was the hour of grim self-avowal. She admitted what had long moved in the back of her mind, striving toward expression, that she hated herself for having married any man for the miserable reason that has driven so many lazy inefficient women into loveless marriages. She should have gone to work. More than one of her father's old friends would have given her a secretaryship. She could have lived on her little capital and taken the four years' course at the School of Mines, equipping herself for a congenial career. If that had not occurred to her she could have taught French, Italian, German, dancing, literature. In a new state like Montana, with many women raised abruptly from the nethermost to the highest stratum, there was always a longing, generally unfulfilled, for the quick veneer; and women of older fortunes welcomed opportunities to improve themselves. She could have taken parties to Europe.

She had played the coward's part and not only done a black injustice to herself but to Mark Blake. He was naturally an affectionate creature, and, married to a comfortable sweet little wife, he would have been domestic and quite happy. In spite of his enjoyment of his club, his cards and billiards, and his buoyant nature, she suspected that he was wistful at heart. He was intensely proud of his wife, in certain ways dependent upon her, but she knew he had taken for granted that her girlish coldness would melt in time and womanly fires kindle. Well, they never would for him, poor Mark. And possessing an inherent sense of justice, she felt just then more sympathy for him than for herself, and placed all his good points to his credit.

She was conscious of no sympathy for herself, only of that deep sense of puzzlement, disturbance, apprehension. Revolt passed. Indications—the abrupt bursting into flower of many unsuspected bulbs in her inner garden: softness, sympathy, a more spontaneous interest in and response to others, the tendency to dream, vague formless aspirations—had hinted, even before she took her newborn vanity to Miss Ruby Miller, that she was on the threshold of one of the dangerous ages (there are some ten or fifteen of them), and that unless she had the doubtful wisdom and resolution to burn out her garden as the poisonous fumes of roasting ores had blasted the fruitful soil of Butte, she must prepare to face Life, possibly its terrible joys and sorrows.

She sprang to her feet and ran upstairs and dressed for the street. At least she had one abiding interest and responsibility, Ida Compton. She was a self-imposed and absorbing duty, and always diverting.

XVI

"OH, you give me the willys!"

"My dear Mrs. Compton! How often have you promised me——"

"Well, if you will stare at me like a moonstruck setter dog when I'm trying to think up 'steen synonyms for one old word without looking in the dictionary! I can't blow up my vocabulary like a paper bag and flirt with you at the same time."

"I have no desire to flirt with you!" said Professor Whalen with great dignity. "It is quite the reverse. You have been playing with my feelings for months."

"Don't flatter yourself. I've been too set on becoming a real lady before leaving for Europe—haven't thought about you."

Professor Whalen turned a deep dull red. His overlapping upper teeth shot forward as if to snap down upon his long rather weak chin. He stared past Ida through the open window. It was May and the snow was melting on the mountains, had disappeared from the streets of Butte; there is a brief springtime in Montana between the snows of winter and the cold rains of June, and today was soft and caressing.

"I'll tell you what is the matter with you," said Ida, cruelly. "It's the spring of the year."

Whalen sprang to his feet. For the first time in his anæmic life he was furiously angry, and he rejoiced in the sensation. "I wish you were a man," he stuttered. "I'd beat you. It would do my heart good."

"If you were a real man you would enjoy beating a woman a long sight more," goaded Ida, who watched him as a man-eating tigress may watch the squirming victim between her paws. She had fed her vanity and amused herself by playing on the little man's pale emotions until she was convinced he really was in love with her. She suddenly made up her mind to force him to "let go," and experience the sensation of being made love to feloniously.

"I am not a brute," announced Whalen, still in the same stifled voice. His face was purple, but he was conscious of a warning whisper that he was in a fair way to lose this remunerative pupil. He dismissed the warning. There is probably no man so insignificant in whom passion for the imperative woman does not develop abnormally the purely masculine conceit. He may despair in solitude, when devitalised by reaction and doubt, but when in her presence, under her inviting eye, and hurried to a crisis by hammering pulses and scorching blood, he is merely the primitive male with whom to desire is to have.

Ida laughed, a low throaty husky laugh. "If you were," she said cuttingly, "you might stand a show."

"It is you that are brutal," hissed poor Whalen.

Ida leaned back in her chair and looked at him out of half-closed eyes. "What induced you to fall in love with me, anyhow?" she demanded in her sweet lazy voice. Whalen clenched his hands.

"I am a man if I am not a brute. You are the most fascinating woman on earth, and you have deliberately tried to entice me from the path of rectitude I have trod all my life——"

"What's that?" Ida sat up straight, her brows drawn in an ominous frown.

"I have resisted you until today, but I yield——"

"What the devil are you talking about?"

"I expected to be tormented to the utmost limit. But I have stood all of it that I purpose to stand." His voice by this time was a subdued roar. "I don't care whether you love me or not. I don't think you could love anybody. I have read that sirens never do. But you are an enchantress, and you have shown plainly enough——"

Ida's frown had relaxed, but her eyes blazed. He misunderstood their expression, as well as the sudden forward thrust of her head. He sprang forward, caught her by the shoulders and kissed her.

"Aw!" Ida's voice was almost a roar. She leaped to her feet, twirled him about, caught him by the back of his collar and the seat of his trousers, and threw him out of the window as if he had been an offensive dog. She flung his hat and stick after him and slammed the window down. Then she stamped her feet in inarticulate rage, and rubbed and bit her mouth. It was one thing to play with a man's passions and quite another to be defiled by them. Ida seethed with the fierce virtue of a young inexperienced and temperamentally cold woman. For a few moments she used very bad language indeed, and struggled with an impulse to run after the "little puppy" and whip him in the street. But, remembering that she was making a heroic attempt to be a grande dame, she finally went into her bedroom and washed her face.

XVII

THERE was a knock on the front door. Ida, smoothing her hair, hastened to open it, glad of diversion. Ora stood there. For a moment the girls looked hard at each other, then burst into laughter.

"What's up?" asked Ida. "You look——"

"My dear, it is I who should ask? Your face is crimson; you look as if you had just given some one a beating, and I met poor little Whalen, dusty, dishevelled, growling like a mad dog—he didn't know me."

"Well, I guess he won't know himself for a while," said Ida drily, leading the way into the parlour. "When he comes to he'll have his work cut out to climb back to his little two-cent pedestal and fit on his battered halo." She related the incident. "What do you know about that?" she demanded in conclusion. "Wouldn't it come and get you?"

"I am afraid you have made an enemy. It is always best to let them down gently, save their pride—and—ah! —it isn't customary to throw gentlemen out of the window!"

"Gentlemen!" snorted Ida. "He's no gentleman. He not only kissed me with his horrid front teeth, but he insinuated that I was just languishing for him, the——" Once more Ida's feelings overflowed in language not intended for print. "It made me so mad I'd have lammed him with the umbrella if we'd been in the hall."

"Ida," asked Ora abruptly, "would you have minded so much if he had been good-looking and attractive?"

"Well—perhaps—I guess in that case I'd simply have smacked him and let him get out quick by the front door. But I don't want any man touching me. I'm a married woman."

"But if you flirt and lead them on——"

"You said once yourself that American men understood the game and knew how to take their medicine."

103

"I also said that they can fall more tiresomely in love than any other men. Of course the Whalens don't count. But do you intend to go on making men fall in love with you and throwing them—metaphorically—out of the window?"

"Much chance I'll get."

"You'll find plenty of chances in Europe. You are a remarkably beautiful woman. And Europeans take what we call flirting for shameless encouragement."

"Well, I guess I'll be getting experience of the world all right. And the Lord knows I'd like to be admired by men who have seen something. I can take care of myself, and Greg don't need to worry."

"I've no doubt of that. Of course you are awfully fond of Mr. Compton, aren't you?" Ora spoke somewhat wistfully.

"Oh, yes; fond enough, fonder than a good many wives, I guess, for he's kind and pleasant, and no earthly trouble about the house. But when a woman marries she gets a kid right there at the altar, and he's her biggest kid till his false teeth drop out on his deathbed, and his great-grandchildren are feeding him through a tube. I don't want any of the other sort of kids, and I guess I'm not what you call the maternal woman, but the Lord knows I'm a mother to Greg and a good one. I'd like to know what he'd do without me—that's the only reason I hate leaving. He never thinks of changing his shoes when they're wet, and half the time wouldn't eat anything but his book if I didn't put the stuff right in front of him."

"Mark knows him almost as well as you do, and will look after him. My maid, who is practically my housekeeper, and an old family servant, will also keep a maternal eye on him."

"He keeps himself tidy," conceded Ida handsomely. "Wants clean things every day, but never knows where to find them. He'll wander out into the kitchen where I'm cooking breakfast and ask where his socks are, and they always in the same drawer."

"I fancy you've spoiled him."

"Not I. I don't hold with spoiling men. They're born spoiled anyhow. I found Greg walking round in a dream when I married, and a pile of socks as high as the door knob he'd thrown away because they'd holes in them so tiny you could hardly see them. I darned every one, you bet, and he's wearing them now, though he don't know it. He's like that, as dainty as a cat, and as helpless as a blind kitten. I am a wife and I know my duty," concluded Ida virtuously.

"I certainly shall give Custer minute directions. I can't have you worrying."

"I'll not worry, once I'm started. Don't you fret! But what's the matter with you, Ora? You look kinder excited, and kinder—well, harassed. How's that out of the new pocket dictionary I've set up in my head?"

"I'll soon have to look to my own vocabulary. Oh—I——"

"Something's up. Spit it out. It'll do you good."

"Dear Ida! If you must use slang, do confine yourself to that which has passed through the mint of polite society. There is an abundance to choose from!"

"Don't you worry; I won't disgrace you. But I must let out a tuck occasionally when we're alone. Greg wouldn't let me go to any of the Club dances, and I scarcely ever see Ruby or Pearl, they're so busy—to say nothing of myself!"

"Very well," said Ora, laughing. "Let me be your safety valve, by all means."

"Fire away."

"Oh—how am I to tell you—I scarcely know, myself ——"

"I guess you're waking up. Ruby, who knows human nature like a book——"

Ora half rose. "Have you been talking me over with Miss Miller?" she asked haughtily.

"Not much. Hardly seen her since we met. But you interest Butte, you know. I guess they talk you over good and plenty. It was only a few days before you called that the Miller girls visited with me all day, and they talked a lot about you. Ruby said that if you'd come to out of the sleeping beauty stage, you'd make things hum, and that her fingers just itched to get at your skin and hair."

"She said that to me once; and I don't mind telling you that I called her in some time ago."

"Oh, I'm not a bat. I've seen you looking prettier every day, and there's only one way to do it, when you've let yourself go. I've had the benefit of Ruby's advice for years, and I don't propose to let myself go, not for a minute.''

''Right you are. And do live your life normally from day to day, developing normally. The awakening process, when the Nature that made you is no longer content to be a mere footstool for the mind, is almost as painful as coming to after drowning. I suddenly have become conscious of myself, as it were; I am interested in many more things—personal things—I seem to want far more of life than I did a few months ago——''

''In other words, you don't know where you're at.''

Ora laughed merrily. ''My present condition could not be stated more patly!''

''Ora, I don't want to pry into your confidence, and you're not one to give much of that anyhow, but everybody in Butte knows that you're not in love with Mark, and never were, nice as you treat him—only because you couldn't be anything but a lady if you tried. Mrs. O'Neil, one day when she was having a massage, told Ruby all about your marriage. She said you were the most bewildered young thing she ever saw, and that Mark snapped you up before another young man could get a look at you. Now, I've known Mark all my life—he beaued my sister who died, for a year or two, and his mother's cottage was just up the hill anyhow; and although he's a good chap and a born hustler, and bound to get rich, he's not the sort of man women fall in love with. You wouldn't have fallen in love with him, if he'd been born a millionaire, and travelled and got Butte out of his system. And if your father had left you well off, you wouldn't have looked at him. There's men, bad and good—that's to say, better —that women fall in love with, and there's men bad and good that they don't, not in a thousand years. Poor old Mark's a Don't all right. You ain't angry at my saying all this, but Mark was like my own brother for years?''

''Oh, no, I am not angry. You are far too matter-of-fact. You might be discussing different grades of ore!''

''Well, that's about it, and the poor ore can't help itself, any more than the slag and gangue can, and Mark's not either of those, you bet. He's good metal, all right, only he didn't come out of the Anaconda mine—What have you turned so red about? My! But you do blush easy!''

"It's this—do you despise me—do you think I did wrong—Oh, I mean I have quite suddenly realised that I never should have married any man for so contemptible a reason. I should have gone to work——"

"Work? You?"

"Why not? Many a delicately nurtured woman has earned her bread."

"The more fool she if she could get a man to earn it for her. That's what they're for. The Lord knows they pride themselves on the way they do it, being the stronger sex, and a lot more words. I guess I'd have married before Greg turned up if I'd met a man I was sure was going to make something of himself. You did just right to take a good husband and take him quick when you found yourself in a hole."

"Yes—but——" Her blush deepened. "You see—" Ora never had had an intimate confidant. It was doubtful if she ever would have; not, at all events, a woman. But Ida, as she herself would have expressed it, could always see through a stone wall when there was a crack in it.

"Oh, shucks!" she said. "Don't let that worry you. If you don't feel that way first you do last, I guess. Most of us are bored to death, but women have stood it for a few thousand years, and I guess they can stand it for a few thousand more. We all of us have to pay high for anything we want. That's about the size of it. Forget it."

"Thanks, dear, you console me." Ora smiled with closed eyes, but she was thrilled with a sudden inexplicable longing; like other of her recent sensations, it puzzled and alarmed her.

"Ora!" exclaimed Ida suddenly. "There's one thing that's just as sure as death and taxes; and knowing men and knowing life don't help women one little bit. It's this: A woman's got to have her love affair sooner or later. If she marries for love she's pretty safe, for ten or fifteen years, anyhow. But if she doesn't, well, she'll get it in the neck sooner or later—and it'll be about the time she begins to sit up and take notice. She's a regular magnet then, too. So watch out."

Ora opened her eyes. They looked like steel. "I have never given a thought to love. There is nothing I want less. I shall continue to make Mark as good a wife as I know how to be——''

''Oh, I'm not saying you'll go off the hooks, like some I could mention in your own bunch, but if the man comes along you'll fall in love all right. Might as well try to stop a waterfall from jumping over the rocks. I'm not so dead sure I do know what you'd do. Pride, and high breeding, and duty would pull one way, but—well, I guess when you marble women get waked up good and plenty, what they call roused, you're the worst kind. A considerable number of other things would pull from the opposite direction, and one of them would be the man.''

''Ida!'' said Ora, aghast. ''How do you know so much? Your opportunities have been very limited.''

''Oh, have they? Wasn't I born and brought up in a mining camp? Butte is some education, believe me. I ran straight all right, not only because the sporting life had no charms for me but because I figured on moving over one of these days to Millionaire Gulch. But it wasn't for want of opportunity, and the same opportunities were handed over by men of your crowd—or fixin' to be. Besides, some women are born wise that way, I guess, and I'm one of 'em. You've been living in a sort of self-made heaven all your life, with only books for inhabitants. I could put you wise every day in the week.''

''It is true that although I saw a good deal of life while my mother lived so much in the world, and always have been deeply interested in the work of the psychological novelists, particularly the Europeans—I—well, I never applied it to my—never thought much about it until lately. I do not seem to know myself the least little bit.''

''I guess it'll be me—Oh, Lord, I—taking you to Europe, not you me. I'll see that you don't get into mischief, for I'd hate like the dickens to have you go to pieces over any man. Not one of them that ever lived since Adam is worth it. They're all right to marry, all things being equal, but to sacrifice your life for, nixie. Any style of man you are partial to? I'll keep his sort off with a broom.''

''I've never gone so far as even to think——''

''Every woman has her style in men,'' said Ida firmly. ''I heard of a woman once who had three husbands and each one had a wart on his nose.''

"Oh, you are funny! I have heard that a woman falls in love with a type, not with the man, and, like all epigrams, that one contains a half-truth. I had two or three girlish fancies; one was an Austrian officer, another a French nobleman—and not impecunious—he wasn't a fortune hunter. The third was a New Yorker who fell in love with my cousin and married her. I had a few heart spasms over him, in particular; possibly because he was quite out of reach. It is true that they were all more of or less of a type—tall and thin and dark, with something very keen and clever and modern in their lean—rather hard faces."

"Hi!" cried Ida.

"What is the matter? You look at me as if you had seen a ghost."

Ida threw back her head and laughed, showing her sharp little white teeth, and straining her throat until the firm flesh looked thin and drawn, over too strong muscles. "Oh, Lord! I was just thinking what a lot of trouble I'm in for, playing dragon to my lily-white lady. I guess about half the men in the world are brunettes, fat or lean. Say, are you going to the Prom? It's only a month off."

"I hadn't thought about it. Probably. I have been asked to be a patroness, and Mark is sure to want to go. Have you decided what to wear?"

"Ma gave me a coral-red silk when I married, and I'm going to make it over and veil it with black net."

"Splendid!" cried Ora warmly. "Bring it up to the house. Mrs. Finley is really an excellent seamstress. We'll all take a hand. It will be great fun. And you will look stunning."

"What will you wear?"

"I expect some gowns from my New York dressmaker in a few days. It will depend upon the state of my complexion, I fancy."

XVIII

ORA received another budget of Ida's philosophy on the day before the Prom; she had taken her a long string of pink coral she had found among her old possessions, and after Ida had wound it in her hair and round her neck, and finally tried on her gown, and then draped Ora successively in various scarves, remnants of her own wedding finery—being almost as interested in the new complexion as Ora herself—they had suddenly come to the conclusion that while in Europe they would assume the mental attitude of girls travelling without a chaperon. They would see the world from the independent girl's point of view, flirt like girls, not like married women (which at least would save their consciences), force men to accept the phenomenon. For a time they discussed the superior advantages of being young widows, but, alluring and even thrilling as were the possibilities evoked, they dismissed the alternative on the ground that it might prove a bore always to be on the defensive; man making no secret of his attitude toward widows. Besides, they felt a delicacy about burying their indulgent husbands even in mental effigy. As counterfeit girls they could crowd enough excitement into six months to serve them in memory during long periods of Butte.

"It will be some bluff," cried Ida. "And believe me, we'll have the time of our lives. And no remorse in mine. I intend to flirt the limit, for I'm just ready to quit being a mother for a while and see a man's eyes kindle when he comes nigh—see him playing about at the end of a string. I didn't have near enough of it even when I had half Butte at my feet—excuse what sounds like conceit but is cold fact. Now, I'm going to light up every man I take a fancy to. I don't care an abandoned prospect hole whether I hurt 'em or not. All they are good for is to give us a good time."

"Ida!" Ora was aghast as she often had been before at these naked feminine revelations. "You talk like a man-eater. I hope to heaven I am not like that down deep."

"Oh, maybe you won't be so bad because you haven't got as much vanity. Mine's insatiable, I guess, and good old Mother Nature taught me the trick of covering it up with the don't-care-a-damn air combined with the come-hither eye. That does the trick. And they get what hurt's going. I don't. You'll cultivate men, thinking it's your vanity waked up, or mere youth, or because it's time to have a fling, but what you really are after is the one and only man. The Companion. The Sympathetic Soul. The Mate. All that rot. He don't exist, kiddo. He's the modern immaculate conception, and he's generally still-born; the bungling doctor being the plain unadulterated male inside of himself. You've got to be your own com-panion, and if you want happiness you can get it by ex-pecting just nothing of men. Use them. Throw them on the ash heap. Pass on to the next. Quit sitting on the watch tower with your eyes trained on the horizon for the prince that is born and lives and dies in a woman's imagination."

"I have seen happy—united couples—who had been married for years."

"Oh, yes; some couples are born to jog along together, and some wives are born man-tamers, and get a lot of satisfaction out of it. But you're much too high-falutin' for that. You'll always dream of the impossible—not only in man but of what he's got to give—which ain't much. And I didn't need all them—those—psychological and problem and worldly novels you made me read, trans-lated from half a dozen languages, either. You take my advice, Ora, and don't start off on any fool hunt for an ideal. Men are just matter-of-fact two-legged animals, and as selfish as a few thousand years of fool women have naturally made them. He does well while he's court-ing because he's naturally good at bluff. But every bit of romance oozes out of him after he's eaten his first breakfast of ham and eggs at home. We can keep up the bluff forever. Men can't. Each one of them's got a kid twin brother inside that plays marbles till he dies and makes you feel older every day. No, sir! If I ever had any delusions, I've got over them good and plenty. And I thank the Lord,'' she aded piously.

''I think that rather adorable, you know: the eternal boy. And I fancy it is all that saves men from becoming horrors; in this country, at least—when you consider the unending struggle, and strain, and sordid business of money getting. They use up all their bluff in the battle of life, poor things. Why shouldn't they be natural with us? . . .''

Ora was recalling this conversation as she sat in her bedroom on the following evening. Her elemental yet uncannily sophisticated friend had a way of crashing chords out of jealously hidden nerves, which no exercise of will could disconnect from the logical parts of the brain. If it were true that what her now rampant ego, too long starved, really demanded was man and romance, she wished she had let herself run to seed until it was too late to reclaim her lost beauty and adventure into temptation. But a glance into the mirror deprived her of any further desire to join the vast sisterhood of unattractive females. Moreover, she had faith in the dominance of her will and common sense, and if her beauty would help her to the mental contacts she craved with brilliant and interesting men, far be it from her to execrate it.

She dismissed the mood of self-analysis impatiently and opened her wardrobe, although half inclined not to attend the Prom. She was one of the patronesses, but her presence was not essential. It was pre-eminently the night of nights for young folks—brownies and squabs—and the absence of a married woman of twenty-six would pass unrecorded. Not a man in Butte interested her personally, nor was she in a frame of mind to be interested by any of the too specialised products of the West. Nor was she inordinately fond of dancing; there really was no object in going to this party save to witness the début and possible triumph of her protégée.

But she felt something more than indifference toward this party. It was as if a gong sounded a warning in the depths of her brain—in her subconsciousness, perhaps, where instinct, that child of ancestral experience, dwelt. But even while she hesitated she knew that she should go, and she took one of her new gowns from a long drawer, and then began to arrange her hair.

It was now some five months since Miss Ruby Miller had taken her in hand, and if the young woman's bank account was heavier her pride as an artist far outweighed it. Ora's hair was soft, abundant, the colour of warm ashes. The skin of her face was as white and transparent, as "pearly" to use its doctor's own descriptive word, as the fine protected surface of her slender throat, her thin but by no means bony neck. Her lips were pink; they never would be red; and after one taste of "lip stick," Ora had declined to have them improved by art. But they were a soft country-rose pink and suited her clear whiteness far better than scarlet. Her eyes, never so clear and startling as now, lighted up the cold whiteness of her face and made her pink mouth look childish and somewhat pathetic. If her lips had been red, her face would have had the sinister suggestion so many women achieve with the assistance of art; as it was she looked by no means harmless as she smiled at herself in the mirror and coiled her hair softly on the top of her head. After some experimenting she had decided that she could not improve upon an arrangement which for the present at least was all her own.

She rang for Custer to hook her gown. It was a very soft gown of white satin draped about the bust with lace and chiffon. It was cut to the waist line in the back and almost as low in front, for her figure was hardly more developed than a growing girl's; and it was unrelieved by colour. She had already put on the string of pearls her mother had hidden when the other jewels were sold in Paris. Altogether it was a costume she would not have dared to wear even two months ago, when a touch of colour on the bodice or in her hair was necessary to divert attention from her spoiled complexion.

Custer had been her mother's maid for many years and had returned with her to Butte. After an interval of employment elsewhere, she had come to Ora as soon as Mark had built his house. She hooked the gown, pinned up a stray lock with an invisible hairpin, shook out the little train, and stood off.

"It reminds me of the way your mother used to look," she said, "and you're even prettier than she was, Miss Ora—now. But I fancy you'll be more comfortable in this gown when you wear it in London. These ladies dress smartly enough, but never as low as the English ladies do, leastways out here. I fancy it's the Western men. They don't seem to approve of showing too much.''

"Well, I think I'll rather enjoy startling the natives. Quick—give me my wrap! I hear Mr. Blake coming. No controversy here.''

XIX

THE Prom was held not in the School of Mines but in The Coliseum, a large hall over a saloon and garage, half way between The Hill and The Flat, requisitioned by all classes when the weather forbade the use of Columbia Gardens. The walls were covered with the School colours, copper and green, flags, and college pennants. The ceiling was a network of electric lights with coloured globes, copper and green, fluttering paper and sprays of apple blossoms, brought from far! ''Cozy corners'' looked like fragments of a lower altitude, and the faithful palm was on duty everywhere. The orchestra, on a suspended balcony in the centre of the room, was invisible within the same elaborate scheme of decoration.

When Ora entered with her husband the Grand March had finished and the instruments were tuning for a waltz. She saw Ida standing directly under the orchestra surrounded by several men who patently were clamouring for dances. Even in that great room full of women dressed from New York and Paris, Ida looked distinctive and superb. Ora smiled proudly, as she observed her, quite oblivious that the throng of men and women and indignant ''squabs,'' who had been discussing the wife of Gregory Compton, had transferred their attention to the dazzling apparition in white. Ida wore her gown of coral silk, whose flimsiness was concealed under a mist of black shadow lace. The coral beads clasped her strong white throat and fell to her supple waist. There was a twist of coral tulle in her black hair, which was arranged in the rolling fashion of the moment, obeyed by every other woman in the room save Ora Blake. And her cheeks, her lips, were as coral as the fruit of the sea. She had powdered her face lightly to preserve its tone through exercise and heat. All the arrogance of youth and beauty and

115

powerful magnetism was expressed in the high poise of her head; a faint smile of triumph curved above her little white teeth; her body was in perfect repose yet as alert as that of a healthy young cat. The waltz began and she glided off in the arm of a young mining engineer from the East. She danced precisely as the best-bred women in the room danced (early in the evening): ease without abandon, dignity without stiffness.

"Heavens, but the American woman is adaptable!" thought Ora. "I never realised before exactly what that time-worn platitude meant. Probably the standards in the Ida set are not so different from ours, after all. As for looks and carriage she might have three generations behind her. Is it democracy or the actress instinct of woman— permitted its full development in this country for the first time in her history?"

This was not entirely a monologue, but addressed for the most part to Professor Becke, one of the most distinguished instructors of the School of Mines, and one of the men she liked best in Butte. He was a tall fair man, with a keen thin fimbriated face, and long fine hands. Ora made a point of asking him to dine with her once or twice a month.

He led the way to two of the chairs on the side of the hall after she had announced that she did not intend to dance.

"But this is the first party we have had for weeks," he said. "They won't leave you to me for long."

"I don't feel in the mood for dancing. Besides," she added with a new daring, "I'm all in white and looking very white once more; I don't want to get warm and spoil the effect."

He stared into her challenging eyes as if he saw her for the first time. In that room, full of colour and of vivid women and young girls, she produced an almost disconcerting effect with her statuesque beauty, her gleaming whiteness, her frail white body so daringly displayed in its white gown. And, oddly enough, to those staring at her, she made the other women look not only commonplace but cold.

Ora smiled to herself; she was quite aware of the impression at work, not only on the scientific brain, but on others more readily responsive; she had considered the prudence of practising on Butte before departing for wider fields.

The Professor changed colour, but replied steadily: "Fancy you two extraordinary creatures loose in Europe! You should take a bodyguard. I can understand Compton giving his consent, for he is the kind of man that wouldn't remember whether his wife were twenty or forty at the end of his honeymoon, and there can be little between them in any case. But Blake!"

"Oh, we'll come home without a scandal," said Ora lightly. "Ida is the reverse of what she looks, and I—well, I am the proverbial 'cold' American woman—that the European anathematises. Ida, of course, looks the siren, and I shall have some trouble protecting her, until she learns how far she can go. But at least I am fore-warned."

"I fancy you will have more trouble protecting your-self!" Professor Becke's voice was not as even as usual. His intellect was brilliant and illuminating, and never more so than when in the society of this young woman whom heretofore he had admired merely as a vivacious and exceptional mind; but, startling as this revelation of subtle and alluring womanhood was, he remembered that he was no longer young and that he had an admirable wife with an eagle eye; he had no intention of scorching his fingers in the attempt to light a flame that would guide him to the rocks even were he invited to apply the torch. But he was a man and he sighed a little for his vanished youth. If he had been twenty years younger he fancied that he would have forgotten his good lady and risked burning his heart out. He moved his eyes away deliber-ately and they rested on Mark Blake, mopping his scarlet face after a lively waltz. He was a kindly man, but all that was deathlessly masculine in him grinned with a cynical satisfaction.

"Who is that?" asked Ora abruptly, and forgetting a faint sensation of pique.

"Ah! Who?"

She indicated a man leaning against one of the door-ways, and looking over the crowd with unseeing eyes. "Heavens! What a jaw! Is he as 'strong' as he looks, or is he one of Bismarck's wooden posts painted to look like a man of iron?—Why, it's——"

"That is Gregory Compton, and he is no wooden post, believe me."

"I haven't seen him for years. *Can* any man be as strong as *he* looks?"

"Probably not. He hasn't had time to discover his master weaknesses yet, so I don't pretend to guess at them myself. At present he is too absorbed in squeezing our poor brains dry——"

"Doesn't he ever smile?"

"So rarely that the boys, who have a nickname for all their fellow students, call him 'Sunny Jim.' "

"What do you think of his wife?" asked Ora abruptly. She hardly knew why she asked the question, nor why she felt a secret glow at the expected answer.

The Professor turned his appraising eye upon the substantial vision in coral and black that tonight had been pronounced the handsomest woman in Butte. "There could be no finer example of the obvious. All her goods are in the front window. There are no surprises behind that superlative beauty; certainly no revelations."

"I wonder! Ida is far cleverer than you think, and quite capable of affording your sex a good deal in the way of surprises, not to say shocks."

"Not in the way I mean—not as you will do, worse luck for my helpless sex. There is no soul there, and, I fancy, little heart. She is the last woman Gregory Compton should have married."

"Why?" Ora tried to look bored but polite.

"Oh—whatever she may have for other men she has nothing for him. She looks the concentrated essence of female—American female—egoism. Compton needs a woman who would give him companionship when he wanted it, and, at the same time, be willing in service."

Ora bristled. "Service? How like a man. Are we still expected to serve men? I thought the world was moving on."

Professor Becke, who, like most men married to a domestic commander-in-chief, was strenuously opposed to giving women any powers backed up by law, asked with cold reserve: "Are you a suffragette?"

Ora laughed. "Not yet. But I just escaped being born in the Twentieth Century. I belong to it at all events."

"So you do, but you never have been in love——" He

broke off in embarrassment; he had forgotten for the moment that this white virginal creature had been married for six years. She showed no resentment, for she barely had heard him; she was looking at Gregory Compton again, and concluding that he might appeal strongly to the supplementary female, but must antagonise women whose highly specialised intellects, at home only on the heights of civilisation, had submerged their primal inheritance.

Professor Becke went on:

"Even a clever woman's best career is a man. If you women develop beyond nature that powerful old tyrant will simply snuff you out."

"Well, man will go too. That may be our final triumph."

"Atlantis over again! And quite in order that the race should perish through the excesses of woman. Then Nature, having wiped her slate clean with a whoop, will begin all over again and precisely where she did before. No doubt she will permit a few records to survive as a warning."

"You may be right—but, although I have an idea I shall one day want to justify my existence by being of some use, it won't be because my sex instinct has got the better of my intelligence. But I refuse to think of that until I have had a royal good time for a few years."

"That is your right," he said impulsively. "You are altogether exceptional—and you have had six years of Butte! I am glad your mine has panned out so splendidly. There is quite an excitement in the Sampling Works——"

"What?" Ora forgot Gregory Compton. "I knew the mine was doing well——"

"Surely you know that your profits in royalties already must be something over a hundred thousand dollars——" He stopped in confusion.

Ora's face was radiant and she never had liked Mark as sincerely as at that moment. "It is just like him! He wanted to wait and give me a great surprise—my husband, I mean."

"And I have spoilt it! I am really sorry. Please don't tell him."

"I won't. And I'll be the most surprised woman in the world when he takes me to the bank to sign my letter of credit. You needn't mind. I'll have the fun of thinking about it for five months—and rolling it up in my imagination. Ah!"

"Compton has recognised you, I think."

Ora had met the long narrow concentrated gaze of her husband's friend. She bowed slightly. Compton made a step forward, hesitated, braced himself, and walked toward her.

"A constitutionally shy man, but a brave one," said Professor Becke with a grim smile, as he rose to resign his seat. "A strong magnet has pulled up many a sinking heart. Good evening, Compton. Glad you honour our party, even if you don't dance."

"I intend to ask Mrs. Blake to dance." Gregory betrayed nothing of his inner trepidation although he did not smile. He could always rely upon the stern mask into which he had trained his visage not to betray him.

Ora, oblivious of her resolution not to dance, rose and placed her hand on his shoulder, smiling an absent farewell to Professor Becke. For a moment she forgot her resentful interest in this man in her astonishment that he danced so well. She had the impression of dancing with a light supple creature of the woods, one who could be quite abandoned if he chose, although he held her as if he were embracing a feather. She wondered if it were his drop of aboriginal blood and looked up suddenly. To her surprise he was smiling, and his smile so altered the immobility of his face that she lost her breath.

"I feel as if I were dancing with a snowflake," was his unexpected remark.

"You look the last man to pay compliments and murmur sweet nothings."

"Are you disappointed?"

"Perhaps I am. I rather liked your attitude—expression, rather—of cool superiority."

"Why don't you use the word prig?"

"Oh, no!—Well, perhaps that is what I did mean."

He stopped short, regardless of the annoyance he caused several impetuous couples. "If you did I shall leave you right here."

"I did not. Please go on. Everybody is staring at us. You took me completely by surprise."

"I? Why?"

"You are the last man I should expect the usual small talk from."

"Small talk? Heavens knows I have none of that. Girls used to talk my head off in self-defence. I merely said what I thought. What did you expect me to talk about?"

"Oh—mines, I suppose." Again, to her surprise, his face lit up as if by an inner and jealously hidden torch. But he said soberly:

"Well, there is no more interesting subject. Never has been since the world began. Where shall we find a seat?"

The waltz was over. The chairs were filling. Young couples were flitting toward the embowered corners.

"Let's go outside," he said abruptly.

"What? On the street? And nobody goes out of doors from a ball room in June."

"Good reason for going. Come with me."

He led her to the cloak room. "Get your wrap," he said.

Ora frowned, but she asked for her heavy white woollen wrap and put it on; then automatically followed him down the stairs and into the street.

"Why don't you get your coat and hat?" she asked, still dazed. "It's cold, you know."

"I never was cold in my life," he said contemptuously. He hailed a taxi. "I must go up to the School of Mines, and ask the result of some assaying," he added as he almost lifted her in. "Then we can talk up there. May I smoke?"

"I don't care what you do."

He smiled directly into her resentful eyes this time and tucked the lap-robe about her.

XX

H^E apparently forgot her during the short drive and stared through the open window of the cab, his thoughts, no doubt, in the assay room of the School, where several students, as ardent as himself, were experimenting with ore they had managed to secure from a recently opened mine. Ora's resentment vanished, partly because she reflected that a new and original experience was a boon to be grateful for in Butte, but more because she was thrilled with the sense of adventure. Her woman's instinct gave assurance that he had no intention of making love to her, but it also whispered that, whether she liked or disliked him when the adventure was over, she would have something to remember. And it was the first time she ever had indulged in recklessness. Butte would be by the ears on the morrow if it learned of her escapade.

When they reached the dark School of Mines he dismissed the taxi, and said to Ora, "Wait for me here. I shan't be a moment."

He disappeared and Ora shrugged her shoulders and sat down on the steps. He returned in a few moments and extended himself over several steps below her.

"Comfortable?" he asked.

"Very!"

"It's a night, isn't it?" he asked abruptly.

He was not looking at her but at the low sulphurous blue sky, with its jewelled lattice, white, yellow, green, blue. There were no tree-tops to rustle, but from the window below came the voluptuous strains of the Merry Widow waltz, mingling incongruously with the raucous noises of the sleepless town: the roaring street-cars, the blasts of engines, the monstrous purr of motor-cats.

"If we could cut out that jungle," he said with a sigh. "Are you warm enough?" He pulled the cloak about the lower part of her body. "I should have taken the rug from the cab——"

"I am warm enough," she said impatiently, and what she longed to say was, "How in heaven's name did you marry Ida Hook?" He had transferred his gaze to the city and she studied his face. Then she understood. In spite of its intense reserve and detachment, its strength and power, its thin sensitive mouth, it was the most passionate face she had ever seen. As a matter of fact she had been at pains to ignore the purely masculine side of men, her fastidious mind never indulging in comparisons. She half rose with a sense of panic. Again he looked up solicitously.

"I am sure you are not comfortable. I could find you some cushions——"

"Please don't. So you love beauty?" She was deeply annoyed with herself, but could think of nothing less banal. He certainly was not easy to talk to.

"Don't you? It would be odd if you didn't. One reason I brought you up here was because I wanted to look at you in the starlight where you belong—the cold starlight—not in that crowded gaudy room full of mere human beings."

"Are you a poet? I have somehow received the impression that you are a mere walking ambition."

"I'm no poet if you mean one of those writing fellows." His tone expressed unmitigated scorn.

"Well, no doubt you have read a good deal of poetry, little as one would suspect it."

"Never read a line of it except when I had to decline it at school—any more than I've ever read a line of fiction."

"Well, you've missed a great deal," said Ora tartly. "Poetry is an essential part of the beauty of the world, which you seem to appreciate. And the best of fiction is the best expression of current history. What do you think when you star-gaze?"

"You mean, can I think at all when I haven't read what other men have thought?"

"No.—No doubt the most original brains are those that have not read too much, are not choked up." Ora made this admission reluctantly, but he had caught her fairly. "Tell me at least what the stars suggest to you. About everything has been said of them that can be said. The poor old stars have been worked to death."

"The stars above Montana are watchfires protecting the treasure below. Perhaps they are bits of her treasures, gold, silver, copper, sapphire, that flew upward in the final cataclysm."

"I don't know whether that is poetical or gross materialism."

"No mines, no poets. Nearly all conquest from the dawn of history down to the Boer War has had the acquisition of mineral wealth as its real object. The civilisation that follows is incidental; it merely means that the strongest race, which, of course, knows the most, wins. If ever we have a war with Mexico, what will be the cause? Mines. Incidentally we will civilise her. Peru, Mexico, India, the Americas—all have been invaded in their turn by more civilised nations, and all after plunder. They gave as much as they took, but little they cared about that. What opened up California? This great Northwest? Prospectors in search of gold. Excuse this lecture. I am the least talkative of men, but you have jarred my brain, somehow. Read the history of mines and mining if you want romance."

"As a matter of fact few things interest me more. I am so glad my mine has been leased for a year only. When that is up I am going to mine it myself. I'll build a bungalow out there and go down every day. Perhaps in time I could be my own manager. At all events, think of the excitement of watching the ore as it comes up the shaft; of running through a lean vein and coming suddenly upon a chamber of an entirely different kind of ore from what you had been taking out. Great shoots full of free gold! Wire gold! Or that crisp brown-gold that looks as if it were boiling out of the ore and makes one want to bite it! Why are you staring so at me?"

His eyes were more widely opened and brilliant than she had seen them. "Do you mean that?" he asked. "I've a great notion to tell you something that I've not told anyone."

"Do tell me!"

She leaned down eagerly. She had dismissed the feeling of panic as something to be forgotten as quickly as possible. But her brain was on fire to penetrate his. She felt an extraordinary mental stimulation. But he relapsed into absolute silence, although he held his head, lowered again, at an angle that suggested he might be thinking intently. She moved impatiently, but he sat still, staring downward, his eyes narrow once more. She noticed irrelevantly how black his hair was, and her white hand went out stealthily as if magnetised, but was immediately restored to order. In the vibrating silence she had another glimmer of understanding. He wanted to tell her something personal, but his natural secretiveness and habit of reserve were engaged in a struggle with the unusual impulse. She shifted the ground.

"I wish you would tell me something of your boyhood," she said abruptly.

He looked up in astonishment. "I never talk about myself——"

"How very egoistical."

"Ego——"

"No, I did not say egotistical."

"Ah!" There was another pause, although he looked at her with a frown. "I have talked to you more than I ever talk to anyone," he said resentfully.

"It is the stars, to say nothing of the isolation. We might be up on one of your escaped nuggets. Remember that I have heard of you constantly for six years—and met you before on one of those occasions when all persons look alike. How could I escape curiosity?"

"I brought you out to look at in the proper setting. I can't say I had any desire to talk to you. I suppose I should not keep you out here——"

"I am much happier and more comfortable than in that hot room. But surely you need more recreation. Why do you never go to dances?"

"Dances? I? I only went tonight——" He, too, apparently, was determined to keep their respective spouses out of the conversation, for he veered off quickly. "It is a sort of religion to attend the Prom even if you only show yourself. I was about to beat a retreat when I saw you. Of course it was my duty to shake hands. Besides, I wanted to see if you were real." And he smiled up into her eyes.

"Do you know that we are flirting?"

"Well, let us flirt," he replied comfortably. "I haven't the least idea what it is, but I am not a bit in love with you, if that is what you mean."

Ora drew herself up rigidly. "Well, you are——" she began, aware that she had a temper. Then she laughed. Why quarrel with a novel experience? Her anger turned into a more subtle emotion. She was well aware of the dazzling brightness of her eyes. She leaned forward and concentrated her mind in an attempt to project her magnetism through them, although again with a feeling of panic; it was too much like the magnet rushing out to the iron.

He returned that powerful gaze unmoved, although an expression of perplexity crossed his own eyes. She was disconcerted and asked lamely:

"Is it true that you used to run away and prospect in the mountains?"

His face lit up with an enthusiasm her fascinations had been unable to inspire; and a richer note came into his voice. "I was eleven the first time and stayed out for six months. Two years after I ran away again. The next time I went with my father's permission. I worked in one of the Butte mines one summer—but otherwise—well, you see, there is a good deal to do on a ranch. This is the first time I have been able to do as I please."

Ora looked at his long slim figure, his brown hands that tonight, at least, expressed a sort of cruel deliberate repose. Whatever they may have been in their ranch days they were smooth and well cared for now.

"Somehow, I can't see you handling a pick," she said doubtfully. "Is it true that you intend to work in the mines all summer?"

"Part of it—when I am not working in a mill or a smelter. I'd be ashamed of myself if I couldn't do anything that another man can do. Some of the best miners look like rats."

He looked like a highly-bred mettlesome race-horse himself, and Ora wondered, as she had before tonight: "Where did he get it? Who were his ancestors?" She had seen dukes that looked like farm hands, and royal princesses that might have been upper housemaids, but her feminine (and American) mind clung to the fallacy that it takes generations to produce the clean-cut shell. She determined to look up his family tree in Holland.

"Well—Custer—my housekeeper—will look after you," she said as naturally as if her thoughts had not wandered for a moment. "Shall you do any mining on your own place before we come back from Europe?"

He started and looked at her apprehensively, then scowled.

"What is the matter? You may not know it but at this moment your face looks like an Indian battle-axe."

To her surprise he laughed boyishly. "You startled me. I have heard of mind readers. Well, I will tell you what I wanted to a while back. But you must promise not to tell—anyone."

"I promise! I swear it! And do hurry. I'm afraid you'll shut up tight again."

"No, I won't. I don't know that I'd tell you were it not that your own mine is just over the border; we may have to consolidate some day to save a lawsuit—No, I will be honest; I really want to tell you. It is this: Close to the northeast boundary line of my ranch is an almost barren hill of limestone and granite. Shortly before I left—last October—I discovered float on the side of the hill. There is no doubt in my mind that we have both come upon a new mineral belt, although whether we are in the middle or on one edge of it is another question."

He told her the story of the storm and of the uncovering of the float. Nor did he end his confidence with a bare statement of fact. He told her of his sensations as he sat on the ragged ground leaning against the roots of the slain trees, his mental struggle, and final resolution. Then he told her of the hopes and dreams of his boyhood, and what it had meant to him—this sudden revelation that he had a mine under his feet—and all his own! He talked for half an hour, with the deep satisfaction that only a shy and silent person feels when talking into a sympathetic mind for the first time. Ora listened with a curious sense of excitement, as if she were overboard in a warm and pleasant but unknown sea. There were times when she felt like talking very fast herself. But she did nothing of the sort, merely jogging him diplomatically when he showed signs of relapsing into silence. Finally he stopped in the middle of a sentence and said abruptly:

"That's all."

"Oh! And you really have made up your mind not to begin work for a year?"

"Quite!"

"But—have you thought—it is only tonight I learned that the engineers who leased my mine have struck a rich vein. Suppose it dips toward yours——"

"It does——"

"Have they put on a big force?"

"Naturally. They are rushing things, as they know they will not get the mine another year."

"Well, suppose their vein runs under your hill—through their side line?"

He stirred uneasily. "I am watching them. So far the dip is very slight. It may take a turn, or go down straight; or," and he smiled at her again, "it may pinch out. Nothing is so uncertain as an ore vein."

"Do you think it will?" asked Ora anxiously.

"No, don't worry. I was down the other day; and did some prospecting on my own account besides. I think you've got a big mine."

"But suppose the vein should take a sudden dip to the right—you don't want them burrowing under your hill ——"

"They won't burrow under my hill," he said grimly. "I should persuade them that there was an even richer vein on their left."

"Is there?"

"I have reason to think so. They naturally would want to avoid the expenses of a lawsuit, and of course they would waste a lot of time sinking a shaft or driving across. Their lease would be pretty well up by the time——"

"You *are* cold-blooded! What of me? I should be making nothing, either."

"You'd make it all later on. How much do you expect to spend in Europe anyway? You must have made a thousand dollars a day since the first car load of ore was smelted."

She was on the point of replying that a woman could not have enough money in Europe, when she remembered the conspiracy to make him believe that a thousand dollars would cover the expenses of his wife.

"Oh, it is merely that I don't like being one of the pawns in your game," she said.

"You'd have all the more later on. Ore doesn't run away."

"How *can* you stay away from your mine? I feel—

after all that you have told me!—that you are wild to get at it?''

"So I am! So I am! But I said I wouldn't and that is the end of it. I want that last year at the School."

"What shall you do with all that money—if your hill turns out to be full of gold? More, I hope, than the rest of our millionaires have done for Montana—which is exactly nothing. You might give the State a complete irrigating system."

"Good idea! Perhaps I will. But that is in the future. I want the fun first——"

"Fun? It is the passion of your life, your great romance. You'll never love a woman like that."

"Of course not." But he was staring at her. He had a sensation of something swimming in the depths of his mind, striving to reach the surface. He changed his position suddenly and sat up. "And you?" he asked. "You have the same vision. Couldn't you feel the same absorbing passion——"

"For ore?" The scorn of her entire sex was in her voice. "Dead cold metal——"

"Every molecule, every individual atom is alive and quivering——"

"I am not interested in chemistry."

He still stared at her. Her cheeks were scarlet, her eyes blazing. She sprang to her feet.

"Ida is the wife for you! She'll never ask much of you and you never could hurt her, not even if you tried. She is fortunate in lacking just that which you could hurt."

"What is it?" He spoke eagerly. He, too, had risen, his eyes still on her face. Unconsciously he held his breath.

"Oh, you wouldn't understand if I told you—and I haven't the least desire to tell you. She will make you comfortable, do you credit when you are a rich man, spend your money royally. That is all *you* will ask of *her*. Now, I'll go back."

He was a step or two below her. Their eyes were on a level. He looked at her sombrely for a moment, then walked past her up the steps.

"You need not call a cab. I shall go home. I should only set them all talking if I appeared in the ballroom again. You can tell Mark that I didn't feel well and that you took me home."

They walked along the high terrace until they found a point of easy descent.

"What have I said to make you angry?" he asked.

Ora laughed with determined good humour. "It was not I. It was merely my sex that flared up. Please forget it."

"I want to thank you for what you have done for Ida," he said abruptly, and it was evident that the words cost him more than his former revelations. "It was a great thing for you to do."

"Oh, Ida has become my most intimate friend. I have never enjoyed Butte so much as in these last few months."

"Has she? And Mark is my best friend." He jerked his head in annoyance; manifestly the remark had been too spontaneous. They were before her gate. She extended a limp hand, but he held it firmly. He was smiling again although he looked depressed.

"Do give me a friendly shake," he said. "I do like you and you will be going in a few days."

"I do not go for five months."

"You can go next week. I'll square it with Mark."

"I don't wish to go next week. Besides, Mark expects some important people here in the autumn, and needs my help. He has a deal on."

"I'll dispossess Mark of any such notion. It's all nonsense, this idea of a man's needing his wife's help in business. It's a poor sort of man that can't manage his own affairs, and Mark is not a poor sort. Now, you are angry again!"

"That would be foolish of me," she said icily. "You merely don't understand. You never could. Do you want to get rid of me?" she asked abruptly.

"Yes, I think I do."

Then Ora relented. She also gave him the smile that she reserved as her most devastating weapon. "I am sorry," she murmured, "but I don't think I can be ready for at least three months. Nor Ida."

"You go next week," he said.

And go they did.

XXI

GREGORY and Mark established their wives comfortably in a drawing-room of the limited for Chicago, asked the usual masculine questions about tickets and trunk checks, expressed their masculine surprise that nothing had been forgotten, told them to be careful not to lean over the railing of the observation car, nor to make themselves ill with the numerous boxes of candy sent to the train, admonished them not to spend too much money in New York, to send their trunks to the steamer the day before they sailed, and give themselves at least two hours to get to the docks; above all not to mislay their letters of credit; then kissed them dutifully, and, as the train moved out, stood on the platform with solemn faces and hearts of indescribable buoyancy.

"My Lord!" exclaimed Ida, as she blew her last kiss. "If Greg was going along I'd have to take care of him every step of the way. I wouldn't trust him with the tickets the length of the train. Men do make me tired. They keep up the farce that we're children just to keep up that other grand farce that they run the Universe. Any old plank to cling to."

Ora kept her sentiments to herself.

If Mark, who was fond of his wife, and more or less dependent upon her, wondered vaguely that he should rejoice in the prospect of six months of bachelorhood, Gregory was almost puzzled. Ida was now no more to him personally than a responsibility he had voluntarily assumed and was determined to treat with complete justice; but at least she made him more comfortable than he had ever been before, and he had trained her to let him alone. Since her rapid improvement her speech had ceased to irritate him; she was never untidy, never anything but a pleasant picture to look at. He had also noted on the night of the party that she was indisputably the handsomest woman in the room and received the homage of men with dignity and

131

poise. He had felt proud of her, and comfortably certain that he could trust her. Altogether a model wife.

Nevertheless as he walked out Park Street after he left Mark at his office (Ida not only had sent his personal possessions to the Blake house but found time to unpack and put them away) his brain, which had been curiously depressed during the past week, felt as if full of effervescing wine.

"Jove!" he thought, "why do men marry? What has any woman living to give a man half as good as his freedom."

His freedom was to be reasonably complete. He had told Ida to expect no letters from him and not to write herself unless she were in trouble. With all the fervour of his masculine soul he hated to write letters. Long since he had bought a typewriter, on which he rattled off necessary business communications so briefly that they would have cost him little more on the wire. He knew that he should hear constantly of his wife's welfare from Mark, and had no desire to be inflicted with descriptions of scenery and shops.

He felt a spasm of envy, however, as he thought of the letters Mark would receive from Ora. *Her* letters, no doubt, would be worth reading, not only because she had a mind, and already had seen too much of Europe to comment on its obvious phases, but because they would be redolent of her subtle exquisite personality. He had once come upon a package of old letters among his mother's possessions and read them. They had been written by his great-great-grandmother to her husband while he was a soldier in the War of the Revolution. It was merely the simple life of the family, the farm, and the woods, that she described, but Gregory never recalled those letters without feeling again the subtle psychological emanation of the writer's sweet and feminine but determinate personality; it hovered like a wraith over the written words, imprisoned, imperishable, until the paper should fall to dust. So, he imagined, something of Ora's essence would take wing on the rustling sheets of her letters.

But the spasm of envy passed. Ora would write no such letters to Mark Blake. Her correspondence with her husband would be perfunctory, practical, brief. To some man she might write pages that would keep him up at night, reading and rereading, interpreting illusive phrases, searching for hidden and personal meanings, while two individualities met and melted. . . . But this yearning passed also. To receive such letters a man must answer them and that would be hell.

He was on his way to change his clothes for overalls and get his blue dinner pail, well filled, from Custer. But before he reached the house he conceived an abrupt and violent distaste for life underground, an uncontrollable desire—or one which he made no effort to control—for long rides over the ranch, and a glimpse of Limestone Hill. It was seven months since he had seen his ranch save in snatches, and he wanted it now for months on end. He was not a town-bred man, and he suddenly hated the sight of Butte with her naked angles and feverish energies. He realised also that his mind insistently demanded a rest. To be sure he had intended to work in the mines for eight hours of the day, but he had planned to study for ten. Well, he would have none of it! Caprice was no characteristic of his, but he felt full of it this brilliant morning. If the air was so light in Butte that his feet seemed barely to touch the ground, so clear that the mountains seemed walking down the valley, what must it be in the country?

He went rapidly to the house, left a message for Mark, packed a suit-case and took the next train for Pony. There he hired a horse and rode to his ranch.

One of the sudden June rains had come while he was in the train. It had ceased, but a mass of low clouds brushing the higher tree tops was almost black. Their edges were silver: they were filled with a cold imprisoned sunlight, which transformed the distant mountains into glass, transparent, with black shadows in their depths. Montana looked as giving an exhibition of her astral body. But as he rode the clouds drifted away, the sky deepened to the rich voluptuous blue of that high altitude; even the grey soil showing through the thin grass of the granite hills looked warmer. Where the soil was thicker the ground was covered with a gorgeous tapestry of wildflowers; the birds sang desperately as if they knew how short was their spring time, affected like mortals by the thin intoxicating air. Even the waters in the creek roared as if making the most of their brief span. The mountains lost their glassy look; blue, ice-topped, they were as full of young and vivid life as when they danced about, heedless that the heaving earth purposed they should wait for centuries before settling into things of beauty for unborn man to admire. They never will look old, those mountains of Montana; man may take the treasure from their veins and the jewels from their crowns, but they drink for ever the elixir of the air. The blue dawn fills their spirit with a deathless exultation, the long blue-gold days their bodies with immortal life, the starry nights, swinging their lamps so close to the snow fields, unroll the dramas of other worlds. They are no mere masses of rock and dirt or even of metal, these mountains of Montana, but man's vision of eternal youth.

Gregory drew rein on the crest of one of his own hills. Below lay the De Smet ranch, and he drew a long breath with that sensation of serene pride which comes to men when they contemplate their landed possessions, or their wives on state occasions. All the arable soil, on flat and hillside, was green; alfalfa, with its purple flowers, filled the bottoms; the winter wheat was rippling in the wind; the acres covered with the tender leaves of young flax were like a densely woven lawn. On the hills and the public range roamed his cattle. All of this fair land, including its possible treasure, was his, absolutely. By the terms of his father's will he paid yearly dividends from the sale of steers and crops to three aunts, now reduced to two. Whether by accident or design, Mr. Compton had omitted all mention of "minerals under the earth." Gregory had not the least objection to making these ladies rich, when his mines yielded their wealth, but he was jealous of every acre of his inheritance, far more of its secrets. All the passionate intensity of his nature he had poured out on his land and its subterranean mysteries, and he would have hailed an invention which would enable him to dismiss every man from his employ. But his head was hard and he always smiled grimly at the finish of his fanciful desires.

He turned his horse toward the distant group of farm buildings, then wheeled abruptly and rode toward Limestone Hill. He had anticipated a long talk with the enthusiastic Oakley on the subject of crops, but he suddenly realised that he was in no mood to talk to anyone and that his secret reason for coming to the ranch was to visit his hill. Oakley would cling to him for hours. One glance had assured him that the crops would have satisfied a state experimental farm. Mining would fascinate him in its every detail, but as far as agriculture was concerned, he was interested only in results.

As he rode toward the hill he frowned at the signs of activity on the other side of his boundary line. A large gasoline hoist had been installed. The waste dump was almost as high as a hill, four "double-sixes"—six-horse teams—stood waiting to be loaded from the ore bins. There were a group of miners' cabins, a long mess house, and a blacksmith's shop. This was the only shadow on his future: he wanted no lawsuits, nor did he want to enter into partnership with anyone, not even Ora Blake.

But he dismissed the matter from his mind, tied his horse, and, although Montanans are a slow race on foot out of deference to the altitude, ran up the hill. A glance told him that his secret was undiscovered. He knelt down and dug up the float, his heart hammering. And then he deliberately let the propector's fever take possession of him. The soles of his feet prickled as if responding to the magnets below; he had a fancy that gold, molten, was running through his veins. But his brain worked clearly. He was aware that his exultation and excitement were not due to the lure of gold alone, but to the still more subtle pleasure that a strong and obstinate nature feels in breaking a vow and deliberately succumbing to temptation. He had vowed in good faith that he would not open his mine until the third of June of the following year. But a week before he had spent an enchanted hour with a woman, and during the rest of that night—he had walked half way to Silver Bow and back—he had wanted that woman more than he had ever wanted anything on earth. He had forgotten his mine.

At first he had lashed himself with scorn, remembering his infatuation for the woman he had married. He felt something of the indignant astonishment of the small boy who imagines himself catching a second attack of measles, before he discovers it is scarlet fever. But it took him only a brief time to realise that the passion inspired by Ora Blake was so much deeper and more various than the blind subservience to Nature that had driven him to Ida (who had not the least idea of being a tool of Nature

herself) that it was far more dangerous than the first inevitable attack of youthful madness could ever be. It
humiliated his pride to have been the mere victim of
the race, the rudimentary male swept into matrimony by
the first woman who combined superlative femaleness with
virtue. Then he wondered if he could have loved Ora at
that time; he certainly felt ten years older to-day.

The word love brought him to his senses. It was formidable and definite. While he had believed himself to be in
the throes of a second fever caught from a beautiful
woman's concordant magnetism, he had felt merely disgusted at his weakness, not in the least disloyal to his
closest friend, whom he knew no woman could tempt him to
betray. But he realised with hideous abruptness that if
he were thrown with Ora Blake for any length of time she
would become so necessary to him through the compre-
hensive appeal, which he only half understood, that he no
more could pluck her out of him by the roots, as men disposed of the superficial passion when it became incon-
venient, than he could tear the veins out of his hill with
his hands.

He had felt the danger dimly when with her, although
he had made up his mind even then to get her out of
Montana as quickly as possible. He vowed anew, with
the first sensation of panic he had ever experienced, that
the same sky should not cover them a week hence. He
knew his influence over Mark Blake.

Then he made a deliberate attempt to banish the subject
from his mind, ordering his thoughts to their favorite
haunts underground. But one little insidious tract, so
difficult to control in all brains still young and human,
showed a disposition to create startling and vivid pictures,
to dream intensely, to cast up this woman's face, fling it
into his consciousness, with an automatic regularity that
was like a diabolical challenge to his haughty will.

He endeavoured to think of Ora with contempt: she had
married a good fellow, but one whom she must have been
compelled by the circumstances of her life to regard as her
social inferior, and who assuredly was in no sense suited
to her—merely from a parasitic dread of poverty. Other
women went to work, even if delicately nurtured. But he
was too masculine and too little influenced by certain
phases of modern thought to condemn any woman long for

turning to man in her extremity. Privately he detested women that "did things"; better for them all to give some man the right to protect them: marriage with a good fellow like Mark Blake, even without love, spoilt them far less than mixing up with the world in a scramble for bread. It would have spoilt Ora, who was now merely undeveloped; hardened, sharpened, coarsened her. He dismissed his abortive attempt to despise her; also a dangerous tendency to pity her.

Before he finished his tramp he had recaptured his poise. What a woman like Ora Blake might have to give him he dared not think of, nor would he be betrayed again into speculation. Doubtless it was all rubbish anyway, merely another trick of the insatiable mating instinct. If it were more—the primal instinct plus the almost equally insistent demands of the civilised inheritances in the brain—so much the worse, the more reason to "cut it out." But when he returned to the cottage in East Granite Street he threw himself on the divan in the parlour and slept there.

XXII

THEREFORE was he in no mood to fight another temptation; rather to take a sardonic pleasure in succumbing. An hour later, in overalls, and assisted by two of his labourers, outwardly more excited than he, for they had worked underground and vowed they smelt ore, he was running an open cut along the line of the float. As there was no outcropping it was mere guesswork; it might be weeks before he struck any definite sign of an ore body, but he was prepared to level the hill if necessary. Until he did come upon indications that would justify the expense, however, he was resolved not to sink a shaft nor drive a tunnel.

They used pick and shovel until at the depth of eight feet they struck rock. Gregory had been prepared for this and sent the unwilling but interested Oakley into Pony for drills and powder. For two days more they drilled and blasted; then—Gregory took out his watch and noted the hour, twenty-three minutes after four—one of the men gave a shout and tossed a fragment into the air.

"Stringer, by jinks!" he cried. "And it's copper carbonate or I'm a dead 'un."

Gregory frowned, but laid the bit of ore gently on his palm and regarded it with awe. He wanted gold, but at least this was his, and the first of his treasure to be torn from its sanctuary. For a moment the merely personal longing was lost in the enthusiasm of the geologist, for the fragment in his hand was very beautiful, a soft rich shaded green flecked with red; the vugs, or little cells, looked as if lined with deep green velvet.

But he turned and stared at the mining camp beyond his boundary line. One of the bits of float he had found last year had been gold quartz. Had it travelled, a mere chip, from the original body to this distant point, or danced here on the shoulders of an earthquake? Float, even under a layer of soil was often found so far from

the ore body, that it was a more fallible guide than a prospector's guess. He walked to the end of the hill, while
his miners shrugged their shoulders and resumed the
drilling.

The great vein of the Primo mine was dipping acutely to
the right. Might it not be wise for him to abandon his
present position and sink a shaft close to the line, trusting
to his practical knowledge and highly organized faculty to
strike the vein?

He stood for half an hour debating the question, listening to the intermittent roar of the engine, the rattle of ore
dumped from the buckets. Then he walked back to the
red gash in his own land. It would be the bitterest disappointment of his life if he failed to find gold in his hill,
but the dominant voice in his brain was always practical,
and it advised him to follow the willing metal for the
present instead of incurring the expense of a shaft and
possible litigation.

" 'Nother stringer!" announced one of the men, as
Gregory arrived at the long deep cut. "Guess it's time
for a windlass."

"Guess it is. Go down to the house and get some
lumber."

He descended into the cut and looked at the unmistakable evidence of little veins. Were they really stringer,
tentacles of a great ore body climbing toward the surface,
or a mere series of independent and insignificant veins not
worth exploiting? He was in a pessimistic mood, but
laughed suddenly as he realised how disappointed he would
be should further excavation demonstrate there was no
chamber of copper ore below.

Four hours later the windlass was finished and four
men were at work. At the end of the fortnight the windlass had been discarded in favor of a gasoline hoist, and
twenty-five men in three shifts were employed upon a
chamber of copper carbonate ore. The nearest of the De
Smet hills began to take on the appearance of a mining
camp; a mess house and a number of cabins were building.
Trees were falling, not only to make room for the new
"town" but to timber the mine when the time came to
sink or drift. At present those of the miners that could
not be housed by the disgusted Oakley occupied tents or
rude shacks. Oakley spent the greater part of his time

escorting the great six-horse teams from the ranch to the public road, as their drivers showed an indifference to his precious crops only rivalled by Gregory Compton's.

Mark took a week's vacation after the first carload of ore had been shipped from Pony to the sampling works in Butte and netted $65 a ton. Gregory, who was working with his men, far too impatient and surcharged with energy to walk about as mere manager, paid scant attention to him during the day; but Mark was content to sit on the edge of the cut and smoke and calculate, merely retreating in haste when the men lit the fuses.

On the third morning, as he was approaching the mine at dawn with his host, Gregory suddenly announced his intention of sending for a manager; he purposed to sink a shaft on the edge of the chamber in order to determine if the present lode was the top of a vein.

"Better take off your coat and go to work," he added. "Do you good. You're getting too fat."

"Getting? Thanks. But I don't mind. You've got several hundred thousand dollars in that chamber by the looks of things, but I suppose that wouldn't satisfy you?"

"Lord, no. That is merely the necessary capital to mine the entire hill—or fight the powers that be when they get on to the fact that I've got another Anaconda."

"Do you believe it? Big pockets have been found in solitary splendor before this."

"This hill is mineral from end to end," said Gregory with intense conviction. "And I want to get to the main lode as quickly as possible."

"By the way," said Mark abruptly, "why don't you locate your claim?"

"Locate? Why, the land's mine. Patent is all right. My father even patented several placer claims——"

"Mining laws are fearful and wonderful things. Judges, with a fat roll in their pockets, have been known to make fearful and wonderful interpretations before this. If you've struck a new copper belt—well, the enemy has billions. Better stake off the entire hill, and apply for patents. You may be grey before you get them, but the application is enough——"

"It would cost a lot of money, and I don't like the idea of paying twice over. This is costing thousands——"

"And you'll soon be taking out thousands a week. But if you need it all I'll lend you the money. It would be a good investment for Ora. You can pay me four per cent. I've a mind to go ahead to-day and begin staking off."

Gregory stood still with his head inclined at the angle which indicated that he was concentrating his mind. "Very well," he said curtly. "Go ahead. And I don't need your money. Stake off every inch of the hill and have a good map made. See that the side lines are flush with the boundary. Of course I'd never have any trouble with you, but Mrs. Blake might take it into her head to sell. Get out a surveyor when you're ready for him. Don't bother me until the thing is done."

Mark took a longer vacation and worked off some twenty pounds. He wished ruefully that Ora would return suddenly, for he doubted that his love of good living would undo the excellent work when he was once more in Butte. He employed a U. S. deputy mineral surveyor, the map was made, Gregory applied for his patents; the lawyers's mind was at rest for the present, although he kept his ears open in Butte.

Gregory sank his shaft ostensibly to determine the dip and width of the vein leading from the chamber, but secretly with the hope of meeting the body of ore already uncovered in the Primo Mine. He was elated with his splendid "find" and sudden wealth, but his old dream never left him for a moment. Indeed he would have been more than willing to miss the pyroxenite if he could come upon a lode of quartz containing free gold. That was what he had visualised all his life. He wanted to stand in his own stopes and flash his lantern along glittering seams, not merely send masses of decomposed grey-black ore to the sampling works and await returns. If he found a vein worth the outlay he would erect his own stamp mill and listen to its music. Such is the deathless boy that exists in all men. Mere wealth meant far less to him than the beautiful costly toy to play with for a while.

The shaft at the end of a month had gone down eighty feet; but had revealed only a lean vein of copper carbonates which made him forget his dreams in the fear that his mine was pinching out. But he persisted, and one morning when he went to the bottom of the shaft after the smoke of the blast had cleared away, and lit his candle, he picked up a lump of yellow ore that glittered like quartz packed with free gold. For a moment his head swam. He knelt down and brushed the shattered rock from several other bits of what looked like virgin gold; and he caressed them as gently as if they had been the cheek of his first born. But he was a geologist. He stepped into the ascending bucket a prey to misgivings. As soon as he examined his treasure in the sunlight he knew it at once for chalcopyrite—the great copper ore of the sulphide zone.

After he had assayed it he philosophically dismissed regret. It ran $26 in copper with slight values of gold and silver. Chalcopyrite ore, as a rule, runs about five per cent. in copper, its commercial value lying in the immense quantities in which it may be found, although it is necessary to concentrate at the mine. If he had struck one of the rare veins of massive chalcopyrite, averaging $25 a ton, he would take out, after it was sufficiently developed, several thousand dollars a day; and, like the carbonates, it could go straight to the smelter. As a matter of fact the vein when uncovered proved to be six feet wide and grew slightly broader with depth. The miners were jubilant over their "fool's gold", and a number of people came out and asked for the privilege of looking at what the foreman, Joshua Mann, declared to be the prettiest pay streak in Montana.

Gregory found his chalcopyrite during the third month after he began to investigate the hill. The chamber already had netted him over a hundred thousand dollars and grew richer with depth. He put an extra force at work on the promising shoot.

In the Primo Mine the luck varied. The two engineers, Osborne and Douglas, exhausted the first lode, struck a poor vein, averaging ten dollars a ton, then ran into a body of the ore netting as high as four hundred dollars. Two months later they came up suddenly against a wall of country rock. Undaunted, they drove through the mass, and struck a lean shoot of chalcopyrite.

XXIII

"WELL, what do you know about that?"

Mark's feet were on the table in the cabin Gregory had had built for himself on the top of the hill. The news had just been brought to them by one of the men who had a faithful friend in the Primo Mine.

Gregory was engaged in biting a cigar to pieces. He waited some ten minues before replying, during which Mark smoked philosophically. "I think this," he said finally, "what those fellows are after is gold, not copper. Better suggest to them to get out an expert geologist— Holmes is a good friend of mine—who will tell them to sink a shaft over on the right, or run a drift from the original stope. All we need is time."

"I'm on. But will they do it? They're not fools and what they're after mainly is cash."

"I think they'll listen to reason. They're not far from the boundary line and there's no possible doubt that the vein apexes here. The moment they cross the line I'll get out an injunction. That would stop them anyhow, hold them up until their lease had expired. And their chance is good to recover the vein on the other side. No doubt it has faulted. Have you noticed those aspens about a hundred yards beyond their shaft? Where there are aspens there is water. Now as there is no water in sight it must be below the surface, and that would indicate faulting. There might be no ore on the other side, but the chance is worth taking. Better have a talk with Osborne to-morrow. He's the least mulish of the two."

"Good. I might offer them some inducement—give them an extra month or two. Even so we'd win out. But they're not the only danger ahead. How long since you've been in Butte?"

"Not since I began work."

"Well, let me tell you that Amalgamated is buzzing.

143

They've got on to the fact good and plenty that you've got the biggest thing in copper that has been struck in Montana for twenty years. Of course they get figures regularly from the sampling works. They know you've already taken out half a million dollars worth of ore—net—and that the new shoot is getting richer every minute. They're talking loud about spoiling the market and all the rest of it. Of course that's rank nonsense. What worries them is a rival in Montana. If your mine was in Colorado or Michigan they wouldn't care shucks. You haven't taken out enough yet to worry them about the market. But if they can queer your game they'll do it. Lucky for you the smelting works need copper just now as badly as you need them. If it were not for that strike in the Stemwinder and the Corkscrew you might be having trouble.''

Gregory smiled, but as he set his jaw at the same time it was not an agreeable smile. ''I'm in a mood to fight somebody—and win. I wanted gold and didn't get it. A row with Amalgamated would relieve my feelings—although I'd rather use my fists.''

''They're mad, too, because you've named your mine 'Perch of the Devil.' That's the old name for Butte, and they look upon it as a direct challenge.''

''So it is. And you don't suppose I'd call my mine Limestone Hill, do you? I shouldn't get half the fun out of it. What the devil can they do, anyhow?''

''That's what I'm worrying about. You never know what Amalgamated has up its sleeve. There was just one man who was too much for them—for a while—and that was Heinze. And they got him in the end. I believe you'd give them a run for their money, and I don't rank you second to Heinze or any other man when it comes to brains or resource. But—well, they've got billions—and the best legal talent in the state.''

''You deserve a return compliment. You may consider yourself counsel for Perch of the Devil Mine.''

''Jimminy! But I'd like a chance at them.'' Mark's cigar was burning his fingers but he only felt the fire in his brain. ''Do you mean it?''

''Who else? Watch them. Put spies on them. Fight them with their own weapons. They've spies among my miners. That doesn't worry me a bit. I merely mention it. Let's change the subject. I've got to sleep tonight. What's the news from Europe?"

"I've got Ora's last letter here; want to hear it?"

"Good Lord, no. Tell me what they are doing. I sent Ida five thousand dollars a few days ago, so I suppose they're flying high. She cabled her thanks and said they were both well."

"Don't you really know what they've been doing?"

"Not a thing."

"Well—let's see. They went over in June. They did France, Germany—lot of places in regulation tourist style —incidentally met several of Mrs. Stratton's old friends. Then they went back to Paris, where they appear to have indulged in an orgy of clothes preparatory to a round of country house visits on the Continent and in England. Ora writes with great enthusiasm of—er—Ida's improvement. Says you'd think she'd been on top all her life, especially since she got those Paris duds, and met a lot of smart people; makes a hit with everybody, and will astonish Butte when she comes back."

"That will please her!" He felt no glow of tenderness, but some satisfaction that he could gratify the ambitions of the woman he had married. He was still too keen on his own youthful dreams, and thankful at their partial fulfillment, not to sympathise with those of others.

Mark left him to accept the more commodious hospitality of Oakley, and Gregory sat for another hour smoking, hoping for the mood of sleep. But the news had excited him, and he preferred to sit up rather than to toss about his narrow bed. The last part of the conversation, however, had given a new turn to his thoughts. Suddenly, unbidden, Ora flashed into his mind and refused to be dislodged. He walked up and down, striving to banish her as he had done before, when, sleepless, she had peremptorily demanded his attention. Tonight she was almost a visible presence in the little room.

He sat down again and grimly permitted his mind to dwell upon his long communion with her on the steps of the School of Mines. He tried to analyse his impulse to take her there. Unconventional as he was it had never occurred to him to do such a thing before, and there were twenty women in the room whom he would have expected to exercise a more potent fascination had he been in the humour for a flirtation. He had been quite honest in telling Ora that he had taken her out merely to look at her under the stars, and in intimating that to make love to her was the last thing in his mind. She had hardly seemed a woman at all there in the ballroom or when he first sat at her feet; his mind was relaxed and the "queer" romantic or poetical streak that he often deprecated had taken possession of it; if he had had a suspicion of anything more he would have fled from her at once, for she was the wife of his friend. As it was he merely had dismissed Mark from his mind and tried the experiment of setting a bit of exquisite white poetry to the music of the stars. . . .

As often as her memory had assailed him he had longed to rehearse that scene; the conversation, desultory and personal; her white profile against the flaming blue sky; the intensity and brilliancy of her eyes, so unlooked for in her young almost colorless face; her pink mouth that changed its expression so often; her curious magnetism, so unlike that of the full-blooded woman—all of that and something more; the strange community of mind—or soul?— that had drawn him on to pour out his secret self into another self of whose contact he was almost literally sensible, —in a sudden desire for comprehension that had been like the birth of a new star in his mental constellation. He had felt the thrill of her sympathy, her understanding, then another thrill of perplexity, fear; then the little quarrel, when he had thought her more adorable than ever, and no longer bearing the least resemblance to a star-wraith, but wholly feminine. When he left her it was with the confused sense that he had sojourned for a bit with the quintessence of womanhood whom Nature had cast in a new and perilous mould.

He went over the hour again and again, hoping to bore himself, to arrive at the conclusion that it had been a mere commonplace flirtation with a coquette who was as cold as she looked. But he found the recaptured scene very sweet. The power of concentration he possessed enabled him to shut out the little room and sit at the feet of the woman whose magic personality had penetrated the barriers he so jealously had built about his soul and given him the first sense of companionship he had ever known.

He was filled with a longing that shook him and hurt

him, to feel that sense of sympathetic companionship, of spiritual contact, again. And far more. He knew that she had loved no man, that all the glory and the riches within her were waiting—and if she had waited, and he had waited, and they had met unfettered that night——

He sprang to his feet. His face in the smoky light looked black.

"God!" he muttered. "God! Have I fallen as low as that? If ever I think of her again I'll cut my heart out. I hope to God the Amalgamated puts up the hell of a fight. What I want is a man's work in the world, not a play actor's."

XXIV

A WEEK later, Gregory, who was down in the bottom of the shaft, received a message by way of a descending miner that a gentleman from Butte, one Mr. John Robinson, requested the favour of an interview, and awaited him in the cabin on the top of the hill. At least such is the polite translation of the message as delivered: "Say, Boss, there's a guy upstairs in your shack what says he's from Butte, and's come out to have a chin with you—some important. Says his name is John Robinson."

Gregory swore under his breath and for a minute his face looked ugly and formidable. But as he stepped into the bucket and gave the signal he permitted his expression to change to one of grim amusement. Mr. Robinson was one of the brilliant galaxy that guided the legal footsteps of "Amalgamated"; that powerful company, financed by Standard Oil, which owned thirty-one of the mines of Butte openly, and exerted a power in Montana far exceeding that of state or nation.

Gregory wore corduroy trousers and coat, and these as well as his face and hands were white with "muck", a mixture of rock-dust and water which spattered everyone in the vicinity of the ore drills; but he wasted no time to clean up before climbing to his cabin to meet the ambassador from Amalgamated.

Mr. Robinson, a portly gentleman, still young, but manifestly the victim of easy fortune, rose from his chair before the stove and greeted his host with beaming smile and extended hand.

"My dear Mr. Compton!" he exclaimed. "It is a great pleasure to meet you again. Of course you have forgotten me for I was two grades above you in the High, when you were a little chap——"

"What have you come here for? Out with it! I've no time to waste. Sit down if you like."

148

Mr. Robinson colored angrily. He knew little of the man with whom he had come to deal, but had always relied upon his urbanity and Western heartiness to "make a hit." He knew Mark Blake and, although he had heard, like others, of Gregory Compton's record at the School of Mines, he had assumed that he was a mere student, and in other respects more or less the same sort of man as his chum. This man looked unlike any he had ever met. He concealed his chagrin, however, and resumed his seat.

"Really, Mr. Compton, you are somewhat abrupt——"

"Get down to business. What does Amalgamated want?"

Mr. Robinson wisely took the cue.

"To buy you out."

"How much will they pay?"

"How much do you want?"

"What do they offer?"

"Well, between you and me, I fancy they might go as high as a hundred thousand."

"Tell them to go to hell."

"How much do you want?"

"A hundred millions."

"Good God, man, are you mad!"

"If you had permitted me to finish, I should have added—in other words, nothing. There isn't money enough inside of Montana, let alone on top, to buy one acre of this ranch."

"But—you know what most mines are—pockety—yours may peter out any minute."

"All right. I take the chances."

"The history of Butte Hill is unique. There will never be another——"

"How do you know?"

"It stands to reason——"

"Why?"

"Oh, Lord, man, if you are indulging in wild dreams——!"

"My dreams concern no one but myself. I'm satisfied with my hill and that's all there is to it."

"I'm afraid not. Look here, you are a fine young fellow with a big future—people talk a lot about you—I don't want to see you crushed——"

"You won't."

"I'm not here to make threats, but you are not so—ah—unsophisticated as to imagine that if Amalgamated sets out to get rid of you, you can stand up against them?"

"They can't do a damned thing and you know it. They might have a few years ago, when a roll could be passed on the street to a judge who was to deny or grant an injunction within a few hours, and at a time when there was no prospect of the referendum and recall; when the people of Montana took the buying and selling of men in the legislature as part of the game, all in the day's work. But Montana has caught the reform spirit that has been sweeping over the rest of the country, and she is also getting pretty sick of corporation power. Now, sir, not only have I a clear title to this ranch, but I've staked off the entire hill and applied for patents. If Amalgamated freezes me out of Anaconda and Great Falls, I'll promote a company and put up a plant of my own. With nearly a million dollars in sight besides what I've taken out, you can figure, yourself, how much trouble I'd have in New York getting all the money I wanted. Amalgamated knows that, and my ore will continue to be smelted in Anaconda. Of course if I were within a mile or so of Butte I might be in some danger. They'd bore through and then claim that my ore vein apexed in one of their properties. But I'm too far away for that."

Gregory saw the other man's eyes flash wide open before they were hastily lowered. Mr. Robinson regarded the point of his cigar.

"Ah, yes," he said. "That's all very true. Luck is with you in a measure, but—well, take my advice and don't fight Amalgamated. They have in their employ some of the most resourceful brains in the country—that are always on the job. Heinze taught them a lesson they'll never forget."

"Let's drop the subject." Gregory rose and opened a cupboard. "Have something?"

He poured whiskey into two glasses. The men smiled as they drank, Gregory sardonically, Mr. Robinson ruefully but with thoughtful eyes. He had what Ida called the quick-rich face, large and round and fat, and it was an admirable mask.

"Like to see the mine?" asked Gregory.

"Why, yes—do you mean it?"

"Why not? If it had any secrets your spies would have turned them over before this. Glad to show it to you."

They went to the shafthead and descended in one of the buckets.

"How far down have you gone?" asked Mr. Robinson, with an air of polite interest.

"We found chalcopyrite at one hundred and ten feet, after a narrow vein leading from the chamber near the surface, and are stoping."

As they left the bucket they were greeted by the cheerful rhythmical sound of hammers on the drills, and by the light of the miners' candles they saw the men working at different points of the dark chamber, two on a scaffolding above.

"Great waste of labor," said Gregory. "I shall install a compressor before long as well as electric lighting. Of course it is only the beginning of a mine."

He saw the ambassador from Amalgamated smile, and turned on his heel. "They'll be loading the holes in a minute," he said. "And I'd like to show you the upper chamber."

When they reached the surface Mr. Robinson declined to go down into the excavation, but stood on the edge watching the busy hive below. "Great sight," he said admiringly. "How deep have you gone?"

"About seventy-eight feet."

"And the end not in sight!"

"Not yet, but of course it's only a chamber."

"You've taken out close on half a million here alone."

"Pretty near. What the devil made you suppose I'd take a paltry hundred thousand for the hill?"

"Oh, just to avoid trouble. You have the reputation of being a very clever man."

"Thanks. It's cold standing round. Wouldn't you like to take a walk? How'd you like to see the Primo Mine?"

As Gregory, who was watching him intently, anticipated, the man's face lit up. "I should like it!" he said definitely. "I hear that they too have struck chalcopyrite. Lost their gold vein."

"They're nosing after it in another direction. When the lease is up I shall consolidate with the Blakes."

"Quite natural. Of course it's the same vein?—the chalcopyrite, I mean."

"Unquestionably. And it apexes in my property."

"Are you so sure of that?"

"Not a doubt in the world. I struck the top of the vein twelve feet below the surface. But it will never go to the courts."

"Of course not."

Gregory, who looked remote, almost blank, lost not an intonation of the other man's voice, nor a flickering gleam in his cunning eyes. His own head was a little on one side, which, had Mr. Robinson had the good fortune to know him better, would have warned him that the young man for whom he had conceived a certain respect was thinking hard and to some purpose.

Douglas, who had a personal liking for his neighbor, unaware that he had been the chief instrument in the upsetting of skillful plans for untold wealth, readily gave permission to visit the mine as soon as the smoke from a recent blast would permit. Gregory and Mr. Robinson walked about to keep warm, the former pointing out the probability of a faulted ore vein under the aspens, and enlarging upon the great fortune bound to be Mrs. Blake's in any case. Then as the man merely remarked, "Yes, charming woman, Mrs. Blake; thought the night of the Prom she was one of the prettiest women I ever saw. No dead easy game there"; Gregory refrained from kicking him and said innocently.

"Good thing the law compels creditors to present their claims within a limited time, or Amalgamated might grab this mine and bore through to my hill. I understand Judge Stratton was heavily in debt to the Anaconda Company when he died."

Mr. Robinson's face turned a deep brick red, and he shot a piercing glance into the narrow noncommittal eyes opposite.

"Of course—it's too late for that, but—Oh, well——" He broke off abruptly and walked toward the shaft as Osborne beckoned. Gregory stood a moment, his head bent forward. He had experienced the sensation of coming into contact with an electrical wave. But he was smiling pleasantly as he joined his guest at the shaft house.

After the visit to the mine, during which he amiably pointed out the dip of the vein toward his own property, and Mr. Robinson succumbed to the charm which never missed fire when Gregory chose to exert it, they walked back to the ranch, where a team awaited the ambassador at the foot of the hill.

"I've had quite a delightful visit," began Mr. Robinson, when Gregory interrupted:

"I've no intention of letting you go. You must have supper at the farm and meet Oakley. I'll send off the rig and drive you in myself——"

"Oh, I couldn't think of troubling you——" Robinson, red again, stood in almost agitated embarrassment.

"No train to Butte till nine-thirty. You don't want to spend four hours in Pony?"

"The fact is——" But whatever he had on his mind died on his lips. He looked sharply into the bland smiling eyes opposite, and concluded abruptly, "All right. Many thanks. Glad of the chance to know you better."

He paid off the driver of the team and they walked toward the ranch house, Gregory commenting on Oakley's genius for dry farming, and expatiating upon the excellence of the crops. Mining was not mentioned again during the evening and the lawyer enjoyed an excellent supper.

Gregory drove him to Pony, and clung to him so closely that he had no opportunity to visit the telegraph office or a telephone booth. They shook hands cordially as the train moved off. When it was out of sight Gregory sent a telegram to Mark telling him to take the first train next morning for Virginia City and meet him in the Court House. He took his car to a garage and spent the night in Pony. On the following morning at nine o'clock he walked into the Tax Collector's office at the County Seat.

XXV

THE County Treasurer, who had just come in, looked blank for a moment, then greeted his visitor with effusive cordiality.

"Always glad to see you, Mr. Compton. It does a poor clerk's heart good just to look at a man who's such a favourite of fortune. Sit down, sir."

"I will. I've a good deal to say."

"Staked off the rest of your ranch? It'll be some little time yet before you get those patents through you've applied for already——"

"What do the taxes foot up on the Oro Fino Primo Mine?"

"Ah—What?" The man's face turned scarlet, then white. He was a young man, clerically able, but otherwise insignificant. "Why——" Then he became voluble. "The Primo mine, over there near your place? It's a new claim, isn't it? Never heard of it before those fellows from New York sank a shaft and struck it rich. Why should there be any taxes before the regular——"

"You know as well as I do that Judge Stratton patented that mine and did the necessary amount of development work, then found it salted and abandoned it. That was twenty-eight years ago. He forgot it, and so, apparently, did this office. It was regarded as an abandoned prospect hole, if anyone thought about it at all. I haven't discussed the matter with Mr. Blake, but assume that he's merely been waiting for his bill. Now, for reasons of my own, I've telegraphed him to meet me here this morning, but in case he can't come I'm prepared to pay the amount myself. How much?" and he took out his checque book.

The treasurer looked as if the cane seat of his chair had turned to hot coals. "Really—that is a large order, Mr. Compton. Twenty-eight years. It will take time to go over the records."

"I'm prepared to wait all day if necessary."

"But why this haste?"

"I have my reasons. They don't concern you in the least. Do they?"

"Why—no—but I am very busy——"

"Then put someone else on the job. I assume that the county is not averse to raking in a tidy little sum in a hurry."

"Really——"

Gregory leaned back in his chair and smiled pleasantly.

"You had a telephone from Mr. John Robinson this morning."

This time the man started visibly, but he made an effort to control himself. "I have just come in——"

"He telephoned to you last night, did he not? What did he offer you to permit him to pay those taxes to-day?"

"I will not be insulted, sir." The man's voice was almost a scream. He heartily wished he had been in training a few years longer, a graduate of the famous Heinze-Amalgamated orgy of corruption, or of the Clark-Daly epoch, when nearly every man in office had been bribed or hoped to be. "I never heard of Mr. Robinson!"

"Of course he reminded you that as the taxes are long delinquent the county has the right to put the property up at public auction, and that in any case Mrs. Blake would hardly be given the usual year in which to redeem it. But why auction when the money is ready to be paid over at once? How much did he offer you?"

"I repeat——"

"I think I can guess. It was five thousand dollars. I'll make it ten. Get to work."

The man, in whom excitement had destroyed his appetite for breakfast, and who had started out in life with the usual negative ideals of honesty, burst into tears. "My God!" he sobbed. "I've heard of the third degree. Your eyes bore a hole through one. They hurt, I say. To think that you should come in here and accuse me of taking bribes."

"Oh, hell, cut it out. Montana may be a great state, but she has her rotten spot like any other. She's been so debauched the last twenty years by open bribery that I doubt if you could lay your hand on a hundred men in her that haven't had a roll anywhere from five hundred to twenty thousand dollars passed to them, and pocketed it. Estimable citizens, too, but a man never knows his weak spot until he has a wad of easy money thrust under his nose—or flung over his transom. You are no worse than the rest. Do you take my offer?"

The County Treasurer recovered himself with amazing alacrity. Ten thousand dollars in a lump never had haunted his wildest dreams.

"All right, sir. It's a bargain. But I want bills. No checques for me."

"I congratulate you on your foresight! But there have been times in this state when checque books were not opened for months. You shall have it in bills. Where are the records?"

"In the vault there."

"I'll sit here. If you attempt to leave the room to go to a telephone I'll drag you out on the Court House steps and tell the story to the town. Now get to work."

"I'll keep my word, sir, and I know you'll keep yours." He went into the vault and appeared later trundling out a pile of records, then sat down at a table and concentrated his mind as earnestly as if corruption had never blighted it. Gregory watched him until Mark entered. Then the two men went out into the corridor, standing where they could see the table. Gregory recounted his interview with Mr. John Robinson, and the present sequel.

Mark listened with his mouth open, an expression of profound chagrin loosening the muscles of his cheerful healthy shrewd face.

"By George!" he cried. "And to think that was the one thing I never thought of. Of course I knew about the delinquent taxes, and intended to pay them when I was good and ready; but what's the use of forking over till you have to? But not to have thought of this! And I pride myself upon sleeping with one eye open—never was caught napping yet!" And for five minutes he exploited his vocabulary of profanity, heaping each epithet upon his own humiliated head.

Gregory laughed. "Merely another proof that two heads are better than one. Do you stand for the ten thousand? If not I'll pay half."

"I'd pay fifty——"

"I'll pay half," said Gregory definitely. "It means as much to me as to you."

"All right. Jimminy, but they're clever!" He was

calmer and his astute legal brain was moved to admiration. "But you are cleverer. I've always sworn by you. They'll get a jolt all right. How did you catch on, anyhow?"

"I fancy I got a wireless. The other man was thinking hard and so was I—had practically nothing else in our minds. Those things will be better explained some day. Perhaps it was merely a good guess."

"You hit the nail on the head all right. I'll have a letter to write to Ora next Sunday! She's had a narrow squeak, and she shall know whom to thank for it."

"Oh, cut that out."

Gregory went to the bank and drew the ten thousand dollars, while Mark kept watch. When the bill was finally made out, Mark examined it critically, and then gave his personal cheque. Three months later the County Treasurer resigned his office on the ground of ill health and bought an orange grove in Southern California. There he and his growing family enjoy a respected, prosperous, bucolic life.

XXVI

GREGORY had scored against the most powerful combination of capital in the world. He knew that they knew he had scored, for he had met Mr. John Robinson as he descended the Court House steps with the husband of the delinquent taxpayer, and he felt reasonably elated. But the keenest and canniest brains are not infallible, and he underestimated the resources of his mighty and now open enemy. Three mornings later, while he was still asleep, Joshua Mann, the miner in his confidence and devoted to his interests, burst into the cabin and shook him.

"There's the devil to pay, sir," he cried. "Amalgamated has staked off a claim between our boundary line and Primo."

Gregory sat up in bed. He never awakened dazed, but with every faculty alert. "What are you talking about? The Primo claim almost overlaps the ranch."

"So anyone would think. But it doesn't. That's the point. Of course the old stakes of the Primo rotted long ago. They must have got hold of the original map. But there it is: a bit of unclaimed land between Primo and the ranch. There isn't much more than room to sink a shaft, but there is, all right. Guess they've got us on the hip." And having delivered his news he relieved his mind with profanity, of which he too had a choice assortment.

Gregory flung on his clothes and accompanied by Mann walked hastily to the edge of the hill. There, sure enough, were the four posts and the flaunting notice of a located claim.

"Must have done it between shifts last night," commented the miner. "Didn't take long and the moon helped. By jing!—if I'd been round with a shotgun! Well, there'll be fun underground sames on top. The moment they break through we'll be ready for 'em. They may get there but they won't stay long. The boys will like the fun; and we'd put our last cent on you—know a winner when we see one.''

"Put on an extra force and make them work like hell. *We must get here first.* When I'm not below you're boss.''

"Thank you, sir. I'll keep 'em on the job, all right.''

"Promise them extra pay. Come up to me at eight o'clock to-night and we'll talk it over.''

He went back to the cabin and telephoned to Mark to come out at once. The lawyer arrived in the course of the morning. The first ten minutes of the interview may be passed over. Then Mark recovered his equilibrium. He lit a cigar, demanded a drink, and elevated his feet to the table.

"We'll just thresh this question out, turn the spot-light on every side of it, present and future. We ought to have done it before, but that first victory was a little too heady. Nothing like a defeat to clear the brain. What's the first thing they'll do? They won't waste time sinking a shaft if they can help it. That's the hardest kind of country rock. They'll try to buy up the lease from Douglas and Osborne. I haven't the lease with me, but most leases carry a clause which permits the original lessees to sub-let. I fancy I could get out an injunction and delay them, however, until the lease expired. But what they can do, all right, is to bribe those two men to give them the use of their cross-cut—the one that has already struck your vein—while they were sinking the shaft. Do you think they'll fall for it?''

"My experience is that most men can be bribed if the roll is big enough. Osborne and Douglas are pretty discouraged, although they've begun to drift across the fault. I'll talk to them, but they're not square men. Amalgamated could pretend to be sinking a shaft against time itself, and be drifting for all they were worth on the Primo vein. I understand that Amalgamated's head geologist has been nosing round for some time and has concluded there's a parallel fissure in their claim and that they can 'prove' apex rights.''

"How deep do you figure they'd have to sink to strike the vein at that point?''

"About two hundred feet, owing to that surface bump.''

"And it apexes here. There's no getting round that—with a square deal. But they figure on proving that they've the main vein, and yours is an offshoot? The case would go to Helena—to the Federal Courts—as Amalgamated was incorporated out of the state. That's bad. If the case could be tried in Virginia City, and there was a good healthy suspicion that the Judge was expecting to retire in comfort, you could apply for a change of venue —result of that odorous chapter in our history when every judge was on the pay roll of either Heinze or Amalgamated. Well, at least there's public opinion to be considered; the state is waking up. Here is one thing we can do. If it comes to a knock-out fight and the case goes to Helena, we can get out an expert geologist of national reputation, whose record shows him to be above bribes, and who will be bound to testify that the vein apexes in your claim. Becke of the School of Mines, will find the man we want. Now, what's your first move?"

"To stope the vein as far as the boundary line, which of course is my side-line, and as far down as possible. If they won in the courts I'd have to fork over eventually, but they'd have to wait for it, and they'll get a good jolt underground."

"You're much too calm. What have you got up your sleeve?"

"I'll tell you that when the time comes. It has nothing to do with the present case. The best thing you can do now is to make the whole thing public and get public opinion behind us. They don't own all the newspapers in the state, and they don't own all the newspapers in the rest of the country, either. Are you on?"

"You bet. Aren't you afraid there'll be a sudden strike among your miners? After all, Amalgamated is popular among the mining class. They pay good wages and treat the men pretty squarely all round. I'll say that much for them."

"I'm not worrying about that. I'll raise the wages of my miners, and they like me. I call every one of them by his first name, and they're men—not a Bohunk among them—and like the idea, too, of a fight under a good captain. If I'd put an Eastern manager in who'd put on dog, it might be different, but I've worked shoulder to shoulder with them, and not one of them has stuck harder to his job. Besides, Mann is devoted to me, and has great influence over them."

"Well, Amalgamated can't queer you in the East, for you get your roll from the Smelting Works. If that went back on you——"

"I'm not worrying about that, either. Torrence is a friend of mine. He's also a Mason. If things get hot he'll give headquarters a hint that my men, their blood being up, are as likely as not to make a bonfire somewhere. Get back to town and give the story to the new evening paper. Its lay is to fight Amalgamated for the sake of notoriety. See that their brightest man writes a story for one of the biggest New York and Chicago newspapers. Now, clear out. I've got to go below."

XXVII

THE next day Gregory visited a mine in Lewis and Clark County which recently had shut down, and bought a compressor at second hand. His miners with the air drills were soon working at five times the rate of speed that had been possible with the hand drills. The contractor in charge of the development work on what was impudently known as the Apex Mine, had installed a gasoline hoist, every new device, and as large a force as it was possible at that early stage to employ with profit. Gregory interviewed Osborne and Douglas, and obtained profuse assurances, but Mann soon discovered that there was an increased force on the Primo copper vein. Their original lease was nearly up but they had accepted Mark's offer of two months' grace; an offer he deeply regretted now, but the papers were signed and sealed. They made a feint of pushing the drift across the fault, but as they employed a small force at that point there was little room for doubt that they had been amply compensated for a doubtful undertaking.

Meanwhile work on the great surface chamber of Perch of the Devil Mine was drawing to a close. It had proved to be a hundred feet long, thirty feet wide, and seventy feet deep, and had netted half a million dollars. Some time since one of the larger houses on the West Side in Butte, built by a millionaire while still faithful to Montana, but whose family now spent twelve months of the year in Europe, New York, or California, had been thrown on the market for less than a third of its cost; new millionaires are not as plentiful in Amalgamated Butte as of old, and that unique camp is still a perch, even for those that make moderate fortunes; if no longer for the devil. It never will be a favourite roost for the gamecock's hens and chicks. The hotels and ''blocks'' are always overcrowded, and even bungalows are in demand by the energetic but impermanent young engineers and managers of the various

162

companies; but "palatial residences," built by enthusiastic citizens who either died promptly or retired in favour of their families, are a drug on that great market they helped to build. When the Murphy house, therefore, was advertised for sale Gregory bought it for Ida and cabled her the news together with five thousand dollars Mark had recently made for him on the stock market.

Above these and other expenditures, he now had half a million dollars to his credit, but he wanted a million more. The new vein was very rich for chalcopyrite, but its depth was problematical, and it might drop in values at any moment. If his belief in his hill was justified and there were huge primary deposits below, there would be no end to his riches; but it would take a year or more to determine that point; and meanwhile he wanted at least a million and a half, not only to meet the possible expenses of litigation, but to mine at depth and to open up his other claims in case Amalgamated, when it reached the chalcopyrite vein, claimed that it apexed in their property, got out an injunction, and forced him to cease work on it.

But he had another and to him a still more vital reason for wishing to make a great sum of money. Half a million dollars, particularly when spectacularly acquired, alters a man's position in his community at once, and the readjustment of his own mental attitude toward life follows as a matter of course; particularly in a country where money not only talks but rules. He was now treated, when business took him to any of the towns, as a permanent capitalist of the great state of Montana; moreover, his romantic attitude toward his hill having been inevitably dampened by its yield of mere copper, his appreciation of its heavy contribution to his bank account was wholly practical. He not only began to forecast himself as one of the small group of front-rank millionaires which Montana has donated to the American Brotherhood of Millionaires, but to be sensible of the sudden and active growth of those business instincts he had always known were dormant in his brain. It had needed but the rousing of his fighting instinct, the success of its first move, and the swift countermove of the enemy, to awaken the permanent desire, not alone to pit his brains against Amalgamated, but to show the world what he could do. In short he was on his met-

tle, and conscious for the first time of his powers and ultimate ambitions.

He had found his mine by an accident. Nature had
flung it into his lap. He was now determined to prove that
he could make money with the resources of his brain as
rapidly as the more famous of the Montanans had made it
in the past, when opportunities were supposed to be more
numerous. There never was a time when opportunity did
not coincide with the man, and of this Gregory was contemptuously aware when he dismissed the usual Wall
Street resource as commonplace, beneath the consideration
of a man living in a state whose resources had barely been
tapped.

When live brains of peculiar gifts think hard and unin-
terruptedly on a given subject they become magnets. Gregory paid frequent visits to Butte and Helena, talking
casually with many men, In less than a fortnight he found
his cue, and, accompanied by a civil engineer, disappeared
for a week.

XXVIII

TWENTY years ago it was the ambition of every Californian, no matter how blatant his state pride, to move to New York. To-day he hopes to live and die in California, the main reason being that the women of his family find themselves members of a comparatively old and settled community, enjoying many advantages and no little importance; given frequent trips abroad they are content to remain at home in houses of modern architecture, and to command a social position that New York has granted to only two or three of California's heiresses and millionaires. Montanans, at present, those that are rich or merely independent, are in the migratory phase of the earlier Californian; but as New York has extended to them an even more grudging welcome than it did to aspirants from the more picturesque state, they visit it, after successive social disappointments, merely for its dressmakers and those exterior advantages that may be exchanged for gold; the majority migrate to "The Coast," more particularly to Southern California. There they not only find relief on the sea-level from an altitude that plays havoc with the nerves, but, in the mushroom Southern cities, social position may be had for the asking, and every advantage for growing children.

Gregory had heard of a man named Griffiths, owner of the Circle G Ranch, a tract of land covering seventy-five thousand acres, who was anxious to sell and move to Los Angeles. As the ranch was practically waterless and thirty miles from a railroad, his only chance of disposing of it was by means of an alluring bargain. He was willing to sell the ranch, his large herds of horses and cattle, and bands of sheep for half a million dollars.

Gregory returned to Butte without the engineer, went directly to Blake's office, and laid his programme before his astounded friend and legal adviser.

He had found Griffiths a man unaccustomed to business but with his mind set upon retiring with a capital of half a million dollars. His efforts in money-making hitherto, had been confined to acquiring rather than disposing of property, and his trading consisted of converting live stock into such cash as was necessary for the purchase of necessities not raised on his property. But he was nearly sixty, his wife and four daughters had besought him for years to sell out and take them to California, and he was now persuaded that he was as tired of life in the wilds of Montana as they were. He was, however, possessed of one fixed idea, to leave each of his "women folks" a hundred thousand dollars when he died. Therefore would he not take a cent less than five times that amount for his fine property; but although he inserted the advertisement that had caught Gregory's eye, so far he had been unsuccessful. One man found the ranch too far from a railroad, another no good for farming, save intensive, as it was without a water supply; still another was willing to pay only a third of the amount down, with easy terms for the remainder.

"It's five hundred thousand cold cash," said Mr. Griffiths to Gregory; although in a burst of confidence later he had said: "What the dickens I'm goin' to do with that great wad of money when I get it beats me! It turns me cold to think of it."

Gregory had remained on the ranch two days, inventorying its stock, buildings, and natural resources. He estimated that seventy-five per cent. of the property was plowland, the rest "rough, wooded, and rolling." There were several sets of buildings on it, and the cattle and sheep sheds were in good condition. The cattle, sheep, and horses could be sold on a rising market for $200,000, thus reducing the cost of the land to four dollars an acre. After asking and receiving an option for thirty days, Gregory intimated that he would like to extend his trip into the mountains in search of float, and hired two riding horses and a pack horse from his host, besides buying of him the necessary food supply. Incidentally, in the course of conversation he learned that there was a river "somewheres in the mountains between thirty and forty miles northeast."

He received more minute directions from a prospector regarding this body of water, which was the object of his trip, and six miles from Circle-G entered a ravine some twenty-five miles long. After climbing one of the mountain sides that bounded the ravine, descending and crossing another gulch, and climbing again, he and his companion saw, far below, between the narrow walls of a cañon, an abundant mountain stream.

The engineer proposed to divert this body of water to Circle-G Ranch. Through the nearest mountain side he should drive a tunnel six hundred feet long, and cross the short and crooked ravine with a thousand feet of flume to a point where it would be necessary to drive another tunnel, about two hundred feet in length. This would conduct the diverted body of water into the long ravine, down which it would flow to a point six miles above the ranch. Here the engineer purposed to construct a dam thirty feet high for the purpose of raising the water to an elevation from which it would flow through a canal or "ditch", to the more level portions of the ranch. A rough estimate of the cost of this project, from headworks to ditch was $300,000.

He returned to Circle-G, told Mr. Griffiths that he had found no float, but nevertheless liked the neighbourhood and was inclined to buy the ranch and sell it in small farms to settlers. He would return to Butte and think it over. If he concluded to buy he would pay a half million dollars in cash, and, if Mr. Griffiths were agreeable borrow back $300,000, for improvements, giving a mortgage at seven per cent. on the forty thousand acres he proposed to make attractive for settlers. He gave no hint of his irrigation project. Griffiths had known of this body of water, but it had never occurred to him nor to anyone else to divert it. He was a stock-grower, pure and simple, with no "modern notions", and Gregory had no intention of enlarging his vision. He would pay the man his price, but he had the ruthlessness of his type.

He had more than one motive for offering to borrow back $300,000 of the payment money; not only should he need it at once, but he feared, after Mr. Griffith's confidence, and knowing his kind, that the old man would withdraw in terror at the last moment, preferring the safe monotonies of his ranch to the unknown responsibilities of a capitalist; like others he had heard that it is sometimes easier to get money than to invest it. Gregory told him to think it over and write to the Daly and Clark Banks in Butte, and to the National Bank of Montana, in Helena, for information regarding his own standing and financial condition. He left the entire family in as hopeful a frame of mind as himself.

On confirmation of the report that forty thousand acres could be put under water by gravity, he should close the deal at once, file a notice of appropriation for forty thousand miner's inches of water, and begin work on the first tunnel. He then intended to lay the matter before one of the great land-selling organisations of Chicago or New York, proposing that he be paid $1,400,000 for the forty thousand acres of irrigated land, subject to mortgage; demonstrating that the land so purchased for thirty-five dollars an acre (or forty-three and a half dollars including the mortgage) could readily be sold to settlers for one hundred, if railroad facilities were provided. As a further inducement, to cover the cost of railroad construction, he would execute a deed and place it in escrow, as a guarantee and evidence of good faith, and accompanied by a contract authorising the land selling company to dispose of the remaining thirty-five thousand acres at ten dollars an acre. The construction of the railroad would add materially to the value of the unirrigated land also, and a pledge of this portion of the property as security that the railroad would be built would be acceptable, because the estimated cost, with liberal allowances, was under $350,000.

The sum paid him by the land selling company would, in addition to the large sum realised by the sale of the live stock, give him at least $1,600,000, or $1,100,000 over the half million originally invested.

Mark listened with his eyes and mouth wide open.

"By George!" he exclaimed, when Gregory finished. "Did you dope all that out yourself? That's the talk of a man who's been in the land business for years. How did you ever think of it?"

"What's a man's brain given to him for—to turn round in a circle? Do you find the plan feasible?"

"It's feasible all right—given a cold half million in hand and brains behind it—plus imagination. That's where you win out. You'll be the richest man in Montana yet."

"I intend to be."

"And the first man born here to make one of the old-time fortunes."

"I hadn't thought of that!"

Mark dismissed enthusiasm and put his own astute brain to work.

"The hitch will be with your land selling company. They might be dazzled, even convinced, but they're cold-blooded, and they never have any too much cash on hand. What special line of argument do you propose to hand out?"

"Several. I didn't go to the Circle-G Ranch without making certain investigations beforehand. In the first place Government statistics prove the productivity of Montana soil without irrigation. I am not the first to discover that this same soil when irrigated is insured against crop failure. In the second place a study of the U. S. Government reclamation projects convinced me that I could, all things being favourable (such as water supply and gravity), put a large tract of land under water at a very small cost compared to the cost under the plan of procedure adopted by the Government. By the plan I have mapped out I can sell both land and water for less than the cost of water alone under the Government direction. But I have a final inducement which I believe will bring the selling company to terms. Those forty thousand acres when irrigated will be peculiarly adapted to the growing of seed peas. This is the best soil in the country for peas. Now the seed houses of the country are in great need of large quantities of seed peas, and the selling company could easily interest these concerns to the extent of securing their financial backing. They would no doubt buy large blocks themselves. Such an opportunity has never been offered them—forty thousand acres under the ditch, and adequate railroad service. This will enable the selling company to raise an initial payment to me of $200,000. And if I guarantee the ditch and the railroad they are in a position to make the same guarantee to settlers to whom they may make sales in a retail way. They'll have no difficulty getting $100 an acre retail; and the seed houses no doubt would invest and become real owners, thus saving the profit now paid to farmers who grow for them under contract. Got it?"

"I get you. But why put all of your own money into

the ranch? Ora has taken something like half a million out of that mine. I could let you have that."

"I'll risk no woman's money. Of course I shouldn't put my own in if I didn't believe it to be a dead sure thing, but there's always risk." He took a packet of papers from his overcoat pocket. "Here are the option and abstract of titles. I wish you would examine them. Say nothing of all this at present—nor for a long time after. I'll spring it when I'm ready—which will be **after** I've disposed of the irrigated land. Will you go out with me when I return to Circle-G? I shall want you to attend to the details of sale and to the location of the water rights."

"I'll go all right. And I'm only living to see what you'll do next."

XXIX

MEANWHILE the story of the Compton-Amalgamated war was the sensation not only of Montana but of the entire country. The Butte morning papers ignored it, but the *Evening Bugle* reaped a golden harvest. The editor himself, who was the Montana correspondent of one of the great New York dailies, made his reputation with the most sensational "stuff" that had gone from the Northwest since Heinze retired from the field. The hill swarmed with reporters. Two Eastern newspapers sent special correspondents to the spot. In less than a fortnight the public knew all there was to know and far more. Perch of the Devil Mine was photographed inside and out, and its uncompromising ugliness but added to its magnetism; which emanated from a "solid hill of metal just below a thin layer of barren soil." The general reader, who admired the colour of copper, conceived that it emerged in solid sheets.

Gregory refused to be interviewed or photographed, but was snapshotted; and his long sinewy figure and lean dark face, his narrow eyes and fine mouth, won the championship of every woman partial to the type. The women's papers, as well as those run by radicals, socialists, and conservative men of independent tendencies, advocated his cause against the wicked trust; nor was there a newspaper in the country, however capitalised, that resisted the temptation to make him "big news." To his unspeakable annoyance he began to receive letters by the score, most of them from women; but he lost no time employing a secretary whose duty was to read and burn them. He appreciated his fame very vaguely, for between his mine and the innumerable details connected with his new ranch, he had little time to devote to newspapers or his own sensations. But although personal notoriety was distasteful to him and reporters a nuisance, he felt more than compensated by the success of his publicity scheme, and the assurance that it was causing the enemy unspeakable annoyance and apprehension.

He paid a visit to Chicago after work had begun on the first tunnel, and spent several days with the interested but cautious officials of the greatest of the land selling companies. Like all silent men, when he did talk it was not only to the point, but he used carefully composed arguments incisively expressed. He indulged in no rhetorical flights, no enthusiasms, no embellishment of plain facts. He might have been a mathematician working out an abstract problem in algebra; and this attitude, combined with his reputation as a "winner", and the details of his cautious purchase of Circle-G Ranch, finally impressed the company to the extent of sending one of their number, who was an expert in land values, to the ranch. Gregory accompanied him, took him to the mountain river, showed him the engineer's report, pointed out the undeviating slope between the river and the ranch, and the land's rich chocolate brown soil of unlimited depth. The upshot was that the expert returned to Chicago almost as enthusiastic as if the original scheme were his. After consultation with several of the seed houses, the land company agreed to buy on Compton's terms, and to pay $200,000 down, $500,000 at the end of sixty days, and $700,000 at the end of four months.

Ora and Ida had asked for an extension of leave, as they had not yet "done" Italy, Spain, and Egypt, and both husbands had given a willing consent; Gregory from sheer indifference; Mark because he was so busy that he no longer had time to miss his wife. He refused to give Ora's picture to the enterprising correspondents, but they found no difficulty with the local photographer. They had not been long uncovering the romantic history of the Oro Fino Primo Mine, and it made a welcome pendant to the still recourseful "story" of Perch of the Devil. Ora's beauty, accomplishments, charm, family history, as well as her present social progress in company with her "equally beautiful friend", the wife of the hero of the hour, became public property.

Altogether, Butte, after several years of oblivion, was happy and excited. So far, although mineralogically the most sensational state in the Union, and the third in size, she had given to the world but four highly specialized individuals: Marcus Daly, perhaps the greatest mine manager and ore wizard of our time; W. A. Clark, who accumulated millions as a moving picture show rolls in dimes; F. Augustus Heinze, who should be the greatest financial power in America if brains were all; and the Sapphic, coruscatic, imperishable Mary MacLane. An outstanding quartette. But Daly was dead, Clark was but one of many millionaires, submerged in New York, Heinze was reaping the whirlwind, and the poet was nursing her wounds. Montana was in the mood for a new hero, and the American press for a new and picturesque subject to "play up for all he was worth."

XXX

ORA and Ida were sitting at one of the little round tables in the pretty green and wicker smoking-room of the Hotel Bristol in Genoa, drinking their coffee and smoking their after-luncheon cigarettes, when Ida, who was glancing over the *Herald,* cried,

"Aw!"

Ora looked round in surprise. Ida often relieved the strain when they were alone by relapsing into the vernacular, but was impressively elegant in public.

"What is it?" she asked apprehensively. "Anybody we know dead? That is about all the news we ever get in these Continental——"

"Dead nothing. Greg's struck a bigger bonanza than I had any idea of, and Amalgamated is after it. They tried to corral your mine for delinquent taxes, but got left. Found a bit of unclaimed land between your claim and the ranch and staked off. They're sinking a shaft and mean to prove that the vein—Greg's—apexes in their claim. Wouldn't that come and get you! Just listen." And she read aloud an embellished but not untruthful tale. "Glory, I hope they don't get him! That would be the end of all my fond dreams."

"I have an idea that Mr. Compton was born to win. At all events you have your new house in Butte, and all the money you can spend for the present."

"Yes, but I want money to spend in Butte, live in that house, and make things hum. However, I guess you're right. I'll bet on Greg. Here come the letters. Hope you get one from Mark as I'd like some real news."

A page with letters in his hand had entered the room. He served the young American ladies first as their tips were frequent and munificent, particularly Ora's. The other people in the room were English and Italian.

Ida's letters were from Ruby and Pearl. Ora's from Mark, Professor Becke, and two of her English friends.

She opened her husband's first. It contained an account of the threatened loss of her mine, her narrow escape, and Gregory's rescue. It was graphically written. Mark fancied himself as a letter writer and never was averse from impressing his clever wife.

Ora's face flushed as she read; she lost her breath once or twice. She pictured every expression of Gregory's eyes as he perforated the clerk; her heart hammered its admiration. She was too thoroughly Montanan and the daughter of her father to be horrified at bribery and corruption. For the moment she forgot gratitude in her exultation that he had triumphed over the mightiest trust in the country. But before she finished the letter she sighed and set her lips. She handed it deliberately to Ida.

"Here is an account of the first development," she said casually. "It will interest you."

Ida read the letter hastily. "Well, they caught him napping after all," she said with profound dissatisfaction. "He dreams too much, that's what. He's got a practical side all right, but he isn't on the job all the time. I'd like to write and tell him what I think of him but guess I'd better keep my mouth shut."

"It was Mark's fault as much as Mr. Compton's—more. He should have had a new map made of my claim; or, if he did have one made, he should have studied it more carefully. Anybody to look at it would assume that it touched the boundary line of your—Mr. Compton's ranch."

"Well, Greg'll get out of it some way. When he does sit up and take notice he doesn't so much as wink, and so far as he knew or cared the rest of the world might have waltzed off into space. Lucky it hit him to buy the house and send that last five thousand before he snapped close on Amalgamated——"

"What does Miss Miller have to say?"

"Nothing much but ecstasies over my house. The Murphys had taste, it seems, so I won't have to do a thing to it. Say, Ora, don't you feel as if you'd like to go back?"

Ora looked up and her face turned white. "Go back? I thought you wanted to stay over here for a year, at least. We haven't half seen Europe yet—to say nothing of Egypt."

"Yes—I know—but sometimes I feel homesick. It isn't only that I want to make Butte sit up; but—well, I suppose you'll laugh, but I miss the mountains. I never thought much about them when I was there, but they've kind of haunted me lately."

"There are mountains in Europe."

"I know, but they're just scenery. Our mountains are different."

Ora looked at her speculatively. It was not the first time that Ida had surprised her with glow-worms flitting across her spiritual night, although she seemed to be so devoid of imagination, or what she would have called superfluous nonsense, as to inspire her more highly organised friend with envy. Her mental and artistic development had been rapid and remarkable but uneven. She yawned through the opera and symphony concerts. She would always be bored by pictures unless she could read a "story" in them, although she had now mastered the jargon of art as well as most of her quick-witted countrywomen. In Florence and Rome she had "struck" after one morning of picture galleries, but she showed a spontaneous and curious appreciation of the architecture of the Renaissance. Ora had expected the usual ecstasies over the old castles of England and Germany, but although Ida admired them heartily, and even declared they made her feel "real romantic," it was for the Renaissance palaces of France and of the cities they visited in Italy that she reserved her instant and critical admiration. Ora, who like most imaginative people played with the theory of reincarnation, amused herself visioning Ida in Burne-Jones costumes, haunting the chill midnight corridors of a Florentine palace, dagger in hand, or brewing a poisoned bowl. If Ida possessed a rudimentary soul, which suffered a birth-pang now and then, Ora had caught more than one glimpse of a savage temper combined with a cunning that under her present advantages was rapidly developing into subtlety. But Ida indulged too little in introspection to develop her inmost ego other than automatically. To mental progress she was willing to devote a certain amount of labour. Whenever they were not on a train or visiting at country houses, she spent an hour every morning with a teacher of either French or Italian; German she had refused to "tackle," but, to use her own phrase, she "ate up" the Latin languages, and her diction was remarkably good. If picture galleries replete with saints, virgins, madonnas and Venuses bored her, she returned more than once to the portrait rooms in the Pitti and the Uffizi galleries, haunted the museums with their mediæval and Renaissance furniture and tapestries, and eagerly visited every palace to which the public was admitted.

And she proved herself as adaptable as Ora had hoped. In England she bored her way through the newspapers until she was able to sustain her part in political conversation. She soon discerned that English people of assured position and wide social experience liked a certain degree of picturesque Americanism when it was unaccompanied by garrulity or blatant ill-breeding. She amused herself by "giving them what they wanted," and was a more pronounced success than Ora, who was outwardly too much like themselves, yet lacking the matchless fortune of English birth. But this did not disturb Ora, who made more real friends, and derived endless amusement observing Ida. On one occasion they visited for a week at one of the country homes of a duke and duchess that had entertained Mrs. Stratton many years ago, and Ida had enchanted these bored but liberal products of a nation that led with too much indifference the Grand March of Civilisation with her Western "breeziness" and terminology (carefully selected), combined with her severely cut and altogether admirable gowns, and her fine imposing carriage. From this castle she went on with Ora to one leased by an ambitious American more English than the English, who permitted herself to indulge in a very little fashionable slang, but had consigned the American vernacular to oblivion in the grave of her ancestors. Here Ida was languid and correct (save at the midnight hour when she sought Ora, not only for relaxation but the instructions she was never too proud to receive); her English slang (which she had "swapped" for much of her own with her various British admirers) was impeccable, and she flirted like a stage duchess.

She estimated the various aristocracies she entered under Ora's wing as a grand moving picture show run for the benefit of Americans, and was grateful to have an inside seat, although nothing would have bored her more than to take a permanent position in their midst. With their history, traditions, psychology, she concerned herself not at all; nor did she in any way manifest a desire to cultivate the intellectual parts of her shrewd, observing, clutching brain. She threw away as many opportunities as she devoured, but on the whole proved herself somewhat more adaptable than the usual American woman elevated suddenly from the humbler walks of life to the raking searchlights of Society. In Berlin and Vienna she repeated her social triumphs, for, although Americans do not penetrate far below the crust of Continental society, smart men abound in the crust; Ida graduated as an adept in flirtation with agreeable and subtle men of the world, yet keeping the most practical at arm's length with a carefully calculated Western directness and artlessness that amounted to genius.

In France and Italy the dazzling fairness of Ora had its innings. A vague suggestion of unreality, almost morbid, and a very definite one of unawakened womanhood, combined with a cultivated mind, ready wit, and air of high breeding, gave her a success as genuine as Ida's and somewhat more perilous. But she soon learned to tread warily, after her theories of European men had been vindicated by personal experience. In fact, after the two girls had ceased to be mere tourists they had taken the advice of one of Mrs. Stratton's friends and enlisted the services of an indigent lady of title as chaperon. Lady Gower had been little more than a figurehead but had served her purpose in averting gossip; and now that her charges were tourists again had returned to her lodgings in Belgravia. As maids also are a doubtful luxury when travelling they had recently dismissed the last of a long line.

On the whole the two girls had got on together amazingly well. They had had their differences of opinion, but Ora was too proud to quarrel, Ida too easy-going and appreciative of the butter on her bread. It was fortunate, however, that Gregory had been able to provide his wife with an abundance of money, for she was far too shrewd, and far too interested in prices, to remain hoodwinked for long. After three months of sight-seeing and *pensions* both had been glad to leave the tourist class and mingle in the more spectacular life of the great world, and that had meant trousseaux in Paris. There Ida had "gowned" herself for the first time, and her delight in her fashionable wardrobe had been equalled only by her satisfaction in driving a bargain. At present they were resting in Genoa, a favourite city of Ora's, after a hard ten weeks in Rome.

XXXI

THEY finished their letters and went up to their rooms to rest, for they had "done" several churches and the Campo Santo during the morning.

"Thank the lord," said Ida, as they walked up the stairs after waiting ten minutes for the lift, "there are no picture galleries in this town that one *must* see. The rest of the programme is streets and architecture, which is worth while. These internal streets make me feel as if I were going right through to China, or whatever is underneath Italy. Genoa, before it had any houses on it, must have looked like Last Chance Gulch, Helena, Montana."

They had reached their connecting rooms. Ida extended herself on a sofa, Ora made herself as comfortable as possible in a chair and lit a cigarette.

"Say, kid," pursued Ida, "you smoke too much. Follow my illustrious example. I go just so far and no farther—one cigarette after each meal because it makes me feel nice and aristocratic. You're the kind that lets a habit run away with you. I deliberate. You drift. See?"

Ora laughed. "Funny thing, nature! Anyone would say quite the opposite of each of us."

"It's like life. Not a blooming thing is just what you figure it out beforehand. Here I wanted the Collins house and I've got the Murphy. And Greg, that I figured on being a millionaire by the time I got back, has gone and tied himself up in litigation, or is heading that way."

"You ungrateful wretch! You came to Europe 'figuring' on making a thousand dollars serve for the entire trip and you already have had eleven thousand. Most rules work both ways. But you don't really want to go back?"

"I do. It's been growing for some time and now it's ingrowing. You can get enough of anything and I've had enough of Europe. Besides, I'd like to get back to a country where lifts are elevators and don't go to sleep a few times on the way up; where it doesn't take an hour to draw a bath, which it does wherever it's pronounced băth; where you can drink plain water, and don't have cheese or garlic or grease in all your food; where you are never taken for what you ain't; where you are never cheated and overcharged because you're an American; where you don't have to see a sight a minute; where you don't have to talk up to people who don't give a hang about anything that interests you; where you are not looked upon as a rank outsider by ancient aristocrats and concierges, no matter how polite they try to be; and where the word democracy means what it is. Over here every socialist—I'll bet every anarchist—would give his front teeth to be a king, a duke, or even a rich bourgeois. That's what's the matter with all of them. Give me America, above all, old Montana. A little money and a lot of 'go' are all you need out there.''

"Oh, Ida! Ida! will you never appreciate the glory of Europe? Is that all you have got out of it?"

"I've squeezed it dry, all right, and I'll take back a lot more than I figured on. Watch me when I'm swelling round Butte, imitating the chaste simplicity of a British duchess—minus the duds they generally sport. There's nothing like Europe to teach you what's what—especially the way we've seen it—put you wise in ten thousand different ways, and fill your mind with pretty pictures—that ain't in galleries. But after all it's just a course in the higher education, and you're outside of it all, every minute. To live you've got to go back to your own country.''

"That's true enough!"

"Could you marry a European and live over here for the rest of your life and never see those mountains again that just seem to belong to you—or even screaming old Butte?''

"No!" Ora spoke with uncommon vehemence. "I couldn't!"

Ida raised herself on her elbow and looked at her friend shrewdly. "I can't see that you've enjoyed yourself so much over here. It seems to me that you've got your fun out of showing me round. You had more real gaiety in you in Butte. You may not know it but you look pretty sad sometimes.''

"Life is sad—mighty sad.''

"Is it? That's a new one for me. I think it a pretty

fine old proposition. What went wrong with you—early in the game?"

"Nothing. Travel is tiring. I'm not as strong as you are."

"You're as tough as a pine knot, for all you look like a lily expecting to be decapitated by the first wind. Well, you won't tell if you won't, but I'll tell you what you need. You've never been in love and that's a sort of ache in women until they've taken a good dose of the only medicine. I rather hoped you'd met your fate in the Marchese Valdobia. He's the sort you once told me was your type, and you seemed to like him pretty well for about five weeks in Rome. The lord knows he was tall enough, and dark enough, and thin enough, and looked as if he had a beastly temper besides. Then you turned him down good and hard. I was sorry——"

"My dear Ida! Are you regretting that I did not have a liaison with Valdobia? I remember your virtuous sentiments in Butte. Perhaps it is time for us to return!"

"Oh, I'm all right. But I'm that advanced I wouldn't mind you having an affair the least bit if it would make you happy——"

"Happy! What happiness do you imagine there can be when you are absolutely at the mercy of a man?—when you never know whether you will see him again or not?—a woman has no real hold on a lover. Matrimony with the man you love may have its agonies, but at least you live with him, you make his home; his interests are yours, he is dependent upon you for comfort and sympathy; there are a thousand ways in which you can endear and enchain him. But a lover, whom you meet in secret for one purpose only, who can give you no real companionship —oh, no! I shall not court that particular form of suffering. Life is hard enough without that! I've known women with lovers and so have you."

"I don't say it would last forever; nothing does, for that matter. But at least you would live for a little while —come down off the unearthly plane you roost on now. Whatever you went through, it would leave you all-round developed and philosophical—in a frame of mind to see and accept life as it is. You need hardening. I was born hard. You're as soft as mush, for all you look like those marble bores in the Vatican, and as romantic as if you'd spent all your life in a castle in a wood with the draw-bridge up. I believe you even keep a diary——"

"Diary——" Ora sat up straight.

"I've seen and heard you writing by the yard, late at night, mostly. It wasn't letters, because we always get those off our chest just after breakfast—fine system. Unless you're a budding author——"

"They were letters!" Ora, who was strung up to a high pitch and merely smoking for relief, felt a defiant impulse to indulge in the impudence of confession. "I've written yards and yards of letters to a man——"

"What? And you don't send them off!"

"I don't know him."

"Good lord, what next? An ideal, I suppose."

"Yes—that's it."

"Do you mean you never saw him—anyone to suggest him—it? What gender has an ideal, anyhow?"

"I saw him—talked with him, once. I said I didn't know him."

"And you're in love with him!"

"Not in the least. He simply jolted my imagination, gave me the idea of what might be—have been. I—it is hard to express—I feel in a sort of mental—spiritual?—affinity with him. When I write I have a queer sense of absolute communion—as if we were talking—I suppose it is because I know he would understand if I could send the letters——"

"And you've never sent one?"

"Of course not. It is—well, just a little private one-sided drama I'm living; a sort of book of which I am the heroine. While I write I am alive. The rest of the time I wonder what I was put on this earth at all for."

"Look at here, Ora, the best thing we can do is to send for old Gower and go back to Rome. You'll be having nerves first thing you know. No, we'd cut out the annex. I'm dead sick of her, and everybody knows we're all right; in Rome they don't care, anyhow. You could have a real romance. We'd take one of those old palaces, haunted, moth-eaten, with one of those antique porters that looks as if he'd let out midnight lovers ten centuries ago, and beds that twenty centuries have died in. That would just suit you. I'd enjoy a second-hand romance first-rate, and be the trusted friend."

"Ida, you are incorrigible! Even if I cared a penny about Valdobia do you suppose I would betray my husband?"

"Rats! Don't you suppose Mark has a girl down on The Flat? Greg has, I'll bet—well, don't look as if you were going to faint. What's the use of being a dog in the manger? Mark'll be the same old devoted when you get back."

"Oh, do keep quiet! And I wish I might never see Butte again. I think I'll write to Mark and ask him to move to New York. He now has plenty of money to wait, and it wouldn't take him long to establish himself anywhere——"

"I thought you loved Montana—wanted to do something big for her——"

"We've been away a long time. I fancy I'm weaned. It is only once in a while that I feel a pull—merely because I was born there."

"Well, Mark won't leave, believe me. He's Western from the cut of his back hair to his love of the free-and-easy. No New York for him except the all-night two or three times a year. Butte's your fate unless you leave him."

"I'll never do that, but I'd like to stay over here for another year or two. Remember, I was brought up in Europe—and—and—I *might* meet the man—If you want to know I've tried. I'd never go as far as you suggest, but I could get something—companionship, perhaps, out of it."

"When you meet the man you'll forget all you ever knew, and men don't companion for a cent when there's nothing in it. I haven't been turning them inside out these last six months for nothing; what I don't know about men wouldn't fill a thimble. Why don't you round up your letter man?"

"That is for ever impossible."

"Do give me a hint who he is. I'm half dead with curiosity. Where'd you meet him?"

"Keep quiet. I'm going to take a nap."

"Well," said Ida, yawning and stretching herself, "so am I, if you've closed up. When we get back to Butte and there's no more sight-seeing on, we'll have to cut out these siestas or we'll get fat, and then good-bye."

XXXII

THEY went out at half past five and joined the dense saundering throng under the arcade of the Via Venti Settembre. All Genoa turns out at this hour with apparently no object but to amble and stare. The two girls, particularly Ora, who appeared to be the only blonde in the city, were almost mobbed. Every other man spoke to them, or rolled his eyes and twirled his moustache. But they preserved a lofty and blank demeanour, and were practically unmolested. The Genoese works almost as hard as the American during a few hours of the day and haunts the afternoon throngs only to amuse himself indolently. If one woman ignores him he passes on philosophically to the next.

"Lord, but I'd like to get a move on!" exclaimed Ida. "Why don't they *walk?* Is this what they call exercise? And I wouldn't mind their ogling and speaking if they only wouldn't pinch. I'll give this side a rest, anyhow." And she dexterously changed places and drew Ora's other arm through her own.

"I love them, pinches and all," said Ora, warmly. "They are like children in one way, and yet they really know how to rest and enjoy themselves, which is more than our men ever do. Even the working-class enjoys life over here. I wonder why they emigrate?"

They had passed round the corner of the arcade and entered the Piazza Defarrari, working their way toward the Via Roma. Ora stopped before one of the cantinas behind the statue of Garibaldi. "Look at those men drinking their cheap wine and gossiping. They look as if they hadn't a care in the world."

"Give me the hustling American," said Ida contemptuously. "I don't call this life. They're just drifting along waiting for the Angel Gabriel to blow his trump. What makes them so lazy and contented? They know they can go just so far over here and no farther. Ancient history made classes and masses, and while they have fun, some of them, thinking they're socialists, they know that most of them will stay put. But the only real fun in life is getting ahead of the next fellow and knowing that your chance is as good as any.''

''What a truly American sentiment!''

''I'm American, all right, and that's the reason I want to get back to Butte, where things hum every minute, and there's no real poverty. Fancy calling these left-overs 'middle-class' like our miners. Every one of those looks forward to being President of Amalgamated one of these days, or striking it rich in the mountains.''

''There are different varieties of happiness, fortunately for several billions that are seeking it.''

''Do you know,'' said Ida, abruptly, as they turned into the Galleria Mazzini from the Via Roma, ''it's queer, but I feel more at home in Italy than I have anywhere else over here, although I had a really better time in England and Germany and Austria. I don't hit it off much with Italians, but—well—I have a more settled-down feeling.''

''That's odd!''

''Why?''

''Oh, I've been romancing about you a bit, fancying you a reincarnation of one of those fascinating abominable women of the Renaissance, who had innumerable lovers and poisoned their husbands, or rivals. You would look quite wonderful in those long velvet or brocaded gowns, with sleeves that come down over the hands, and pearls twined in your hair.''

''That's not a bad idea. Maybe I was, although I don't see myself with lovers or thinking anybody worth swinging for. Several American reincarnations must have changed my habits; but I don't mind looking the part. Good idea —when we get back to Paris I'll have several of those Renaissance costumes made. They won't go out of style, either. Greg can fork over the pearls later.''

''You'll be a picture. I wish I had thought of it before. Don't you think you are capable of jealousy?''

''Nixie. To be jealous you've got to have a fearful crush; and thank the lord I don't love anybody but myself and never shall.''

''That is often the secret of love for some man—of most

men's love for a woman, I imagine! Perhaps it creates the most powerful delusion of all.''

"Well, none of it in mine. Me for the great society act. I'm going to be the grandest dame in Montana, and when I've wrung that dry I'll move on to New York. Greg says he won't, means to live and die in Montana, but I guess he'll manage to stand it if I desert him occasionally. If he's got a hill full of copper he won't know whether I'm in Butte or the Waldorf-Astoria. You look better, Ora; you ought to stay out of doors more and watch these funny old crowds. You've got a nice colour, and smile as if you meant it—Oh! that's it, is it? Well, thank goodness, I've got a front seat——''

"What on earth are you talking about?''

"Pretending you haven't seen him? I like that!''

Ida felt the arm within her own stiffen. "Valdobia! Don't leave me for a moment.''

"I won't, although, believe me, the rôle of gooseberry is no cinch.''

"I've played it for you often enough.''

"You have, and I'm a dead game sport. Lord! he looks more bad-tempered than ever. Probably every meal he's eaten since you left has disagreed with him, including maccaroni.''

"He's not bad-tempered. Hot-tempered, no doubt, but I'm sure he's kind and quite amiable. He's rather grim, and of course he's lived pretty hard and is disillusioned. That is all.''

"That's right, stand up for him. Bad sign—or a good one! He's seen us!''

Valdobia's eyes flashed recognition, although he lifted his hat with unsmiling lips, and made no effort to push his way through the crowd. Ora favoured him with a glance of chill indifference as she returned his salutation, but she noticed that he made the young Genoese patricians look provincial. He not only was tall and gracefully built, his carriage military, but he had the air of repose and distinction, as well as the keen, tolerant, detached glance, of the man who has spent his life in the great world, and, on the whole, subordinated his weaknesses to his brain. It was evident that he was dressed from Conduit Street, and at first glance, in spite of his dark colouring and fine Roman features, his nationality was not obtrusive; he looked the cosmopolitan, the man-of-the-world, who might have made his headquarters in any one of her great capitals. As a matter of fact, while in the diplomatic service he had lived in several, including a short sojourn in Washington; but after coming into a large inheritance through the death of his father and of an energetic uncle who had boldly gone into business and prospered, he had travelled for a year in Africa and India and then settled in Rome.

If he was too indifferent or too wise to hurry he managed to make his way consistently toward them, although a crowd had formed about a bulletin board to read the latest news from the seat of war. He stood opposite them in three or four minutes and shook hands politely with both.

"At last!" he said. "I called at the Bristol, and have been looking for you ever since." He had a warm deep voice but his tones and manner expressed less than his words.

"You don't have to look far in Genoa," said Ida, giving him a cordial smile and handshake to cover Ora's chilling welcome. "If the whole town turns out for what it calls exercise, each quarter seems to keep to itself. We see the same faces every day."

Valdobia fell into step beside Ida, who at once began to chatter questions about their common acquaintance in Rome. She grinned mentally as she rattled off titles, recalling the wiry little figure of her mother at the washtub, and her father with his "muck"-spattered overalls and blue dinner pail; but Valdobia, too accustomed to titles to note whether Americans were lavish in their use or not, replied naturally and refrained from glancing at the woman who had given his self-centred ego the profoundest shock it had ever received. He was now thirty-eight. In his early manhood he had loved with the facility and brevity of his race. Then for six years, after his return to Rome, he had been the lover of a brilliant and subtle woman ten years older than himself, who, for a short time, inspired in him the belief that at last he had entered the equatorial region of the *grande passion*. This passed off, and she became a habit, which lasted until, with the decline of her beauty, she lost much of her finesse, as well as her control over both temper and complexion. It had taken him a year or more to regain his liberty, and when he did, after scenes that he fain would dismiss from his memory, he determined to keep it. His long experience with a woman of many characteristics and one or two noble qualities, before she gossipped and inflamed them to death, had thoroughly disillusioned him, and since his release his gallantries had been lighter than in his youth. When he first met Ora Blake he was attracted merely by her cold fairness, redeemed from classic severity by her brilliant seeing eyes, which so often sparkled with humour, and amused at her naïve and girlish attitude of happiness in temporary freedom; so successfully practised by herself and Ida. He had supposed her to be little more than twenty, and had wondered if her husband were even busier than the average American, to let her run away so soon. When she told him she was twenty-seven, and had been married seven years, he found himself speculating on the temperament of a woman whom time and life had left untouched. Shortly after, he received a biographical sketch of her from Mrs. O'Neil, also of Butte, who was wintering in Rome and entertaining such of the aristocracy as she met at her Embassy. It was some time since his thoughts had dwelt upon any woman when alone, and when he found himself sitting by his window in the evening dreaming over his cigar instead of amusing himself in the varied life of Rome after his habit, he was at first amused, then angry, finally apprehensive. He had no desire for another period of torment, followed by the successive stages that finished in impatience and satiety.

He tried flirting with her, making her talk about herself, focussing her mind on the years she seemed determined to ignore, in the hope of discovering that she was commonplace. But Ora, who found him more interesting than any man she had met in Europe, also a conquest to be proud of, continued to make herself interesting—and elusive—with a skill and subtlety that so closely resembled the frank ingenuousness of the West, that the man accustomed to the patented finesse of European women experienced the agreeable sensation of renewing his youth. He felt himself falling in love like a schoolboy, and meditated flight. He remained in Rome, however, and made a deliberate attempt to fascinate her. Then one day when Ida was pouring tea at the Embassy, chaperoned by Lady Gower, he found Ora alone, indisposed after a sleepless night, and lost his head. Ora, who was in no mood to let him down gently and reserve him for conversational pleasures, dismissed him abruptly, and had not seen him since. She had regretted her impatience, for he was always worth talking to, her feminine liking for his type was very strong, and she had amused herself fancying that if she had not permitted another man to rule her imagination she might have found her fate in this one. But as he had presumed to follow her when she had banished him summarily, she greeted him with cool civility and resumed her study of the kaleidoscopic crowd.

Suddenly she moved her head in a fashion that suggested the lifting of one of the little ears that lay so close to her head and were not the least of her points. The ear was on the side next to her companion in arms. Could it be that Ida was flirting with Valdobia? Mrs. Compton's manner and speech were as correct as her smartly tailored suit and hat of black velvet and the calm pride of her bearing, but she was talking with sweet earnestness to the Roman about himself and expressing her plaintive gratitude that he had cared to follow them to Genoa, where she at least was very lonely. It had not been possible for Ora to see the flash of understanding these two had exchanged after Valdobia's first puzzled glance, but she did see many heads turn to look at the handsome and well-matched couple. Even the Italian women did not smile ironically as they so often did at the too obvious American tourist. Ida not only had delivered herself of every exterior trace of commonness, but would no more have appeared on the street looking the mere tourist than she could be betrayed into adopting the extreme of any new style by the persuasive Parisian. She saw Ora's head come round her shoulder, and her voice deepened to the soft husky tones she reserved for decisive moments with her agitated admirers, then dropped it so low that only the man, with his head bent, could hear the words. At this stage of the flirtation's progress Ora noted that the approving glances of the sympathetic Italians were accompanied by significant smiles.

They had reached the end of the long Galleria for the second time and turned. The crowd was thin. The restaurants were filling. Shutters were rattling down over

the windows of the tempting shops. Said Ora abruptly,
"I think I'd like to dine in one of these cafés—the Milano. The Bristol dining-room is a little Ritz, and it's a bore to dress."

Valdobia leaned forward with a pleasant smile. "I should like nothing better, but you must dine with me."

"Why not? What do you say, Ida?"

"I'd love it. The food is good and the crowd more interesting."

They entered the bright café and seated themselves at one of the side tables, the two girls on the bench against the wall, Valdobia in the chair opposite. A number of the tables were already occupied, several by stout comfortable couples, but the majority by men with their hats on, playing dominoes or reading the evening papers. Opposite the door was a long table set forth with the delicacies of the season: raw meat, winter vegetables, oranges, and kicking lobsters.

Valdobia, assiduously waited upon by the proprietor himself (whose wife, surrounded by several of her children, smiled benignantly from the cashier's desk), ordered a special dinner; a light soup (the table d'hôte soup was a meal in itself), spaghetti, inimitably cooked veal in brown butter, salad, freshly caught fish, ices, and a bottle of the host's most precious Chianti.

"I never could have pictured you in a Bohemian restaurant," said Ora, smiling brilliantly into the face of her host. "Have you ever been in a place like this before?"

"About as often as I have weeks to my credit." He looked steadily into her snapping eyes. "You have studied Italians to little purpose if you've not discovered their partiality for their native cooking. These plain little cafés are the last strongholds in our large cities. Even the restaurants where the business men go for luncheon are queer imitations of London or Paris."

"We like to come here because the men pay no attention to us. It is men of your class that know how to make us thoroughly uncomfortable."

"Quite so. Every class has its own code. In ours it may be said that the women set the pace. They demand open admiration and we are gallant enough to give it. This class bothers itself little about the unattainable, and

merely throws you the passing tribute they would throw
to the Queen, or to a beautiful work of art.''

''Which they appreciate. Would that our working-
classes did. On this side the masses are as likely as not
to spend their holidays in a picture gallery or a museum.
Ours can think of nothing better than a saloon.''

''That may be the fault of your great country. The
crude mind is easily trained. Give your working-people
more galleries and museums and fewer saloons—or cantinas
with their light wines, and beer gardens, instead of rum
and whiskey. But it is unfair to expect a new and heterogeneous—almost chaotic—country to compete with twenty
centuries.'' Two pairs of American eyes flashed, and he
continued suavely. ''I fear that the old standards of
my own people are in danger of being demoralised by
socialism and the new craving for raw spirits. That is
becoming a serious question with us.'' He turned to Ida.
''It is far more odd to see you without your usual train
of admirers—both of you. How do you stand it?''

''Oh, we're merely recuperating,'' said Ida lightly, and
smiling into his admiring eyes. ''We will return to the
fray refreshed and more dangerous than ever.''

''How much longer shall you stay here?''

''A week or two. Then we go on to Paris. After that
Egypt, Spain, or some other old place.''

''But not without seeing Monte Carlo? You must let
me show it to you.''

''I suppose that is an old stamping ground of yours?''

''I go once a year, although, like a good many other
pleasures, it has lost its irresistible fascination. But I
shall enjoy seeing you catch the gambling fever.''

''I'm not very susceptible to microbes, but I don't doubt
Mrs. Blake will gamble the clothes off her back. That
would be the good old Montana style.'' And she told him
something of life in Butte before it indulged in one of its
spasms of exterior reform, and of the present life on The
Flat.

''I must see your Butte,'' he said enthusiastically. ''An
English friend of mine has a ranch in Wyoming, and I
may go out there next year.''

Ora stood this until the fish had been removed; then she
emerged conclusively from the cold and nervous apathy
that had possessed her for several days, and began to

sparkle. Ida was no match for her when she chose to exert herself, for that native product only really shone when able to employ her own rich vocabulary. She subsided with a smile and devoted herself to the excellent dinner, while Ora entertained their fastidious host with bright little stories of the adventures they never failed to experience, being two young women who travelled with their eyes and ears wide open. Valdobia, now satisfied that he had recaptured the interest of his lady and been in a measure forgiven, gave her all his attention; although not a man disposed to conversational exertion, he took pains to interest her in return. They discussed the news of the day and the latest books; and his deference to her opinions was very flattering, although he did not permit a flash of his eyes to betray his passionate delight at being once more with this woman whom he thought lovelier and more desirable than ever. Ora wore a blue velvet suit, not too dark, and a little hat of the same shade with a long feather that nestled in her warm ashen hair. Her cheeks were as pink as her lips, and she held her chin up as if drinking in the elixir of her native air. She looked very young and wholly without guile.

She continued to enchant him until they were in the Bristol, and the lift stopped at the first floor. Then she abruptly bade him good night, and ascended to her room, while the others went into the smoking-room and ordered coffee at one of the smaller tables.

"Well?" said Ida, smiling. "I'm not the sort that talks in circles except when I'm on parade. I'm glad you've come. Ora was fearfully down about something. I believe she likes you better than any man she has met over here. A little flirtation will do her no end of good."

Valdobia coloured. He was as practical as most Italians, but by no means given to the direct method of speech with women. Love simplifies among other things, however, and after a moment he put down his cup and looked her straight in the eyes.

"I think I shall take you into my confidence," he said. "I know that you are honest and that I can trust to your discretion——"

"You bet."

Ida relaxed her spine with her speech and settled herself comfortably.

"And you could give me great assistance. I want to persuade your friend—may I call her Ora to you? It is a beautiful name and I have said it so often to myself——"

"Ora goes."

"I want to persuade Ora to divorce her husband and marry me."

"Aw—that is—Good Lord!" Ida sat up straight and nearly dropped her cup. "That's a large order."

"Rather. But I—now—want nothing less. I am sick of the other sort of thing, even if she were not too good for it. I want to marry—and she is the only woman I ever have wanted to marry."

"Hm. You Italians haven't the name of being the best husbands in the world. How long would you be faithful to her?"

"I have no intention of ever being anything else."

"That's what they all say—think, no doubt."

"I shall be." He spoke with intense conviction.

"Well, perhaps—you've lived your life. I should think you men would get mighty sick of dancing about and never coming to anchor. But divorce? There's Mark, you know."

"Her present husband?"

"Yes, and a rattling good fellow. He married Ora when she didn't know which way to turn, and she is really grateful to him, and as fond of him as if he were her own brother. I don't think she'll turn him down."

"Women have been known to desert their brothers before this! I mean to make her love me, and if I do—how she could love a man!—I fancy I can persuade her."

"I like Mark and I don't want to see him thrown down. He's not what you might call in love with Ora—he got discouraged pretty early in the game. But he's fond of her and proud of her, and he has ambitions. She could help him a lot."

Valdobia lit another cigarette.

"Better have a liaison and get over it. Then he'll never know, and what men don't know don't hurt them."

"I shall do nothing of the sort. I mean to marry her. Will you help me or not?"

"Ora'd look fine all right in that old palace of yours. It would suit her a long sight better than Butte, or even Washington—let alone Helena; Mark wouldn't mind a bit being Governor of Montana. Have you got a castle in the country?"

"I have several."

"Fine! I'd visit you every year."

"No one would be half as welcome."

"I've been away from America so long and seen so much, and Butte seems so far away, that I've kind of lost my bearings. If you'd come over there and lay your siege, I guess I'd fight you to the last ditch."

"Permit me to remind you that we are in Italy, a state several centuries ahead of yours in civilisation, even if we lack your facile divorce laws. I know something of Mr. Blake from Mrs. O'Neil. Can you picture Ora finishing her life with him?"

"No, I can't, and that's a fact. I wonder there hasn't been a grand bust-up before this. It will come some day. Why not now?"

"Quite so."

"And Mark could get a dozen girls to suit him better, make him nice and comfy. He'll never get any real companionship out of Ora, fine as she's always treated him. A man like that needs a running mate."

"I shall waste none of my mental energy in sympathy for Mr. Mark Blake. American husbands, so far as I have been permitted to observe, are accustomed not only to being deserted for months and even years at a time, but to periodical divorce."

"It's not quite as bad as that, but Mark has the elasticity of an india rubber ball, and that's a fact."

"Good. Will you help me?"

Ida hesitated an instant longer, then, dimly conscious that her answer in a measure was dictated by a profound instinct she made no attempt to define, exclaimed, "It's a go. I believe it will be all for the best. Shake." And she gave his hand a hearty grasp.

"You are a brick," he murmured, with a sensation of gratitude he had rarely experienced. "But there is one thing more. Please give her no hint of this, for the present at least. Tell her, and make her believe it, that I have not come here to trouble her, that she need never fear to trust herself alone with me. Tell her that I only want to enjoy her society and make things pleasant for her."

"Right you are. Ora's not the sort you can rush. But

don't overdo it and make her think you've altogether got over it. Sometimes that piques and works out all right and sometimes it don't. She's as proud as Lucifer and might get over her fancy for you while she was still mad.''

"You do know your sex! I'll use all the art I've ever acquired.''

"Respectful devotion without humility, and pained self-control. That's your lay.''

He laughed heartily. "We'll drift for the present.''

"Well, now, drift out. I want to go up and sound her. I'm simply expiring to know what she's thinking about at the present moment.''

XXXIII

WHEN Ida reached her room she put her ear to the closed door leading into Ora's, and heard the scratch of the hotel pen.

"May I come in?" she asked softly.

There was a rattle of paper, the snap of a trunk lid, and then Ora said in tones as dulcet, "Come in, dear."

Ida entered and found Ora extended on the sofa.

"What did you run off like that for?" she asked, as she selected the least uncomfortable of the chairs in the fresh and artistic but hardly luxurious room. "The poor man was as glum as a funeral until he'd had two cups of coffee and several cigarettes."

"I was tired. And I really think he has followed you."

"You don't think anything of the sort. His heart was in his patent leathers when he met us, and I just tided him over. He gave me a message for you. Shall I deliver it?"

"Why not?" asked Ora languidly.

"He wants me to impress you with the fact that he's not come here to make love to you, just to enjoy your exhilarating society——"

"Is he over it?" Ora's eyes flashed upward.

"Not exactly, but he has no intention of making any more breaks, and being cut off from the solace of your company now and then—principally now, I guess. He's got to see you or go off to India and shoot tigers. But he's really much nicer than I had any idea of, and is anxious to give us a good time. Life is a desert, kid, with all the men we know in the next town. Men were invented to amuse us, so do continue to thaw. You did bravely when you got started, and no harm will be done. If you can't fall in love with him you can't, and he's prepared

197

to take his medicine. He's a good sport. A man like that can behave himself when he sets his mind to it."

"Is he indulging in the hope that I can be made to care for him?"

"Men are so conceited that they always hope for the best. But he'll not worry you, that's the point. It will be fine to have him pilot us about; perhaps he'll get us inside of one of those old palaces in the Via Garibaldi. And he'll take us to Monte Carlo. How do you feel about it?"

"I don't care whether he goes or stays, but on the whole I am rather glad he is here. He has brains and I like to talk to clever men that have seen the world."

"And don't keep me hitched to your elbow all the time, for mercy's sake. I hope he'll dig up some friend of his here who will beau me. Give him a chance and remember he is a gentleman and has passed his word."

"Is this a plot?" Ora laughed. "Don't worry. I won't bore you any more than I can help. I fancy I am quite safe, for he never really can see me alone, as we have no salon here. Besides, in long days of sight-seeing he'll no doubt recover, and we shall become merely the best of friends."

"That's what I'm figuring on. Now, cut out those love-letters and come down to earth."

Ora sat up in her indignation. "Love letters! I've not written a line of love."

"What in the name of goodness do you write about then to this lover in the air?"

"Oh, I just—*talk*—about everything that interests me— the things one says to a familiar spirit—that is if there were such a thing—but otherwise has to keep to oneself always."

"And you don't call them love letters, because you leave out the 'darlings' and 'dears'? Good thing the man will never see them. Good thing for more reasons than one. Men hate long letters. If I'd disobeyed orders and inflicted Greg, I never would have got that house and the extra ten thousand."

"And yet he was in love with you once?"

"Thought he was. Just had the usual attack of brain fever men always get when they can't have the girl they want without marrying her. Lasted about a month. Greg cares too much for other things for any woman to last more than a few minutes in his life, anyway. Just the husband for me.''

Ora was swinging one foot and looking at the point of her slipper.

''I shan't destroy those letters,'' she said finally, ''because they have meant something to me that nothing in this life ever will again. But I'll write no more.''

They remained in Genoa for ten days longer. Valdobia, who had taken rooms at the Miramare, gave them a dinner and they met several of his Genoese friends, but none of the men was blest with Ida's critical approval. Her demand for the admiration of men was merely a part of her insolent pride in her beauty and magnetism and her love of power; she had little natural coquetry, and wasted no time on a man who bored her or was not ''worth while.'' She particularly hated soft dark eyes, and the two unfortunate young scions of the aristocracy of Genoa invited by Valdobia, had peculiarly lovely orbs that they rolled exceedingly. But it was a merry party, for no people can be gayer than the Genoese, and they played baccarat until two in the morning; a new experience for the Americans. During the hours devoted to the game Ida had the satisfaction of observing that two pairs of flaming dark eyes had apparently forgotten the existence of woman. Even Valdobia, who held the bank twice and lost a good deal of money, became very keen on the table, although he kept Ora beside him and taught her all that one can learn of a game of chance. The stakes ran very high toward the end, Valdobia lost several thousand francs, and Ora five hundred. She would have lost more, no doubt, for she found it an interesting and exciting experience, but Valdobia dictated her stakes, and she meekly obeyed. Ida, who had been wary, came out even.

''You don't catch me dropping good money when I don't get something good enough in return,'' she announced as they entered her room at the hotel. ''It's fun all right, but like most things that are off on a side-track from your main purpose in life, just to be nibbled at. I prefer bridge anyhow.''

''Do you? I think I like the game of chance. I don't mind losing——''

"Well, I do. It made me sick to see you lose five hundred francs, and if it hadn't been for Valdobia you'd have lost as much more. I couldn't sleep a wink if I'd lost a hundred plunks."

Ora laughed. "It would be great fun to see you really excited and carried away about something. I hope you will have visions of sudden wealth at Monte Carlo and forget the world."

"Not much!" said Ida contemptuously. "I'll be rich, all right, but it'll be because I take no chances. I knew whom I was marrying, and he'll make the millions. You'll never see me spend a cent unless it brings in good interest, like clothes, and tips, and entertaining. And the only thing that could excite me would be if Amalgamated got the hill, and Greg had to go to work to make his fortune as a mining engineer. But I'm not the kind to get wrinkles worrying. Lord! Don't the people in this town ever go to sleep?"

Their windows were close to the Via Venti Settembre, although on a short side street. It is possible that the afternoon throngs are replaced by a different set in the evening, and these again by lovers of the night; but certain it is that the more inviting of the streets are rarely deserted until dawn, and the later the revellers the more noisy they are; following a universal law of nature. When the light-hearted Genoese has sung all his songs to the stars and chattered at the top of his voice for several hours, he stands still and screams. The girls put their heads out of the window, wondering if anyone were being murdered below. A group of young men were standing in a circle and outscreaming one another.

Ida slammed the long windows together, fastened the catch and covered them with the heavy shutters. "Me for beauty sleep," she said; "I like air all right, but I like quiet better. Good night."

Ora left her window open and lay thinking for a long time. She liked the new excitement of gambling, and she was divided between regret and gratitude that for the last five days she had enjoyed thoroughly the society of the man who would have been the chief exponent of the type she admired had he possessed more primitive strength of personality; had he been obliged to develop his native forces in a fierce battle with life instead of having been from birth one of her favourites. But he was a man, brave, unsoftened by luxury, quick, keen, resourceful, modern to his finger-tips, an almost perfect companion. What more could any woman ask? Ora wondered just what it was she did ask. She felt very grateful to him, however. Her regret was that her unreal life seemed to be over, or slept profoundly when she perversely and tentatively summoned it. That life had been terrible in its intensity, only retreating now and again when real events crowded, or she deliberately tried to interest herself in a new and charming personality. But all men sooner or later faded to the transparency of wraiths beside the vital figure that dominated her imaginative life. Would Valdobia accomplish the miracle? At least he gave her peace for the moment. She fell asleep smiling and deliberately thinking of him.

XXXIV

ON the following day they lunched at a large restaurant opposite the Bourse, a favourite resort of the two girls; it amused them to watch the keen clever business men of Genoa at their midday meal in leisurely conversation and enjoyment of their excellent food and wine; contrasting them with the American who took five minutes for lunch, achieving dyspepsia instead of nutriment, and possibly accomplishing less than a race which has been commercial and acquisitive since the dawn of its history. There is little real poverty in Genoa and great wealth.

They had come too late to secure one of the tables overlooking the Piazzi Defarrari, and were facing the windows, at one of the longer tables, when Valdobia, who sat opposite, rose with a word of apology and went behind them to greet a man with a pleasant English voice.

"Lord John Mowbray," whispered Ida. "He's all right, but, lord, I'll be glad to get back to a country where a few men are plain mister."

Nevertheless, as the Englishman bent over her with a delighted word of greeting, she lifted her heavy eyes to his with the expression of one whose long suppressed hopes have blossomed at last.

"I wish I could join you," he said ruefully, "but I am with a party of friends."

"Get rid of them after lunch," murmured Ida, "and come with us. We are going to explore all those interesting little streets down in the gulch—that is to say the ravine, or whatever it was once—and it would be jolly to have you along."

"I will," he said, with fervour, "and I know what a gulch is. My brother is ranching in Wyoming, and I may join him there in a few months. I believe he also has interests in Butte."

"Good! We'll begin to get friendly right now. So

long.'' Valdobia returned to his chair, and she asked,
"Is he a brother of your Wyoming friend?"

"He is, and no doubt we'll go out together. Your
Northwest must be the realest thing left in the world."

"It's that, all right. And it will be no end of fun having you out there!" She smiled sardonically, and Ora
coloured and moved restlessly. She was vaguely aware
of a new drama unfolding, and had no wish to analyse it.

Mowbray, to Ida's satisfaction, not only deserted his
friends after luncheon, but permitted them to go on to
Rome without him and lingered in Genoa. He was a fair
well set-up young Englishman, with a nonchalant manner
and an inflammable heart. Ida had met him at a country
house and amused herself "landing him," but as she had
left England immediately after, and hunting had claimed
all his ardours, she neither had seen nor heard from him
since. Although she meant to keep him at her elbow as
long as he served her purpose, she knew him to be a shy
youth under his natural buoyancy and quick intelligence,
and did not disturb her placid mind with visions of
"scenes." On the whole she liked Englishmen better than
any of the men she had met in Europe, for they had more
pride and self-control where women were concerned; if
things went deeper with them they were less likely to
offend her cold purity with outbursts of passion; which,
she confided to Ora, "made her sick."

To her delight Valdobia took them one afternoon to call
on an elderly relative who lived in one of the great palaces
of the Via Garibaldi. They were escorted up to the top
floor; the rooms on the other *pianos* were either closed
or emitted the chill breath of the tomb. Their destination
was a large lofty room, inadequately heated by a stove in
one corner; their noble hostess was fortified against the
cold by several shawls and a foot-warmer. She had invited
three other aristocratic relics in to look at "the Americans," and, although the principessa and her friends were
more polite than they would have been to intruding bour-
geoises of their own country, it was apparent that they
could find little to say to two young women from a land
of which they had a confused and wholly contemptuous
apprehension. They knew that its chief title to fame was
its original discovery by a Genoese, that the lower classes
emigrated to it a good deal, and that many American

women, who spent far too much money on their clothes, visited Europe and occasionally married above them. More than this they neither knew nor cared to know. So far as they were concerned new countries did not exist.

Conversation languished. Ida was suppressed, and divided between a desire to laugh and to scream. Ora, with a heroic effort, talked about the mistake the average American made in seeing so little of Genoa; but, having laid aside her furs out of politeness, she was shivering, and unable to drink the strong coffee which immediately succumbed to the temperature of the room.

She sent an appealing glance to Valdobia, who was smiling to himslf. Lord John, who had been honoured by a chair beside his hostess, treated with the consideration due his ancient lineage, was delivering himself of spasmodic clauses, with one eye on Valdobia.

"Jimminy!" whispered Ida, who now felt quite at home with her fellow conspirator, "if you don't get us out of this quick I'll have high-strikes, and Ora'll get a cold and be laid up for a week. I always keep her in bed when she has a cold."

Valdobia rose instantly. "We have an engagement in half an hour," he said to his mother's second cousin. "Perhaps you will permit me to show these ladies over the palace?"

"Oh, do!" exclaimed Mowbray, acting on instinct, for he was too cold and too unnerved to think. "I'd like jolly well to see it myself; must be rippin'."

The permission was given with some graciousness, and the party bowed themselves out. As they descended the grand staircase, they heard a buzz of voices behind them, as of several elderly ladies talking at once.

"We'd be roasting on red hot coals this minute if there were any in that refrigerator," said Ida, "but I don't care so long as we are going to see the real part of the palace."

An aged major domo showed them through the magnificent reception rooms, built for entertaining a proud and gorgeous aristocracy in the days when Genoa was known throughout Europe as "La Superba." They were hung with tapestries or cordova leather, and filled with priceless pictures, porcelains, enamels, gold and silver ware, and massive furniture. Valdobia told them dramas sentimental and tragic which had been enacted within the walls of the historic house. But they had to stamp about to avoid a chill, and were glad to emerge into the warmer air of even the narrow street.

"Well," announced Ida, as they walked rapidly out of the Via Garibaldi into the broad sunshine of the Piazza delle Fontane Marose, "if that's a sample of your ancient aristocracy no more of it in mine. My curiosity is satisfied for good and all. Why on earth don't they live like human beings?"

"Or steam-heated Americans?" asked Valdobia, smiling. "Console yourself with the assurance that you are the only Americans that have ever crossed that threshold."

"It doesn't console me one little bit, and I feel pneumonia coming on. Let's walk as fast as we know how!" And accompanied by the willing Englishman she started off with a stride that soon left the others far behind.

"It is true," said Valdobia disgustedly, "that this older generation does not know how to live, not in any sense. They possess the greatest wealth in Italy, and they hoard it as if poverty stared them in the face. They have only to turn on the electric lights once a week and provide a simple supper to make Genoa one of the most delightful cities in Europe, but they won't even do that. They have the finest jewels in Italy and never wear them except on the rare occasions when the King and Queen visit Genoa and command them to the royal palace. Thank heaven there is a younger set, equally well born, that live in the new apartment houses or in those villas up on the hills, and are neither too economical nor too antiquated in their ideas to enjoy life. Those old people are divided up into intimate little sets and spend their lives gossiping about the rest of Genoa or talking of the past. But I do hope you did not take cold."

"I didn't, and I really enjoyed it!" said Ora, smiling mischievously. "I amused myself thinking what would happen if I told our uncomfortable hostess that my father's sister had married a Roman relative of her husband; but I wouldn't have relieved the situation for the world. I suppose they are fumigating themselves."

"I don't doubt it. They think they are aristocratic and are merely provincial."

"How different you are!" Ora looked at him admiringly. "One hardly could believe that you belonged to the same race."

"I don't. I am a Roman, and a citizen of the world. No doubt you, too, have a root that runs back into the dark ages, but today is all that counts with us. I mean that in more senses than one!" And, although he smiled, he gave her a quick side-glance.

"I hope so. I am well aware that you are enjoying yourself immensely." Ora felt it quite safe to flirt with him in the open street.

"Do you like me a little better?"

"Rather. Friendly companionship is my chief idea of happiness, now that I am more or less tired of books."

"Is it? May it be my good fortune to initiate you into a higher! You have everything to learn!"

"Have I? I wonder!"

"What do you mean by that? Have you ever been in love?"

"Not the least little bit!"

"You said that rather too vehemently. It is my turn to wonder." This time he looked hard at her and his face was grim. He had a way of setting his jaw that reminded her of the man whose haunting memory had made her alternately happy and miserable during many long months. She looked away hastily.

"The kind of love you mean I have not the very least knowledge of. You must believe that."

"Of what other kind, then?"

"Oh, all women dream, you know," she said lightly. "They have a sort of ideal that consoles them for missing the realities of life. You come quite close to it," and once more she sparkled her eyes at him.

"I have no intention of letting you flirt with me," said Valdobia calmly. "My flirting days are over. I shall remain the best of your friends until you love me or send me to the other end of the world."

"Well, don't become serious and spoil everything."

"I shall not lose my head, if that is what you mean," he said drily. "I find the present state of affairs very pleasant. Let us overtake the others and go for a drive."

XXXV

"WELL," said Ora, when she and Ida had returned to the hotel to dress for dinner, "did you have a queer feeling when you were prowling through those dim old rooms, furnished three or four hundred years ago, and the scene of all sorts of romance and tragedy?"

"I had a queer feeling all right. Had visions of rheumatism, sciatica, pneumonia, and a red nose for a week. I suppose those wonderful velvet gowns they wore—in pictures, anyhow—were padded inside, and they slept in them; didn't take them off all winter. If I lived in one of those palaces today I'd surely lose all my good American habits."

"Didn't you have any haunting sense of mystery—of having been there before?"

"Nixie! No wonder I murdered if I ever was. However," she added thoughtfully, "there's no telling what I might have felt if they'd had a furnace in the house. There was something wonderful about it, all right—being in those musty old rooms, that fairly smelt of the past. I guess they'll haunt me as some of those Roman palaces have that are not shown to the public. But don't put weird ideas into my head, Ora. They don't gee with Butte. The severely practical is my lay."

"Don't you think there could be romance and tragedy in Butte?"

"Oh, plenty of shooting, if you mean that; and mixing-up. But people don't stay jealous long enough to get real tragic about it; they just get a divorce. We've improved on daggers and poisoned bowls and rings, and the rest of it. Good old Butte!"

They all dined at the Bristol that night, and soon after nine o'clock had the smoking-room to themselves. Ida, indeed, carried Mowbray off into the reading-room. Ora sighed as she found herself alone with the handsome distinguished Roman of the type that even in minor exponents

207

so often compelled her response. Why didn't she love him? He was proving himself the ideal companion. There was apparently no question to which he had not given some thought, and he knew far more about the subjects that appealed to her than she did herself. They discussed the ever-fascinating sexual problems impersonally, delicately, and exhaustively, a feat in itself, an experience Ora never had enjoyed before; for while it drew them together it apparently neither disturbed Valdobia nor altered his attitude toward her. His analyses of politics and of the fashionable authors of the day were the acutest she had heard or read, and he enlarged her knowledge of the world by his anecdotes of life in the different capitals of Europe that he knew so well. He could be personal without egotism, and his sense of humour was keener than her own. While he treated her ideas and criticisms with deference he forced her to look up to him and to feel only pleasure in his masterful mind and great experience.

Tonight he made her talk about herself; and, artfully beating about her life's most significant chapter, she expressed herself with a freedom and veracity which she found another novel and fascinating experience; her confidences to Ida were superficial and sporadic. She could feel his sympathy and understanding flow toward her, although he uttered no sentimental platitudes, and let only his eyes express a little of what he felt. But for the hour she glowed with a sense of utter companionship, her mind was stimulated to the pitch of excitement; she caught herself wishing that they could have these long intimate talks for the rest of their lives, and that he would sometimes hold her hand to complete the sense of perfect understanding.

When they parted at midnight and she walked slowly up the stairs alone—Ida had dismissed Mowbray an hour since—she sighed again. Why didn't she feel the pull? What was the nature of that mysterious current that seemed to vibrate between two people only out of the world's billions, and was quite independent of mental identities? Certainly passion was not the only source. If she had been free and never had met Gregory Compton she would have married Valdobia and given him all he craved; for his magnetism was by no means confined to his brain. Why could not she love him as it was? She had not been the heroine of one of those passionate love-affairs that leave a woman cold for several years, perhaps for ever. The intensity of emotion she had experienced during these months in Europe had been one-sided, a mere madness of the imagination. She had yet to realise that a woman can live more profoundly and completely with a man in her imagination than when in daily contact with his discouraging weaknesses, his inability to reach her impossible standard, and impinged upon by the disintegrating forces of daily life.

Such women as Ora Blake, endowed with a certain measure of creative imagination, yet spending their maturing years unnaturalised citizens in a cross-section of life which barely brushes their aloofness in passing, develop as unnormally as those that cultivate this exotic garden of the mind for fame and fortune. If they find a mate while the imagination is still as young as their years, these highly organised women, with every sense and faculty keenly alert, and stimulated by mental contact as others may be by drugs and wine, have the opportunity at least to be the happiest beings on earth. If they marry a brute, or are forced to fight the world for bread, a wide channel is dug in the brain through which flow the normal and crowding thoughts of the average, commonplace, adaptable woman; which is perhaps the best of all educations for life.

But Ora had married a kind prosaic man who soon learned to let her alone, and kept her in a comfort that burdened her days with leisure. If she had been unimaginative no harm would have been done. She either would have grown fond of her essential husband and become a domestic angel, or consoled herself with society and bridge. But, misplaced in life, she belonged to the intellectual aristocracy of the earth, who are the loneliest of its inhabitants, unless they can establish an invisible bond with their fellow-beings by offerings from that mental garden which is at once their curse and their compensation for the doubtful gift of life.

Ora was too indifferent to the world to care to weave this gossamer bridge, and had grown accustomed to mental solitude. But she had never placed any curb on her imagination. In the days when her only solace was books it enabled her to visualise the *mise-en-scène* of the remote or immediate past, the procession of the traveller, or the abstractions of science; as if she were in one of those theatres where the great modern manager threatens to atrophy what imagination is left in the world. It even enabled her to enjoy fiction whose scene was a land of which she had no personal knowledge; a rare gift in the American, whose demand for familiar settings and characters keeps our literature commonplace. And she could at will shut her eyes and wander in Europe when Butte became insufferable.

Her surrender to the obsession of Gregory Compton had been gradual; she had fought it, not only out of loyalty to her husband and her friend, but because the future menaced terrors against which she had no desire to pit her strength. But she had finally cast defiance to the future, and dismissed her phantom loyalty with a shrug. Mark no doubt had consoled himself for her defection long since; to Ida a husband was a money-maker pure and simple. She herself would never see Gregory Compton again if she could avoid it; or, if life took her inevitably back to Butte, no doubt her infatuation would have been cured by mental satiety, and she would be able to greet him with the indifference that is ever the portion of the discarded lover.

Having arrived at this reasonable conclusion, she had dismissed cynicism, cowardice, and qualms, to limbo, and entered upon one of those exalting, tormenting, incredibly sweet, and profoundly depressing mental love affairs, which, lacking the element of comedy inevitable in all actual relations between men and women, obsess the mind and detach it from life.

After she parted from Valdobia, puzzled and wistful, she recalled one week during which she had been completely happy. Ida was visiting friends uncongenial to herself, and she had gone alone to Bruges. In that ancient city of almost perfect beauty, she had given the wildness in her nature uninterrupted liberty. She had written letters that no woman yet has sent to a man without regretting it, for in this stage of man's progress, at least, he wants little of the soul of woman. It is possible that the women who live in their imaginations are the most fortunate, after all, for they arbitrarily make man the perfect mate he possibly may be some centuries hence. At all events Ora imagined Gregory Compton with her unremittingly, deliberately ignoring the depression that must descend upon her when once more companioned by his wife. It had seemed to her that her step had never been so buoyant, her body so light. People had paused to stare at the beautiful young American with her head in the air looking as if she were about to sing. It had been a wonderful, an almost incredible experience, and she never had been able quite to recapture it even when alone in the night. But she had wondered sometimes if life held any happiness as real as that had been, and she wondered again as she switched off her light and flung herself into the bed that had witnessed so much despair before Valdobia had appeared and put a quietus on her imagination. She wondered also if the passion of the soul were so much greater than the common experience of man and woman that its indulgence must forever make life itself unreal. She felt that this question threw some light on her problem, then dismissed the subject peremptorily. She might regret that extraordinary love affair, with its terrors and its delights, but she would bury it once for all; and she fell asleep with the wise remark:

"What fools we are! Oh, lord, what fools!"

XXXVI

AFTER this she discarded what was left of her crust, and emerged like a butterfly. The present was delightful, she would enjoy it without analysis or retrospect. She met several clever and interesting men, but had eyes for no one but Valdobia. They explored Genoa until they knew it almost as well as the natives, spending hours down in the long twisted streets, so narrow that no vehicle had ever visited them, and swarming like the inside of an ant-hill. Harrowing adventures were impossible, for the Genoese masses if discourteous are neither a lawless nor an impertinent race. Ora and Ida might have roamed alone, and been unmolested save by the enterprising shop-keepers that dealt in filigree. They rode over the steep hills in the trams, and took long motor drives in the brilliant winter sunshine to the picturesque towns and villages down the Riviera. Then, on a Saturday morning, they bade good-bye to the ancient city and took the train for Monte Carlo.

The girls established themselves in a small hotel opposite the Casino Gardens, the men in the great hotel that lies between the Casino and the International Sporting Club.

"I suppose we really should have sent for Lady Gower," said Ora, doubtfully, as they hooked each other up for dinner. "It's stretching the point rather to come to a place like Monte Carlo with two men. We'll be sure to run into a dozen people we know."

"Oh, bother! I love the idea of feeling real devilish for once. Besides, anything goes at Monte Carlo, and everybody is interested in gambling and nothing else. What good would old Norfolk-Howard do us, anyhow, asleep on a sofa. She never could keep awake after ten, and nobody'd know in those big rooms whether she was there or not. We're Americans, anyhow, and I'm having the time of my life. Lord John is a perfect dear."

212

"Well, at least I am thankful that you are no longer in a hurry to return to Butte."

"Butte'll keep, I guess. The more experiences I take back the more they'll think of me. Gives me backbone to feel a real woman-of-the-world. Besides, kid, it's good philosophy to drink the passing moment dry. Amalgamated may bust us any minute. You look prettier every day, and I'm not going off either."

She wore a severely cut gown of black velvet, the corsage draped with coral-coloured chiffon. Her first evening gowns, cut by the ruthless Parisian, had caused her many qualms, but they had been growing more décolleté ever since; and so superb were her neck and shoulders that she had ceased to regret her lack of jewels. Ora had refrained from buying any, although she longed for sapphires; but she always wore her pearls. Tonight her gown was of a misty pale green material from which she rose like a lily from its calyx. She still wore her hair massed softly on the top of her head, and although not as tall as Ida, and far from being as fully developed, was an equally arresting figure. No two women were ever more excellent foils, and that may have been one secret of their amicable relations.

They dined with their cavaliers at one of the fashionable restaurants, then, after an hour in the Casino rooms, which were not at all to their taste, with their ornate walls and dingy crowd, went by means of lifts and underground corridors over to the International Sporting Club. Valdobia and Mowbray had put them up at this exclusive resort during the afternoon and they entered the roulette rooms at once. Here the walls were chastely hung with pale grey satin, and all the colour was in the company. The long tables were crowded with smart-looking men and women of both worlds, although only the ladies that had stepped down from ancestral halls dared to show a grey hair or a wrinkle. The cocottes were so young and fresh as well as beautiful that to Ora and Ida they looked much like girls of their own class. All, young and old, were splendidly dressed and bejewelled; and if there was excitement in their brains there was no evidence of it in their calm or animated faces. They might have been a great house-party amusing themselves with some new and innocuous game.

Our party walked about for a time dividing their attention between the spinning balls, the faces of the players, and the gowns of the women; even those of the cocottes were not eccentric, although worn with a certain inimitable style. Their ropes of pearls were also the longest in the room. A number of the most notable men in Europe were present, princes of reigning houses, and statesmen high in the service of their country.

In spite of the absence of that feverish excitement which is supposed to pervade these gambling rooms of Monte Carlo (and which is absent from the Casino even when a man shoots himself and is whisked out), Ora wandered about in a curious state of exaltation. The cool splendour of the rooms, the atmosphere of high breeding and restraint, the gratification of the æsthetic sense at every turn, the beauty of the women and the distinguished appearance of the men made it a romantic and memorable scene. Notwithstanding the constant clink of gold, the monotonous admonitions of the croupiers, it was a sort of worldly fairyland, this apotheosis of one of the most perilous of human indulgences. These people might be gambling for greed or mere excitement, being blasé of other mundane diversions, but they were at the same time so frank and so reserved, so pleased and so indifferent, that they produced the illusion of sojourning on a plane high above the common mortal with his commonplace loves and disasters and struggles to exist or shine. No wonder that men came here to forget the burdens of state, women Society's conservatisms or the inconstancy of man. For the hour, and the hour generally lasted until four in the morning, they lived in a world apart, and a duchess sat next to a cocotte with a serene indifference that amounted almost to democracy.

"I don't know that romantic is the word I should use," said Valdobia, laughing; Ora had uttered some of her thoughts aloud; "but I think I know what you mean. The people that come here can afford to lose; their minds are almost as carefully composed as their costumes; they are both pleasantly reckless and frivolous; this is their real play-time; the world beyond these four walls is obliterated; if they lose they shrug their shoulders, and if they win they experience something like a real thrill; in short, being soaked in worldliness, it is their only chance to feel primitive—for gambling was practised by the most ancient tribes of which we have any knowledge. At the Casino most of those people are subconsciously wondering how they are going to pay their hotel bills and get out of Monte Carlo, calm as they manage to look; but here—well, here you see the quintessence of the world's frivolity. No wonder it creates a heady atmosphere. Do you want to gamble?''

''Of course I do.''

''Well, put a louis on the red. I'll follow your stakes. Perhaps we'll bring each other luck.''

They staked and won, staked and won again, seven times running without removing their winnings from the red. Then Valdobia said, ''Don't tempt fortune too far. The luck may turn to the green any moment. Suppose we try ours *en plein.*'' He selected the number 39, and once more they won. Ora, her hands full of gold, turned to him with blazing eyes. Her cheeks were crimson. Valdobia laughed.

''You mustn't look so happy,'' he said teasingly, ''or these old stagers will know that you are what your friend calls a hayseed. Better change all this gold into notes.''

''Notes? I want my gold. Paper never did mean anything to me.''

''What a child you are—ah! I must leave you for a moment. The Duc——'' he mentioned a prince of his royal house—''wishes to speak to me. Don't try *en plein* again. That rarely happens twice. Put a louis at a time on the red.''

He left her. Ora deliberately placed not only her double handful of gold on the red, but pushed forward the pile that had accumulated before her. Red came up and doubled her winnings. She added to her already imposing hillock the gold shoved toward her, and, with a quick glance at Valdobia, who was deep in conversation with his prince, took a thousand franc note from her châtelaine bag and laid it on top of the gold. Once more she won, and met the sympathetic smiles of the croupiers, who in the Sporting Club, at least, are very human persons. She was about to add another thousand franc note, when Valdobia returned. He swept her gold and notes off the red just as *rien ne va plus* sounded above the buzz of conversation behind the tables.

"What on earth are you doing?" he asked angrily. "I don't like to see a woman gamble like that."

Ora pouted and looked like a naughty child.

"But I want to gamble. Give me my money. What have you to say about it?"

"I brought you here—and I shall not bring you again if you are going to gamble like that old Frankfurt banker over there. Why not follow the example of Mrs. Compton, who is decorously putting five franc pieces on the green at the next table?"

"Oh, Ida! I like the sensation of doing big things. You just said we enjoyed letting loose our primitive instincts."

"Is that the way you felt? Well, here are three louis. Stake one at a time. I shall change the rest into notes and give them to you at the hotel."

He kept his eye on her, and she staked her gold pieces one after another and lost.

"Now," he said, "come into the bar and have a glass of wine or a lemon squash. I want to talk to you."

They found seats in a corner of the bar behind a little table, and Ora demurely ordered a lemonade. "I suppose you are going to scold me," she murmured, although her cheeks were still flushed and her eyes rebellious. "What difference did it make? I am not poor, and I had won nearly all that I risked, anyhow. You have seen women gamble all your life. One would think that you were a hayseed, yourself."

"Shall I be quite honest? I fancy I was jealous. For the first time I saw you completely carried away. I had hoped to furnish that impulse myself!"

"It is a wonderful sensation," she said provokingly. "I doubt if anything but gambling could inspire it."

"Do you?" But he knew that it was no time for sentiment, and asked curiously, "Are you so fond of gold? I never saw such a greedy little thing."

"Remember I've walked round over gold for the best part of my life, and have a mine of my own. It fascinates me, but not because I care much about riches—I like the liberty that plenty of money gives; that, to my mind, is all that wealth means. But I loved the feeling of being possessed, of being absolutely reckless. I should have liked to know that my whole fortune depended upon that spinning ball. That would have been worth while! It makes one forget everything—everything!''

He looked at her with half-closed eyes. ''You have a secret chapter in your life,'' he said. ''Some day I shall read it. But I can't make up my mind whether you are a born gambler or not.''

Ora shrugged her shoulders. ''To tell you the truth I shouldn't care if I never saw a gambling table again. I have had the sensation. That is enough. I will admit I was rather disappointed not to lose that immense stake. Lucky at cards, you know.''

''And you think you are unlucky in love?'' Valdobia laughed, but his face was still grim. ''How many men have you had in love with you already?''

''That doesn't count!''

He turned pale. ''What do you mean by that?''

''I mean that I don't believe I am destined to happiness. Don't you think we know our lines instinctively?''

''I know that you are trying to torment me. You are still excited and angry, so I shall not permit your words, significant as they are, to keep me awake tonight.'' He was smiling again, but she saw the anger in his own eyes, and said impulsively:

''I rather like you better than usual tonight. You have made me do something I didn't want to do, and anger is becoming to you.''

''The eternal female! Well, God knows, I wouldn't have you abnormal. What is this?''

A page was standing before the table with a telegram in his hand. ''Pour M. le Marquis de Valdobia,'' he said.

With a word of apology Valdobia opened the telegram. Ora, watching him, saw his face turn white.

''What is it?'' she asked anxiously. ''I do hope it is not bad news.'' She felt a sharp pang at the possibility of losing him.

He rose and looked at his watch. ''My mother is very ill,'' he said. ''A train goes in an hour and ten minutes. I must take it. But there is something I want to say to you before I go; I may be detained in Rome. Will you get your wrap and come into the gardens for a few moments?''

''I am so sorry,'' murmured Ora, with real sympathy. ''Of course I will go.''

He took her to the cloak-room. ''Wait here for a moment," he said. "I must telephone to my man to pack and meet me at the train; and tell Mowbray not to look for us later."

He left her, and Ora watched the passing couples, trying not to think. She was a little frightened, but still too excited to shrink from a possible ordeal.

XXXVII

H E returned in a few moments, and they left the Club
House by the main entrance and strolled toward
the gardens; then he suddenly led her to the terrace.
There were many people walking in the tropical scented
park of the Casino, but the digue above the Mediterranean
was deserted. Monte Carlo can be cold in May but it can
be as warm as July in February, and the night was mild
and beautiful. The sea under the stars was almost as
blue as by day. The air was very still, although a band
was playing somewhere, far away. From the other side
of the bay came the faint humming of an aeroplane. There
was to be an aviation meet on the morrow, and no doubt
one of the airmen was about to make a trial flight.

They sat down on one of the benches, and Valdobia
folded his arms, then turned and leaned his elbow on the
back of the seat and his head on his hand.

"I am not quite in the mood for love-making," he said,
"after the news I have received; but I can't go without
letting you know why I followed you to Genoa—without
some sort of an understanding."

Ora looked at him out of the corner of her eye. His
face was set and determined, but she concluded that he
was not the man to be dangerous when grieving for his
mother.

"What is it?" she asked softly. "I know, of course, that
you—like me."

"I love you, and I want to marry you. I wish you to
divorce your husband and marry me. Don't give me your
final answer now," he continued, as Ora interrupted him.
"It is not a question to decide in a moment. But while I
am gone think it over. You do not love your husband.
I know all your arguments from your friend. She made
them when I first gave her my confidence. They don't
weigh with me for a moment. You will never spend your
life with that man, good as he may be. As for obliga-

tions, you discharged them long ago. I can make you happy, and I believe that you know I can."

"I don't know." Ora, stunned for a moment, felt thrilled and breathless. "Oh, I don't know!"

"I have begun to feel sure that you have loved another man, or fancied that you loved him. Would it be possible for you to marry him if you divorced your husband?"

Ora hesitated, then answered, "No."

"Why is he not your lover?"

"That would be impossible, even if I would do such a thing, and you know I would not."

He gave a sharp sigh of relief. "I *felt* that he had not been. Why is it impossible?"

"There are complications. I cannot explain them. But he could not be less to me if he were dead."

"Does he love you?"

Ora hesitated again. "I have sometimes felt—no, of course, it is impossible. I let my imagination run away with me, that was all."

"You mean that he never told you—that he doesn't write to you?"

"I met him only once, and I have never seen his handwriting."

"Well, dismiss him from your mind. You have imagination and have dreamed, because your demands upon life are very great, greater than you know; and oddly enough, considering your opportunities, fruition has eluded you. But the time has come for you to live; and you could live!"

Ora looked down at her hands. They were ungloved and looked very white and small. Valdobia suddenly covered them with one of his own, and bent his face close to hers. She saw that he had forgotten his mother, and gave a little gasp.

"Ora!" he said. "Don't you know how happy I could make you? I not only could teach you love, of which you know nothing, but we could always be companions, and you are the loneliest little creature I have ever met."

To her astonishment she saw two tears splash on his hand, and winking rapidly discovered that they had fallen from her own eyes. As she would have detested to see a man cry, she melted further, and whispered,

"Oh, yes, life with you would be very delightful. I

know that. I fancy the other man, even if I could marry him, would make me miserable. He—American men that amount to anything give their wives very little of themselves.''

''And you would be lonelier still! I have known American women that loved their busy husbands—that *seeking* type. They interested me, poor things—rushing madly about trying to fill their lives. If you join that sisterhood it will kill you. I am not an idler, for I have business interests to which I devote a certain amount of time, but I have leisure, and I not only should give you the companionship you have craved all your life, but I can offer you the world in all its variety. Now dismiss this man, whoever he is, from your mind. Even were I beside the question, it is your duty to yourself as a woman of character, not a sentimental schoolgirl.''

''Yes, that is true.''

''That sort of thing is morbid, besides being quite beneath a woman of pride and dignity. But women often romance about some dream-hero until they have found the right man. Can you doubt that I am the man for you? You were made for Europe, not for America, and for a man that can give you everything—everything!''

''Yes, I know.'' She moved restlessly. ''If I could only feel just one thing more for you! I hardly know what to call it—I like you better than anyone in the world. I almost love you. Why don't I?'' Her voice was suddenly full of passion and she clasped both of her hands about his own. ''If you could only make me, I should worship you.''

He glanced about rapidly. They were quite alone. He put his arm round her and she felt it vibrate. His face was flushed and his breath short. She could feel his heart thumping against her head, and she was fascinated for more reasons than one: she knew that it was many years since any woman had roused him to strong emotion, and it was the first great passion that had ever been close to her save in her stormy imagination. She was enthralled for a moment, and some of the wildness in her own nature stirred. But it was too soon, she must have time to think. She cast about desperately and found her inspiration.

''We have been here a long time!'' she said hurriedly. ''You will miss your train. Your mother may be very ill.''

He dropped his arm, and stood up.

"You are a woman of infinite resource," he said. "And no little cruelty. Will you consider what I have asked you—seriously?"

His anger as well as his power to control himself always fascinated her, and she also experienced a spasm of contrition. She rose and gave him her hand; her eyes were frank and kind.

"Yes," she said. "I will consider it, and think of you always—and miss you horribly. Will you telegraph to me every day?"

"Two or three times a day, probably. And don't think I am really angry with you. If you are cruel it is only because you don't understand. I am glad that you do not, for it is only women that have loved greatly that have forgotten how to be cruel. Come. I must take you to your hotel."

PART II

PART II

I

TWO weeks later Ora and Ida sailed from Havre. Gregory had cabled, and the *Herald* had published a dramatic account, of the wounding of Mr. Mark Blake in the tunnel of his wife's mine. The engineers' lease had expired and he had closed down the mine temporarily. The sinking of the inclined shaft in the "Apex" had proceeded very slowly owing to the uncommon hardness of the rock; it would seem that Nature herself had taken a hand in the great fight and enlisted for once on the side of the weaker power. Although when Osborne and Douglas had turned over the mine, their cross-cut almost had reached the point on the vein which the new shaft expected to strike, Gregory had risen twice in the night and walked along the hill beyond his boundary, reasonably sure that all the blasting was not in the shaft, his keen ear detecting muffled reverberations slightly to the east and at a greater depth. He communicated his suspicions to Mark, and on the following night they examined the lock on the Primo shaft house and discovered that it had been tampered with. They went down by way of the ladder; and in the cross-cut on the chalcopyrite vein they found miners working with hand drills. There was a desperate hand-to-hand fight with the manager and shift boss; the miners, who were bohunks, proceeding phlegmatically with their work.

The four men had wrestled out into the station at the foot of the shaft, where they had drawn their "guns"; each had been wounded, but only Mark seriously. He had received a ball in the lung and another in the leg. The night was bitterly cold and it was some time before Gregory and the two antagonists could get him to the surface. He had insisted upon being taken to a hospital in Butte; and, between loss of blood, shock, and pneumonia, his condition was precarious.

The girls, who had left Monte Carlo two days after Valdobia's sudden departure, received the news in Paris, where they were replenishing their wardrobes. Ora, torn with remorse, and terrified with vague and tragic visions of the future, was in a distracted condition; but Ida, although she sincerely lamented the possible demise of her old friend, did not lose her head. She gave final and minute orders to tailors and dressmakers, instructed them to send the trousseaux in bond directly to Great Falls, Montana, devoted a morning to the selection of hats both for herself and her friend, and packed all the trunks. Mowbray, always willing to be useful, bought their tickets and escorted them to Havre. Ida thanked him with something like real warmth as they parted at the head of the gangplank, and promised him the "time of his life" when he came to Montana in the summer.

"Now, buck up," she said, smiling into his disconsolate face; "you know I'm not flirting with you. We're the best of pals. I'll be glad to see you, all right, and perhaps I'll find a nice little heiress for you."

"Oh, don't!" Mowbray tried to arrange his features for the benefit of the passersby. "You know I'm fond of you no end. Why——"

"Get along now. That's the last whistle. Good-bye, and write me nice gossippy letters. It's only a few months, anyhow."

Mowbray walked down the gangplank with his head in the air, and, as he turned on the dock to lift his hat, Ida noticed that his face, whose charm was its boyish gayety, looked suddenly older, and almost as determined as Valdobia's.

"Oh, Lord!" she thought, as she turned away, "men! They're as alike as lead pencils in a box. But I guess I can manage him."

Ora stayed in bed for two days; reaction left her physically exhausted and she slept most of the time. On the third day Ida peremptorily dressed her and took her on deck. A wireless from Gregory, announcing that Mark was holding his own, further revived her, and before they reached New York another wireless was still more reassuring. A few years before, when the ores of Butte Hill were roasted in the open and the poisonous fumes were often as thick as the worst of London fogs, pneumonia ran its course in twenty-four hours to the grave, but in these days the patient had a fighting chance despite the altitude. The Butte doctors were experts in pneumonia, so many of the careless miners were afflicted, and Mark not only had a sound constitution but never had been a heavy drinker. There was every reason to expect him to pull through, as Ida assured her friend whenever they were alone; but she managed to meet several agreeable people, and kept herself and Ora companioned by them throughout the voyage.

Valdobia was still in Rome; his mother was dying. He had written daily to Ora and she had read and reread his letters. They said neither too much nor too little; but he was one of life's artists and he managed to pervade them with an atmosphere that was both sweet and disturbing. His telegram, when he had read the news of her husband's misadventure in the newspapers, was a masterpiece. If he was unable to grieve over the possibility of Mr. Blake's abrupt removal from a scene where he was the one superfluous actor, too well-bred to betray his relief, and too little of a hypocrite to be verbose in condolence, his attitude was so finely impersonal, and it was so obvious that he knew exactly how she felt, that Ora liked him more than ever if only for rousing her stricken sense of humour.

She had thrust his letters and telegrams into the depths of her steamer trunk, but after she had made up her mind that Mark would recover (her lively imagination picturing him hobbling among the orange groves of Southern California while she guided his footsteps and diverted his mind), she retrieved the correspondence and read it every night when alone in her stateroom. Valdobia's devotion not only gave her courage, but his strong imposing personality stood with a haughty and confident menace between herself and Gregory Compton. She refused to think on her future, beyond the long convalescence of her husband, but had it not been for her meeting with Valdobia and her deliberate installment of his image on the throne of her adventurous imagination, she doubted if she would have had the courage to return to Montana. As it was there were moments when the poignant mental life she had led with Gregory Compton reached a long finger from the depths to which it had been consigned and sketched his image in her mind as vividly as if he stood before her; while her whole being ached with longing and despair. But her will was strong; she banished him summarily and reinstated the Roman who was so like and so unlike the man compounded of the old world and the new in the mortar of the Northwest.

Ida, with an unexpected delicacy, refrained from curiosity, and although she had too much tact to avoid all mention of Valdobia, only alluded to him casually. She left Europe out of the conversation as much as possible, and amused Ora, when they were alone, with the plans of her campaign in Butte. When they reached quarantine Ora was horrified to find herself surrounded by reporters. The Paris *Herald* had published the story of her mine as well as her picture and Ida's, but they hardly had been sensible of their notoriety until, on the steamer, they were among Americans once more. It was manifest that they were "big news" in their own country, and Ora fled to her stateroom, leaving Ida to face the reporters alone.

Ida was undaunted; moreover she was quick to seize her first opportunity to dazzle Butte. She made herself amiable and interesting to the young men, her natural cunning steering her mid-stream, in this her first interview: an ordeal in which most novices are wrecked on the tropic or the arctic shore. She thanked them as warmly for their news that Mr. Blake had left that morning with his doctors and nurses in a private car for Southern California, and expected his wife to go directly to Los Angeles, as if Ora had not received a wireless to that effect an hour before; she modestly told them something of her social experiences abroad, answered the inevitable questions regarding suffrage, excused Ora, "who was naturally upset", and expatiated upon her happiness in returning to live in Butte. They thought this odd, but were so delighted with her mixture of dignity and naïveté that they rushed to their respective desks and told the world that the wife of Gregory Compton had been the guest of princes and was the handsomest woman in America.

Ora was almost gay at the prospect of going directly to California, although she was obliged to make the journey alone. It was early in the afternoon when they landed. Ida established Ora in the first Overland Limited that left the Grand Central Station, and returned to the Waldorf-Astoria, where she had engaged rooms for a month. She had no intention of returning to Butte ignorant of New York. Westerners of wealth, old and recent, visited New York casually several times a year; and not to know it, even with Europe to her credit, stamped a woman with the newness of the new-rich who wore all their jewels all the time. Ida had seen many women make fools of themselves and had no intention of leaving any penetrable spaces in her armour. She spent every morning in the shops, or in the establishments of the exclusive dressmakers tailors and milliners that were patronized by the fashionable women of Butte and Helena, giving them liberal orders. She saw all the new plays, heard the more famous of the opera singers, and even attended three symphony concerts. She drove in the Park every afternoon or joined the throngs on Fifth Avenue; and she took tea or lunch in the different hotels and restaurants devoted to fashion. Sometimes she sat in the gangways of her own famous hostellerie, recalling with a tolerant smile her early crude ambitions—had they died less than a year ago?—to trail her feathers up and down Peacock Alley. She wore one of her severest tailored suits upon these occasions, and maintained an air of stately detachment that somewhat counteracted the always startling beauty of her face and figure. No man took his courage in his hand.

One afternoon she sat longer than usual, for she had set her teeth that day and walked through the Metropolitan Museum. She fell to musing, and with a more sustained introspection than was her habit, upon the changes that had taken place within herself during the past year; wondering "how deep they had struck", if she really were as altered as she must appear even to the raking eye of Butte; or if she merely had developed her native characteristics while polishing her surface and furnishing her mind.

She also endeavoured to analyse her attitude toward returning to her husband, but gave this up, although puzzled that it was not more obvious. But her mind was clear on one point. If Gregory desired her society he must spend his week-ends in Butte; nothing would induce her to return to the De Smet ranch. She had not even a spasm of curiosity to see the famous Perch of the Devil Mine.

II

IDA was not given to imaginative excursions, but during the three days' journey from New York to Butte, she made no acquaintances, resting in the seclusion of her drawing-room; and after she had read all the magazines her mind began to people itself. Although the ladies of Butte, whom she now regarded as equals, moved along the central highway, Gregory was always turning the corners, and she visualised him most frequently advancing hurriedly toward the station as the train entered—both late, of course. She rehearsed the meeting many times, never without a pricking sense of awkwardness, for she now fully realised that when a woman and her husband have not communicated save on the wire for nearly a year, the first interview is liable to constraint. He always had been difficult to talk to. Would he be bored if she tried to entertain him as Ora would entertain Mark: with such excerpts of their many experiences as a confiding husband might appreciate? She never had understood him. Out of her greater knowledge of the world and men should she be better able to fathom the reserves of that strange silent nature—or did she really care whether she could or not? Although she had made up her mind to greet him at the station with the warmth of an old friend, and flatter him with her delight in returning home, she had not the faintest idea how she should carry off the long evening—if the train were on time.

It was not. Probably no Northwestern train has arrived on time in the history of the three railroads. Ida's train, due at seven in the evening, arrived at midnight. Her Pullman was at the end of the long dark platform, and as she walked slowly toward the station building—which looked like the bunk house of an abandoned mining camp in the desert—searching for some one to carry her hand baggage—porters being non-existent in the Northwest—she saw neither Gregory nor any other familiar face. For the first time in her life she felt a disposition to cry.

230

But as she tossed her head higher and set her lips, a young man approached and asked if she were Mrs. Gregory Compton. He was a pleasant looking youth, and she was so grateful to be called by name that she forgot her new reserve and replied emphatically that she was.

"I am your chauffeur," he said. "Your new car arrived a few days ago, and Mr. Compton 'phoned me to meet you. Have you any hand baggage?"

Ida indicated her portmanteau and hat box in the dark perspective and went on to inspect her car. It was a handsome limousine, lighted with electricity, and for a moment she took a childish pleasure in examining its fittings. But as the man returned and piled her baggage in front she asked irrepressibly:

"Is Mr. Compton not in Butte?"

"No, ma'am. He hasn't been in Butte for weeks. Lively times out at the mine, I guess."

"And my house? Had I not better go to a hotel?"

"Oh, the house is all right. Mr. Compton's secretary 'phoned to an agency, and they put in three or four in help. I guess you'll find everything all right."

Ida entered her car, but scowled at its luxuries. By this time she was "mad clean through." "The famous American husband!" she thought, gritting her teeth. "Best in the world—not. If it's my horse, my dog, my wife with an Englishman, it's business first last and always with an American. European men are courteous whether they mean it or not, but Americans only remember to be polite when they have time. Ten months and he can't leave his mine long enough to meet me when I arrive at midnight!"

Her pleasure in returning to Butte had turned as flat as spilt champagne. She did not even glance at the gay electric signs and midnight activities of Broadway as her car rolled through that sleepless thoroughfare toward the West Side. But when her chauffeur, who had ignored the speed limit, stopped abruptly before a large house of admirable architecture and blazing with lights, her face flushed with excitement and she forgot her recalcitrant spouse. The door was opened at once and two maid servants ran down the steps. They were young, neatly dressed and capped, and it was evident that their service was dictated not only by curiosity but by sympathy.

"Welcome home, ma'am," one of them, a Swede, said shyly as Ida stepped to the pavement. 'It's too bad your train was so late. The cook's got a nice hot supper for you.''

Ida, who was not easily touched, felt as grateful to these smiling girls as to her friendly chauffeur, and for a moment was tempted to "come down off her perch" and revel in human companionship. But she knew that it "wouldn't work"; she merely thanked them graciously and ascended the wide steps of her new home, that palatial residence of cream-colored pressed brick of her unswerving desires. While the maids were taking her bags and boxes upstairs, she walked through the large rooms of the lower floor. Everything was in the best modern style of furnishing, the prevailing tone dim and rich, with Eastern rugs on the hardwood floors; French tapestries and carved oak furniture and stained glass in the library—also a few books; paler tapestries set in panels in the immense drawing-room, and many beautiful pieces of furniture carefully selected with an eye to both contrast and mating. Out of this room opened a dining-room that looked like a baronial hall, and although the Murphys had taken their silverware they had left their china, imported from Limoges, and their glass ware, made for them by a Venetian firm that had supplied Ida's grandes dames for thirty years. In short it was one of those stately and sumptuous interiors, furnished by the best houses in New York, which one associates exclusively with the three or four great cities of the United States, and is always unwarrantably surprised to find in the newer cities of the West.

Ida made a pretence of eating her dainty supper, remembered that she was now a grande dame and visited the kitchen to say an appreciative word to the cook, then ascended to her bedroom divided between anger and a depression so foreign to her temperament that she barely recognised it for what it was.

The large upper hall had been fitted up as a billiard room, and with a continuous divan broken only by the doors of the bedrooms. Ida threw it an appreciative glance, but it merely emphasised the fact that there was no man in the house, and she did not linger. Mrs. Murphy, evidently a brunette, had furnished her bedroom and dressing-room in primrose yellow and much lace. Ida approved both as unreservedly as she had the rest of the house, thankful there was nothing to alter; like many women she had consummate taste in dress and none whatever for house decoration; although unlike most of these disparate ladies she was quite aware of her deficiencies. She knew when a room was all that it should be, but could not have conceived one of the details, much less the unimpeachable combination. The sex instinct teaches those subtleties of personal adornment likely to allure the male, and arrest the anxious eye of other females, but ancestral brain cells are necessary for the more civilised accomplishment.

Ida's eyes fell on the telephone beside her bed and lingered. She forgot her beautiful room and the successive throbs of gratified ambition, in an overwhelming desire to call up Gregory and tell him what she thought of him. But she was a woman in whom calculation was stronger than impulse, and in the past year she had learned to control her temper, not only because a carefully nourished refinement had crowded out some of the weeds of her nature, but because her ever-growing intelligence despised lack of self-control in all things. So she merely undressed herself, her eyes wandering every few minutes to the telephone. It was incredible that he did not ring her up. That, at least, would take but a few moments of his precious time.

However, she fell asleep immediately after her bath, and it was the telephone bell that awakened her at eight o'clock. This time she frowned at it, for she wanted to sleep; but she sat up, put the receiver to her ear and asked languidly: "Well?"

A strange man's voice replied: "Is this Mrs. Compton?"

"Yes. Why am I disturbed so early?"

"I'm sorry—this is Mr. Compton's secretary speaking—but Mr. Compton told me to call you at eight o'clock. He always comes in for breakfast at this time—here he is."

"Hello! How are you? What time did you get in?" Gregory's voice was elaborately polite and as eager as any lover's of yesteryear.

"Are you interested?" Ida's heart beat thickly, but her tones were crisp. "I arrived at midnight. Really, I expected you to meet me. That is generally considered the decent thing to do."

"Oh! I'm sorry it was impossible. I can't leave the mine at present. How did you like the house?"

'I am enchanted with it—and with the limousine. When are you coming in?"

"I can't say at present. I dare not leave for a moment. You will find a deposit to your credit at the Daly bank."

"Thanks. Would—shall I run out?"

"Better not. There is always danger of rows."

"But of course I'm wild to see the mine. You forget how famous it is."

"Better wait awhile. It really isn't safe."

"Very well. How's your wound? Where were you hurt, anyhow?"

"Not worth mentioning, as I cabled you, and I suppose you got my telegram in New York saying I was all right again. Sure you got everything you want?"

"I am overwhelmed by all this luxury, and your generosity."

"Glad you like it. Has Mrs. Blake gone to California?"

"She went directly from the steamer. How is Mark getting on. I've had only notes from Ora."

"All right. He doesn't write but has telegraphed once or twice. He'd better stay below several months. Write Mrs. Blake to persuade him to take things easy. He had a close call. I can get along without him for awhile, but I can't afford to lose him. Will you see to this?"

"I'll write Ora today. She's in no hurry to return to Butte—was delighted at the prospect of going to California, and intends to take Mark to Santa Barbara, where she knows a lot of people."

"Ah! Good. Well, I must get some breakfast. Amuse yourself."

"And you won't be in for several days?"

"Afraid not. Good-bye."

Ida set the receiver back on the table, but it was some minutes before she lay down again. She sat thinking, with compressed lips. Born with intuitive knowledge of men, she had, as she once remarked to Ora, turned a goodly number of them inside out during the past year. Gregory Compton did not intend to live with her again. She knew this as conclusively as if his kind matter-of-fact tones had expressed the direct message. Before she left home it never had occurred to Ida to wonder if her hus-

band still loved her or not, and she had learned to accept
his consuming masculine interest in matters mineralogic
as all in the day's work. Now she wondered if he had
ceased to love her then or since. That he took no further
interest in her as a woman, although amiably determined
to do his duty as her legal provider, would have been almost patent to an imagination as riotous as Ora's; to Ida,
practical and clear-sighted, there was not a loophole for
delusion.

In a few moments she relaxed the tension of her body
and lay down.

"Well!" she thought impatiently, "what's the matter
with me, anyhow? Isn't it what I always hopefully looked
forward to? Did I ever pretend to be anything but resigned—or to be in love with him after the first few weeks?
I guess I'm spoiled with too much devotion, that's what.
Seeing too many men lose their heads. Much their old
heads are worth. But I guess I don't like being turned
down for once. Goose. It's my lay to cut out pique and
sing a song of thanksgiving that I've got pretty nearly
everything I ever romanced about and set my mind on.
It's a pretty good old world when things come your way,
and women'll never be happy till they learn to put men
in the same place that men put us—on a handy little side-
track. I've got a whole parlour car instead of an upper
berth like some poor devils, so I'll quit whining. But if
there's another woman in the case, let them both look out
—that's all!"

III

IDA slept for two hours longer and rose in a philosophical mood. As she more than once had remarked to Ora, "nothing in life is just what you figured it out beforehand"; and this, one of life's most unwelcome lessons, it had not taken her twenty-six years to learn. She had, in fact, accepted and docketed it while women twice her age were nursing their illusions.

She had expected to be met at the station not only by her husband but by Ruby and Pearl, to say nothing of reporters. "She had slunk in like a nobody," and her husband declined to feed the fires of her vanity, blazing so merrily these last ten months. Never mind. She had the genius of quick readjustment and a sharp eye for the next move in the great law of compensation.

"And believe me," she thought, as she put the finishing touches to her smart morning street costume, and taught the admiring Swede how to pin on a veil, "the gods have provided the goods pretty liberally, and I don't belong to the immortal order of female jackasses. Nine-tenths of women's troubles, mental and physical, sprout in that hothouse corner of their skulls they call imagination. None of it in mine. Let us eat and drink, for to-morrow we shall die. Wait till I'm launched in Butte. And just wait till I give a dinner party to the second son of an English duke. Tra la la!"

Before the morning was over even philosophy had folded her wings. If life had been niggardly yesterday she gave with both hands today. When Ida arrived at the bank she was received with exceeding deference by the vice-president and informed that he had recently invested two hundred thousand dollars in her name, acting on instructions from Mr. Compton; and that as a large part of it was in mortgages the interest in some cases ran as high as eight per cent. The money had been placed in his hands for investment shortly after the great land deal, details

236

of which had reached the public ear in due course and greatly added to the prestige of Gregory Compton. In fact it had invested his remote and ambiguous personality with an almost sinister significance. As Ida listened to the story of this transaction (she barely had opened a newspaper in New York and knew nothing of it), she found herself wondering if it could be true that once she had possessed this man of whom even bankers spoke with bated breath. It was patent that they stood in awe not only of the rapid and masterly strokes which had increased his little patrimony by something over two millions in less than a year, but of his colossal luck, his sensational reputation as a "winner", and his open defiance of the greatest of all great trusts.

It seemed to Ida, as she sat in the vice-president's office listening to his classification of her husband with Marcus Daly, W. A. Clark, and F. Augustus Heinze, the three commanding figures heretofore in the financial history of Montana, and to predictions that Compton would go farther than any one of his predecessors, that she might have known Gregory in his extreme youth or in some previous existence; but that this man who now not only ranked first in the eyes of all Montana, but had focussed the attention of a continent, no longer touched her life save as a fairy god-father. It was the first time that she had appreciated his fame. She had been absorbed in Europe and its diversions—and diverters; the new wealth had been accepted as a matter of course; her imagination had not been powerful enough to visualise at a distance what her mind grasped the moment the facts were presented to her in the measured yet glowing terms of a bank's president.

"He always did feel himself a cut above me," she thought grimly as she left the building and walked down Main Street. "And now, I suppose, he thinks Perch of the Devil is Mount Olympus, and that he is some god. It would be fun to put a nick or two in his halo—but never mind: I've got a cool two hundred thousand— *and* a palatial residence, *and* a limousine—sounds like a fairy tale. There's nothing mean about him, anyhow."

When she reached her beautiful home she found four reporters awaiting her. They apologised for not meeting her at the train, but as hour after hour had passed with discouraging reports, they finally had gone home to recuperate for the next day's labours. Ida dismissed the last of her regrets, and told them all that she wished Butte to know at once, showed the women the contents of her trunks, which the maids were unpacking, promised to let them know when the newer Paris wardrobe arrived, and finally gave them lunch. Reporters are the quickest people in the world to detect affectations, assumptions, and false values, and the most merciless in their exposure; but, although these four were on the alert, they could find neither traces of original commonness nor imitation of the British aristocracy. Ida apparently had consigned the slang of her former class to the limbo of careless grammar, and she was so simple and natural that they failed to discover how clever she was; they agreed, as they walked down Broadway, that she was merely a marvel of adaptability, like so many others that had done credit to the great state of Montana, to say nothing of the fluid West in general.

But, although Ida could be anything she chose when occasion demanded, she always sought relief from the strain as quickly as possible. Immediately after the departure of the reporters she telephoned for her limousine and drove to the large "Block" in the heart of the business district where Miss Ruby Miller kept the looks of the Butte ladies up to par. As she left the elevator she saw that the familiar door was open as usual and the old screen before it. She tapped discreetly, and Miss Ruby came out into the hall, removing the cold cream from her hands with her apron.

"Ide!" she cried rapturously, throwing both arms about her friend's velvet shoulders. 'Glory be, but I'm glad to see you and you do look fine——"

"How mean of you not to meet me——"

"We had it all fixed and supper here, but gave it up at ten o'clock. For all we knew you might not get in till morning, and you know how we work——"

"Well, I'll forgive you if you both come to dinner with me tonight. I want to have one good old time before I sit up and play the grande dame act for weeks on end——"

"I guess you're one now without any playacting. You look the real thing all right. And I guess we won't see so awful much of you now——"

"Do you mean because I'm harnessed up to a bunch of money——" began Ida in high indignation.

"Oh, I know you'll always feel the same, but grand dames and our sort don't gee at the same table. The West is democratic but it ain't too democratic. Don't think I'm jealous. You're just where I'd like to be myself, and I'm proud that one of us has got to the top so quick. My! But Mr. Compton's a wonder. To think that I ever dared call him Greg—even behind his back. Well, he'll be just as proud of you as you are of him. Pearl'll want to see your hats."

"She can copy them all. Be sure to come early."

She felt warmed by the little interview, but as she went down in the elevator she admitted to herself that her future intercourse with her old friends must be sporadic, no matter what her loyalty; and she wondered if her new friends would take their place; or even be to her the half of what Ora had become in the long intimacy of travel. She shrugged her handsome shoulders. If you elected to mount in life, you must pay the toll. Were she abruptly returned to the old cottage in East Granite Street certainly Ruby and Pearl would not compensate her. No, not for a moment. You may slip back in life if you are not strong enough to hold on, but you do not deliberately turn back even for the friends of your youth. Neither does Progress halt and sit down to wait for its failures to catch up. Ida leaned back in her limousine and met the interested eyes of many pedestrians of both sexes as her chauffeur drove her about for an hour to get the air, and incidentally to be looked at.

Today she was in a mood to enjoy Butte, and she deliberately summoned the long anticipated sensations. She revelled in the gaunt grey ugliness of Anaconda Hill which flung its arrogant head high above the eastern end of the great hill itself; in the sensation of driving over miles of subterranean numbered streets, some of them three thousand feet below, to which that famous mass of rock and dirt and angular buildings was the portal. She leaned far out of her car to admire the glittering mountains that looked like blue ice topped with white, and decided that they were far more original and beautiful than the Alps of Austria and Switzerland; certainly they tugged at her heartstrings and at the same time filled her with an unprecedented desire to sing. She noticed for the first time that the violet foothills against the nearer mountain east of the city seemed to close the end of the streets as the Alps did in Innspruck, and gave the ragged overgrown camp clinging to its high perch in the Rockies a redeeming touch of perfect beauty.

She drove out to Columbia Gardens, bought flowers from the conservatory for her rooms, and wandered about recalling the many gay times she had had in the dancing pavilion. But her eye was suddenly arrested by the steep mountain behind, then dropped slowly to the base. It was there that she had promised to marry Gregory Compton. She remembered his young passion and her own. She had never felt anything like it again; nor had he ever been quite the same. Was it one of those "supreme moments" novelists so blithely alluded to? The logical inference of that old bit of bathos was that such moments had no duplicates. She felt faint and dizzy for a moment; then walked back to her car, smiling grimly as she realised that she had experienced a fleeting echo of that vast unattainable desire women live and die cherishing or bewailing. "Poor things! Poor things!" she thought, with the first pang of pity her sex had ever inspired. "No wonder they go in for suffrage, art, work, any old thing. Home," she added to the chauffeur.

She peremptorily dismissed all thought of the past during the drive back to town and reverted to her pleasure in once more feeling a part of her surroundings, hideous though they might, for the most part, be; instead of walking with alert critical eye through what always must seem to her the animated pages of ancient history. But her complacency received a sudden shock. The car was rolling along Park Street when her eye rested upon a man's face vaguely familiar. She had bowed graciously and the face was behind her before she realised that the man was Professor Whalen, and that, for a second, she had looked into a pair of pale blue eyes that sent her a swift message of hate.

Ida shuddered. The warm light air of her beloved Rockies turned cold and heavy. "I feel as if I'd stepped on a snake and just missed getting bitten," she thought, putting her sensations into a concrete form, after her habit. "I had forgotten the little viper was alive, and

I wish to goodness he wasn't." She had flouted superstition always, but she could not shake off the sense of menace and evil that had vibrated from the man until she was within her own doors once more. Then she became as oblivious of Whalen's existence as during that late exotic period when everything connected with her old life had seemed too crude to be real.

The parlour maid handed her a note that had arrived an hour before from Mr. Luning, Mark's partner. Mrs. Blake, he wrote, had bought a present for Mrs. Compton in Paris and sent it to the care of her husband's firm. Mr. Luning had gone the day before to Great Falls to clear it in the Custom House, and now had the pleasure of forwarding the boxes, etc.

"Good gracious!" exclaimed Ida, "what can it be?"

"There's four big boxes in the back hall, ma'am."

Ida lost no time. If Ora had given her a present it must be worth looking at, and she went as rapidly as dignity would permit to the nether regions and ordered the boxes opened. The present proved to be a magnificent silver service, from many dozens of "flat ware" to massive platters, vegetable dishes, flower, fruit and bon-bon pieces, and candelabra. The delighted servants made a shining display on the dining-room table, and after Ida had gloated over it for a time and informed her audience that it was copied from a royal service in the Louvre, she went suddenly up to her bedroom. This time she did shed a few tears, and as she looked at her handkerchief in some wonder she decided that there was at least one person that she loved, "hard-headed" as she was, and that Ora Blake had found the one soft spot in her flinty heart and wormed herself into it. She went to her desk immediately and wrote Ora a letter that was almost tender, admitting that she missed her "like fury", and begging her to return soon.

"Greg telephoned this morning," she concluded, oblivious that she was betraying the fact that she had not seen her husband, "and told me to tell you to keep Mark down below for several months. But his lungs must be well by this time or he'd be dead. And the rest of him will mend all the sooner in this magnificent air. Heavens, but it's good to breathe it again! It makes one feel as if the atmosphere of Europe hadn't been aired for a century. I've got a wonder of a house and a jim dandy of a limousine, but ever since I came I've felt kind of home-sick, and I've just realised it's for you, old girl. So, come home. Once more ten million thanks.''

And when Ruby and Pearl dined with her that night she realised that all her old zest in their society was gone. Ida Hook, at least, had ''passed on.''

IV

IT was on the morning of this same day that Gregory
sat alone in his cabin uncommonly idle, for he still
spent the greater part of his time underground, when not
away on business connected with his new investments and
deals. For the last week he had not left the hill, and although he was on the alert to hear his geological acumen
vindicated, he was in no mood to find pleasure in his mine.
His conscience, an organ that troubled him little, was
restive. In spite of his liberal disbursements, he knew
that he had treated Ida unfairly. He had long since made
up his mind to obliterate her from his personal life, and,
if the truth must be told about a man who had snapped
his fingers in the face of the most formidable combination
of capital in the world, he was afraid to meet his wife.
Vanity, he argued, in such women takes the place of
warmth, and he had no mind to burden his memory and
resource with an endless chain of subterfuges; nor had
he any relish for the bald statement that since he could
not have the woman he wanted he would have none; and
that his mine, as complex and mysterious, as provocative of
dreams, as capricious and satisfying as woman herself—
to say nothing of hard work and increasing power—was to
fill his life.

Ida might rage, stamp, scream, with her hands on her
hips, her superb eyes flashing. Worse still, she might weep,
lamenting that he loved her no longer—if he made her
hurried friendly calls. Far, far worse, he might suc-
cumb to her beauty and superlative femaleness and hate
himself ever after. His was to be a life of unremitting
and constructive work; he must keep that blue flame
burning on the altar in his sanctuary. If he never paused
to draw it up into his consciousness he must know it was
there.

Better stay away until she understood all that it was
necessary she should know, wore out her pique in private,

and accepted the situation. But he would have felt better this morning if he had heard that her train had arrived early in the evening. He might be ruthless, even where women were concerned, but he was also sensitive and capable of tenderness.

But he was not thinking of Ida alone. He was listening for the footsteps of Joshua Mann, and in a few moments he heard them, as well as the angry growl of his foreman's voice. Mann entered without ceremony.

"I've been looking for you, sir. We've the devil's own luck again——"

"Apex struck the Primo vein?"

"No, and won't for fifty feet yet. But—well—I hate to say it—we've lost our vein—cut off as short as if it had been sawed. Of course, it's faulted, and God only knows where its dropped to—or how far. A prettier shoot of ore was never uncovered. What's worrying me is that—oh, hell!—just suppose that's what Amalgamated is sinking on. My head's going round. Can I have something?"

Gregory waved his hand toward the cupboard where his visitors found refreshment. When Mann had braced himself, his employer tapped a large sheet of paper that lay on the table.

"Come here," he said. "I made this map some time ago, and calculated to a day when you would lose the vein. I guessed our vein had faulted before Amalgamated got busy. But don't worry. They're either on a parallel vein or on a mere fork." His pencil moved along the vein already stoped, travelled over the fault line and recovered a vein further down. "Hundred feet," he said. "With air drills and unless the fault breccia is uncommonly hard, which I don't think is the case, we should find it in less than three weeks. They can't get through that rock for at least a month. Even then they may not touch us, but then again they may, and we must be there first. Cut across the fault at once and follow it on the footwall side to the east. Get well into the footwall. If you don't recover the vein inside of a hundred feet I'll stand to lose a thousand dollars and you'll be the winner."

"I guess not," said Mann admiringly. "But, by jing! I was worried. You never can tell about them faults. When the old earth split herself up and got to slipping she not only lost one side of herself sometimes, but twisted about as if she was having fun with the apex law of Montana in advance. But I figure out that you're like old Marcus Daly—you've got a sort of X-ray in your eye that sees the ore winking below. So long.''

He departed to carry encouragement to the anxious miners, and Gregory went out and walked along his hill. By this time he knew every inch of it, and had found indications of ore in his other claims while superintending the development work necessary before perfecting his patents. If Amalgamated sank on his present vein and the courts enjoined him from working it until the matter of apex rights was settled, he would simply go ahead and sink through the carbonates in his other claims to those vast deposits of chalcopyrite with which he was convinced his hill was packed. He knew the geological history of every mine in Montana, and while he had given up all hope of finding gold on his estate save in small incidental values, he believed that he possessed one of the greatest copper deposits in the Rocky Mountains. And now that even one vein of his hill was threatened, he dismissed his old dreams with a shrug and transferred his undivided affection to the exciting treasure the earth had given him. There were few surprises in gold mines. A great copper mine might make geological history. In two districts, Butte and Castle Mountain, copper glance, an ore of secondary enrichment, had been found far down in the sulphide zone below chalcopyrite, chief of the primary ores. He believed that he should find glance at a depth of nine hundred feet. If there were masses of it he should take out millions in a year, for chalcocite was the richest of the permanent copper ores of this region, running as high as 79.8.

He had been on amiable terms with the manager and engineer of the Apex Mine since the battle underground, and he crossed the claim unmolested to make his daily inspection of the Primo shaft house. But there had been no further attempt to use the cross-cut, although the Apex people had managed before they were discovered to drive to the point upon which they expected to sink.

Gregory walked up the hill beyond to look at the cottage just completed, which was to be occupied by the manager and foreman of the Primo Mine as soon as Mark reopened it. He had been about to begin operations, cutting across

the fault Gregory had demonstrated—a fault parallel to
the one in Perch of the Devil—when he was shot nearly
to death.

The cottage was situated in a clearing in the pine woods,
somewhat apart from the cabins, which were being reno-
vated and made comfortable for the miners. Gregory was
so positive that the pyroxenite vein would be recovered just beyond the row of aspens, some sixty feet below
the tableland, that Mark, who believed his friend to be an
inspired geologist, was preparing for a long period of
mining; although if it had been a quartz mine Gregory,
sure as he was of his judgment, would not have permitted
him to put up a mill and concentrating plant until suffi-
cient ore had been blocked out to warrant the expense. But
pyroxenite went direct to the smelter, and a cottage could
always be rented.

The little bungalow had two bedrooms besides one for
a Chinese servant, a bathroom, and a large living-room
with a deep fireplace, a raftered ceiling, and pine walls
stained brown. Gregory, as he realised how cosy it would
be when furnished, wondered that he had been satisfied
with his two-roomed cabin for so long. He had been too
absorbed to think of comfort, but today he felt a desire for
something more nearly resembling a home than a perch.
He looked through the windows at the sibilant pines, the
pink carpet of primrose moss, the distant forests rising to
the blue and white mountains; and then he sighed as he
glanced slowly about the long room and pictured it furnished in warm tones of red and brown, wondering if either
of the men would be married. It would be an ideal home
for a honeymoon.

He twitched his shoulders impatiently and went outside.
To his surprise he saw a wagon ascending the hill laden
with lumber, the seats occupied by the contractor and car-
penters that had built the bungalow.

"What's up?" he asked, as the contractor leaped to
the ground.

"Another bungalow. Perhaps you could suggest a site.
It's to be near this, and the same size. We had a telegram
from Mr. Blake yesterday."

"But what does he want of two cottages?"

"Can't say, sir, unless he means to come out here to
get well."

"That's nonsense. He knows he could stay at my house on the ranch."

But Gregory was not in the habit of thinking aloud. After indicating a site he swung back to his hill, angry and apprehensive. Could it be possible that Mark intended to spend the summer at the mine and bring his wife with him? As soon as he reached his cabin he sat down at his table, and after getting his friend's present address from Luning, telephoned a long distance message to Pony to be telegraphed to Mr. Mark Blake in Santa Barbara. Its gist was that the weather was abominable and that Mark must not think of anything so foolish as to bring his weakened heart and lungs to this altitude. His services would be imperative later when his solicitous friend locked horns with Amalgamated, and meanwhile he was, for heaven's sake, to take care of himself and remain on the coast until he was in a condition to work day and night.

He received an answer that afternoon.

"No intention of leaving here for two months. Lungs pretty good, but shall wait for leg to heal. Ora wants present cottage for herself as she intends to spend summer at mine. Will you be on the lookout for a manager? He can live in the lessee's shack until the new cottage is built. Might begin operations at once. Hope this not too much trouble. Mark."

This message was transmitted over the telephone, and, to the excessive annoyance of the operator, who happened to be the belle of Pony, Gregory asked her three times, and with no excess of politeness, to repeat it. The third time he wrote it out and stared at the words as if the unsteady characters were recombining into a sketch of the infernal regions.

"Good God!" he thought. "And I can't get away!"

Was Mark mad? Was she mad? Then he realised the blissful ignorance of both regarding the drama he so often had swept from the stage of his mind, that secret dweller in the most secret recesses of his soul. Doubtless Ora never had thrown him a thought since they parted at her gate. He remembered her expressed intention to live at her mine when the lease was up, her desire to adventure underground, her intense appreciation of the romance of mining. He closed his eyes, his face relaxed. So long as she cared nothing for him there was no danger; he might daydream about her a bit. At least—at last!—he should see her again, talk to her, work with her, help her as no one else could help her. If the association he would have avoided was inevitable why not welcome it as a brief oasis in what must be an arid life, so far as mortal companionship was concerned?

But he was not the man to dream long. Presently he opened his eyes, set his jaw until it looked a yard long, put on his overalls, and went underground.

V

BUTTE long since had made up its mind as to the social future of Mrs. Gregory Compton. That Ida's mother had been a laundress and her father a miner concerned the ladies of Butte as little as many similar outcroppings of family history peculiar not only to Montana but to all regions of recent exploitation and rapid growth.

In the hearty welcome extended to the newcomer, with either the money or the personality to command its attention, Butte more nearly resembles London than any other city in the world. To pasts she is indifferent, provided they are not resurrected as models for a present; she asks no questions of a pretty, amiable, amusing woman who pays her the compliment of sojourning in her midst, so long as the lady exercises an equal reticence—assuming reticence to be her virtue—and plays the social game with *savoir faire*. Distractions on that high perch are few, social life ebbs oftener than it flows, many of the large houses are closed for the greater part of the year, and only the very young, who care not where they are so long as they may dance, find life in an overgrown mining camp as satisfactory as their elders find New York.

But the hospitality of Butte is genuine and founded largely upon common sense. Most of the women composing its society have enjoyed wealth for many years; they have travelled extensively; and if they continue to make their homes in Butte it is solely on account of their own business interests or those of their men. They argue that to deprive themselves of even the casual diversion, assuming the exclusive airs of large and resourceful communities, would merely put them on a level with thousands of other small towns slowly stagnating, be unworthy of their worldly experience, and of the large free spirit of the Northwest which has pervaded that isolated camp since they came with their husbands or fathers to take a hand in its history.

As for Mrs. Gregory Compton all they knew of her in her present stage of development was favourable, although several had a lively remembrance of the rosy black-haired Ida Hook delivering her excellent mother's laundry work at their back door, and receiving more or less of her "cheek." But they had heard, at the time, of her lessons with Professor Whalen, and of Ora Blake's coincident interest. Of her social advantages and triumphs in Europe the press had kept them informed; she returned to Butte, in fact, as one new-born. Moreover, she now owned one of the finest houses in the city for entertaining, they knew that she had elected to shine in Butte rather than in London (that Mecca of so many quick-rich women without position in their own country); and above all she was the wife of Gregory Compton, the man in whom Montana was beginning to feel assured it could take an unequivocal pride, not only for his diabolical cleverness, but because he was as "straight" as the Twentieth Century in the United States of America would permit. Butte felt devoutly grateful to Ida for being and returning, and, with that utter lack of affectation that characterised it, began calling two days after her arrival.

Ida would have been glad to have had Ora's support and advice during this ordeal—which caused her far more apprehension than ducal week-ends. But she summoned all her acquired knowledge and tact, fortified it with her native and supreme confidence in herself, and made no mistakes. Butte was charmed with the severe rich gowns that set off her haughty head and warmly colored face and the long, flowing, yet stately lines of her beautiful figure; charmed also with a manner that was both simple and dignified. She showed no enthusiasm at being taken up so promptly, neither did she quite accept it as a matter-of-course. If her talk ranged freely over common acquaintance in London, the Paris dressmakers of the season, the new opera, the plays of the moment in New York, it was without glibness, and she took a firm hold on the older and more important women of the community by confiding to them that she should not make her first venture in the difficult art of entertaining until her friend Mrs. Blake returned to help her through the novitiate. Many of the younger women were the wives of Amalgamated officials and attorneys, or of men in a relationship to that mighty power but one degree further removed; but the men individually were too broad-minded to cherish a personal grudge against Compton, and they were, moreover, quite as eager as their mates to meet his handsome wife.

During the ensuing fortnight Ida dined out every night, went to a bridge party every afternoon, as well as to several luncheons, teas, and dances. She wore a different costume every time she appeared in public; but although there was at the moment nothing in Butte to compare with her gowns she never produced the effect of outshining the other women by anything but her beauty and individual style. In short her success was so immediate and so final that, although she liked these ladies of her native town even better than she had anticipated, her rapid conquest soon lost its novelty, and she wished that Ora would return; not only because she missed her increasingly, but because to entertain in her great house would give her a new and really poignant excitement, and lift her definitely from the ranks of the merely received.

Gregory telephoned every few days, and never twice at the same hour. When she found herself restlessly awaiting the ring of the instrument, she dashed out of the house angrily and took a walk. If she found upon her return that he had called her up, she felt that he had given her the excuse to telephone to him, and she soon learned at what hours she could find him either in his cabin or down in the mine, where he had a booth. She was furious at what she called her raging female vanity, and if she could have found another man to assuage it she would not have hesitated to press him into service at whatever cost to himself. But, as happens more often than not, there was not an unmarried man in Butte old enough to be worthy of a fastidious woman's notice. She would have yawned in the face of "Brownies", and, although more than one roving husband would have placed himself at her disposal, she was the last woman to court scandal or even gossip. She longed for the advent of Lord John Mowbray, whose gayety would distract her mind, and whose devotion make her forget that she was a neglected wife. She could throw dust into the eyes of Butte by pretending to be his matrimonial sponsor.

But for the first time she wished that she had children. The great house seemed to demand the patter of small feet, the slamming of doors, a row of naughty faces peering over the banister of the second floor. It was terribly silent. And yet she had felt settled down in that house at once, so long had one of its kind been the object of her unswerving desire; its atmosphere already seemed to hang listless with ennui. She subscribed to both the state and city suffrage fund, for she felt a new sympathy for women who were trying to fill their lives, and sincerely hoped they would invent some game that would make them independent of men.

Seventeen days after her return she was sitting in the library, trying to forget her solitary luncheon in a novel when she heard the front door bell ring. Her servants were amiable but not too competent, and she waited impatiently and in vain for one of them to answer the summons. She restrained the impulse to open the door herself. This was now an obsolete custom among her new acquaintance; although having the front door shut in one's face while the colored maid took one's card to the lady of the stately mansion was hardly an improvement, and this had been her experience a day or two ago. She rang the bell in the library. Still there was no sign of life from the high-priced young women who doubtless were gossiping over the back fence. Ida's curiosity overcame her. The hour was too early for callers. It might be a cable. She stole to the front door and peered through its curtain of Honiton lace. Then she gave a war whoop which would have horrified her servants—who, careless as they were, stood in awe of her—flung the door open, caught Ora in her arms and almost carried her into the library.

"Good Lord, but I'm glad to see you!" she cried. "I'm just about dead of lonesomeness. Why didn't you telegraph? I'd have met you if your train didn't get in till two in the morning."

Ora laughed and disentangled herself, although she kissed Ida warmly. "I just got in—came here on the way from the station and sent my bags to the house—but I always did hate to be met. How beautiful your house is."

"It's all right. But it's about as cheerful to live alone in as one of those palaces in the Via Garibaldi! My, but I'm glad you're here. You're the only person I ever missed, and being a real lady for weeks on end is telling on my plebeian health. I didn't have any relief even in New York. How's Mark?"

"Quite well, except for his broken leg."

"Is he here?"

"Oh, no—I left him in Santa Barbara—that is to say at the Club House at Montecito, the fashionable suburb. He has a jolly circle of friends there, and has no desire to travel any further until he can walk."

Ida put her hands on Ora's shoulders and turned her round to the light. "What's up?" she demanded. "You look fine, as pretty as a picture—but—different, somehow."

"I've left Mark."

Ida glanced into the hall. The opening of back doors indicated that one of the maids had condescended to remember she was a wage earner. "Let's go upstairs," said Ida; and as they crossed the hall she said to the girl who was hastening to the front door with a propitiating smile, "You're just about ten minutes too late, as usual, and the next time it happens you lose your job. I'm not the sort that sits down and wails over the servant question. This house will be run properly if I have to send East for help. Now put on your hat and run down to Mrs. Blake's house and bring up her bags, and tell them to send her trunks here"

"Yes, you're going to stay with me for the present," she said, as Ora protested. "Don't say another word about it."

Ora shrugged her shoulders, and when they were in Ida's bedroom she took off her hat and coat and wandered about aimlessly for a few moments. Ida was almost breathless with impatience and a curious sense of apprehension that vaguely recalled the strange terror Ora had inspired on the day of their meeting. Ora wore a blue frock, and Ida noticed that the yellow room did not dim her fair radiance. If possible she was holding her head higher than usual, her skin "gleamed" more than ever, there was a curious light in her always brilliant eyes, half defiant, half exultant.

"Do sit down!" said Ida sharply, cutting short Ora's voluble approval of the room. "There, that's right," as Ora flung herself into a chair. "Now, fire away. You're brimming over with something. Do you mean that you've left Mark for good and all?"

"Yes."

"Told him so?"

Ora nodded.

"Did you tell him about Valdobia, or what? For heaven's sake open up."

"No, I—I thought I wouldn't tell him everything at once. I told him that I meant to spend the rest of my life in Europe, and that it was only fair to himself to divorce me—he can do it easily on the ground of desertion—and marry some one who would make a real home for him—make him happy."

"Ah! Mark's the sort women marry but don't fall in love with. And what did he say when you handed him that?"

"He was rather broken up."

"Really! And you? I always had an idea that when it came to the point you wouldn't do it. You have high-falutin' notions about honor, noblesse oblige, and all the rest of it, to say nothing of being really soft, as I once told you. There's only one thing that would make you hard—to everyone else—and that's being in love——"

"That is it!" exclaimed Ora eagerly. "I've made up my mind to marry Valdobia. I wasn't so sure when I left Europe, but you know what separation often does——"

"Yes," said Ida dryly, "I do. Well, Mark will have to take his medicine, I guess. I've never doubted, since Valdobia joined us in Genoa, that he was the man for you. It's fate, I guess. But tell me what Mark said, after all. Did he consent?"

"There was nothing else to do. He knew I meant it. I broke it to him by degrees. Besides, he knew how it was long before I left for Europe. He had practically given me up. Of course he was fond of me—I had become a habit and made him comfortable, besides being useful to him—but—well, I gave him six years—my youth!" she burst out passionately. "What wouldn't I give to wipe out those years, be twenty again and free! I tried to make him understand that I was no longer in the least like the bewildered undeveloped girl he had married; and that I bore as little resemblance to the intellectual automaton I made of myself later. I told him that I was awake once for all, and that rather than live again with a man I couldn't care for I'd be boiled in oil. Then he understood.''

"I should think he might! Of course he asked if there was another man?"

"Yes, but I told him that was neither here nor there; that in any case I should leave him and live in Europe."

"Poor Mark! Tied by the leg, and lost in the shuffle!"

"You know as well as I do that I have nothing in me for Mark and that if I cared as little for Valdobia it would only be fair to give him a second throw for happiness. When I left him he was quite resigned, and we have agreed to remain the best of friends. I shall leave him my power of attorney as before, and he will continue to manage my affairs."

"How much more sensible we are in our Twentieth Century! No doubt he will visit you in the Palazzo Valdobia when he takes a whirl at Europe."

"Why not? But tell me you think I did right, Ida?" Ora's voice was very sweet and plaintive.

"You did what you were bound to do, I guess, when you met a man that could throw a lariat round the neck of that romantic imagination of yours. Right? I don't know. I guess I've got the same old streak of Puritan Americanism in me, although if other people want to have *liaisons* and divorces it's none of my affair. Women will do more and more as they damn please, I guess, men having set them such a good example for a few centuries. But I simply hate the idea of losing you. I want you right here in Butte. Lord, I've almost forgotten my slang!"

Ora laughed with something like her old merriment. "Oh, you'll have me for an escape valve for a while yet. Valdobia's mother is dying of some lingering horrible disease. It wouldn't be decent for me to go to Rome, and I should be lonely anywhere else. So, I've made up my mind to stay here during the summer at least, and realise a dream I used to indulge in before I ever knew I could fall in love." Once more she looked straight at Ida, this time with the slow expectant smile of a child. "I'm going to reopen my mine and run it myself—of course I shall have a manager. Mark has written, or telegraphed, to Mr. Compton to find one for me—but I shall live out there and go down every day, and make believe I am doing something, too—at all events realise that it *is* my mine.

Mining has always—that is, always did fascinate me more than anything else on earth. I shall be devoted to Valdobia when I am married to him, but I simply must have that adventure first——"

"For heaven's sake don't go dotty like Gregory over a hole in the ground. If you get that bee buzzing round in your skull I pity poor Valdobia. If it were not for his mother I'd cable to him to come out——"

Ora's face set with a hardness that arrested Ida's observant eye. "Don't you do anything of the sort. Mark said once about my father, 'It was characteristic of him that when he quit he quit for good.' I am always discovering more and more of my father in me. I'll live that old dream and it will finish when Valdobia and I both are free. Then I shall wipe it off the slate—consign it to limbo." She sprang to her feet and stretched out her arms. "I am going to do exactly as I please as long as I am free. Of course I am mad about Valdobia—you know that I wouldn't marry him if I were not—but I am mad too about liberty and my mine. This is my only chance. And I am a Montanan, born in the Rocky Mountains. I want something of the life that has made my state famous before I become a European. I've never had anything of her but Butte. I want the wild mountains—I want, above all, the mine that has given me my freedom. I'm going to wear overalls and go down into the mine every day."

"A sweet sight you'll be!" said Ida disgustedly. "And the miners—Oh, they'll just love the idea of having a woman at their heels! What on earth has got hold of you? It's the only time I've ever known you to get off your base. Why, there's nothing a woman can do at a mine unless she's a graduated mining engineer, and nothing then that a man couldn't do better. You'll be in the way and you'll soon be bored to death yourself. If you're so crazy about Montana why don't you do some of those great things for her that your father suggested? And how do you reconcile your marriage to an Italian with your devotion to your father's memory?"

Ora turned away her head. "My father gave me too much of himself to expect me to play the rôle of ministering angel to anything. I intend to invest in Montana the greater part of all that I take out of my mine. If it gives me one of the great fortunes I shall endow my state in some way—as Mark may suggest. But I cannot live here. That is for ever settled. When I go to Europe I shall never return—not even to America. I shall forget my life here, everything connected with it—everything! One side of me is already European. I shall become wholly so."

"Somehow," said Ida slowly, and with the sensation of being so close to something that she couldn't see it, "I don't get the idea that you're so mad about Valdobia. Long since I figured that when you did love a man you'd be a sort of white pillar of flame about him. I firmly believe that Valdobia is the man for you, but, well—he fell too quickly. He didn't make you suffer, never kept you guessing for a minute. The women that turn men's heads are a good deal like men themselves; they've got to be hurt hard and kept on tenterhooks before they are in a condition to accommodate the virus. You are fond of Valdobia, and well you may be, but mad isn't the right word——"

"Oh, yes it is! It is!" Ora was walking up and down the room. "You must believe that I love him as I never dreamed I could love anybody——"

"Hi!" cried Ida. "Your letter-man! That's what! You were more nearly in love with him than you are with Valdobia, and because, for some reason or other, you couldn't get him. Where is he?"

Ora's eyes looked large and blank. "That! I had quite forgotten it. It was the last of a long line of mental love affairs. Those always evaporate even from the memory when the real man comes along." She sighed heavily and sat down once more. "I know that I shall be happy with Valdobia, only I am not happy now. That is so far off! And of course I feel badly about poor Mark. But I couldn't help it. Not to do it would have been worse. And I should go off my head meanwhile if I didn't have this mine. Do you think I could remain here in Butte and go to dinners and bridge parties? I should scream in their faces. I must have work. Be sure I can find something to do at the mine—I suppose there are a laboratory and assay office. And there will always be the excitement of hoping to find free milling gold—at present what could be more exciting than to drift for that lost vein?"

"It wouldn't keep me awake nights. But have your

own way. I don't want you down with nerves, and that will happen if you don't look out."

"If I don't get my own way."

"Exactly. But I wish your way marched with mine. I've missed you like fury—Say!—here's an idea: I'll go back to Europe with you now if you like, and stay until you marry. There are lots of places we planned to go to and didn't——"

"Ida, you are a dear! And you longed so for Butte. Why it would be like tearing an author from his unfinished magnum opus. Besides—well—you have a husband——"

"Oh, Lord! Gregory is running the Universe at present. Women don't exist for him. Shall we go?"

Ora shook her head. Her face had turned from white to pale. "No. I must spend these last months of my freedom here in my state. And that lost vein—it pulls me. I *must* have that life for a few months—for the first and last time. You—you—might spend your week-ends with me."

Ida scowled and turned away her head. She had no intention of admitting even to Ora that Gregory deliberately avoided her. "Not I. I hate the sight of the De Smet ranch. Go, if you like, but I feel sure you will come in often. And before you go I wish you would do me a favour."

"Of course I will."

"Let me give you a dinner. I want to begin that sort of thing and you'll furnish the excuse besides helping me out."

"Very well. Have it soon. I want to go to the mine as quickly as possible. I shall begin to send out the furniture for my bungalow tomorrow."

"A week's notice will be enough. I'll write the invitations today. There's another reason I want to give this dinner. Gregory hasn't been seen anywhere with me— hates going out. But I shall make him understand that he must come to my first dinner—or people will be talking—and I hate people prying into my affairs. Besides, it will be his duty to you as the wife of his best friend. (He needn't know you've left Mark yet awhile.) I'm not hankering for the rôle of the neglected wife; and I'm sick of making excuses. For all Butte knew I might not have laid eyes on my husband since my return."

And although she spoke bravely Ora knew that she had not. "We'll have the dinner," she said warmly. "And it will be great fun to get it up——"

"Now, come this minute and go to bed. You are to stay with me as long as you are in this camp, and I'm going to tone you up, and make you rest as we used to in Europe every afternoon—hard work in this altitude but it can be done. I've got to go to a bridge party now, and you are to sleep. If you feel rested when I get back, I'll call up two or three of your old friends and ask them to come informally to dinner. So long."

She closed the door of her best spare room on Ora and walked slowly back to her own, her brows drawn; once more quick with a sensation of profound uneasiness, of being close to something that she could not see. But it was not her habit to ponder for long over the elusive and obscure. "Guess I'm worried about Ora's health," she thought impatiently, and rang for her maid.

VI

TWO days later Gregory received the following note from his wife:

DEAR GREGORY:

Ora is here, and before going out to the mine has promised to help me through the ordeal of my first big dinner. Entertaining goes with this house, and although I am beginning somewhat sooner, perhaps, than is necessary, I have my reasons. I have asked twenty-four people, the most important of the older and the younger married sets. The dinner is to be at eight o'clock Tuesday. I want you to come. You have been very generous, but there is one thing more that you can do for me and I feel that I have the right to demand it. If you no longer care for me, that is something I cannot help; nor you either for that matter. But so far as the world knows, I am your wife, and if we are never seen together there is bound to be disagreeable gossip. I don't want to be gossipped about. It is vulgar and it complicates life. The Butte women I most wanted to know are all right, but the town has the usual allowance of fools and scandal-mongers. By showing yourself at my first dinner in your own house you will muzzle them. You can arrive in time for dinner and take a late train back to Pony, if there is one. But please come. I am sure if you think it over you will admit that I am merely proving my new knowledge of the world in asking for your formal protection.

IDA.

Gregory read this note hastily when he found it in his morning mail-bag in company with many business letters, to which he also gave scant attention: he was in haste to go underground. There was still no sign of the lost vein, and nineteen days of the three weeks' limit he had set himself were gone. But they broke into it that same afternoon. He barely left the mine until the following morning, but he finally sought his cabin and bed satisfied that the recovered vein of copper pyrite was, like the original, six feet thick and as rich in values. When he awoke he remembered Ida's note, and although it had provoked a frown of annoyance when he read it, his spirits were now so ebullient that he not only admitted the justice of her demand, but would have granted almost anyone a reasonable request.

Moreover, as he reread the note, its restraint and dignity struck him forcibly, as well as its remote likeness to the Ida Hook he had wooed in Nine Mile Cañon. Certainly she had made the most of her opportunities!

And apparently she had recovered from her first disappointment, or pique—if, indeed, she had felt either—and he assumed that the last year, crowded with exceptional experiences, had made her over into something like a woman of the world. No doubt among her many accomplishments she had acquired self-control. (That she might also have acquired finesse did not occur to him.) He dismissed the fear that she would make a scene—and himself thoroughly uncomfortable. On the whole it would be interesting to see Ida as a bird of paradise. He remembered her in shirtwaists and serviceable skirts, and recalled that he had sometimes thought it a pity she should not have the plumage worthy of her beauty and style.

And if the fates had willed that he must meet Ora Blake again he preferred that the first interview should be in public.

He rang up Pony and in the course of half an hour was connected with Butte.

"Hello!" he said cordially, as he heard his wife's voice. "Got your letter, but couldn't find time to answer before. I'll come to the dinner with pleasure."

"Oh, I am so glad." Ida's tones were crisp and cool. There was none of the husky warmth that Gregory suddenly remembered; nor any of the old common inflection. "Are your evening togs at Mark's?"

"Yes, will you send for them?"

"I'll have everything here in one of the spare rooms. The maid will show you up if you are late. It takes me hours to dress."

"All right. Say—Ida—I wish you'd persuade Mrs. Blake to give up that idea of coming out here. It won't work. She'll only be in the way of the men, and if there was a big row on would be one more responsibility for her manager. I suppose she knows I've opened up her mine. Besides, it's no place for a woman anyhow. There are only a few women—miners' wives—in my camp; none in the others."

"I've told her all that. But—well—you don't know Ora. Gambling—taking long chances—is in her blood, I guess. You should have seen her at Monte Carlo. You must take in Mrs. Cameron, but I am putting Ora on your left as it is time you two got acquainted. Try to dissuade her. I want her to stay here with me."

"I'll do my best. How are you getting on? Butte still panning out?"

"I adore Butte and find nothing to change. It's too wonderful—to have all your old dreams come true like this! I hope your mine is behaving. I heard a rumour the other day that you had lost your vein——"

"Just found it again!"

Ida noted the exultant ring of his voice, and was about to laugh when she changed her tactics swiftly. "Good! I know just how fine you feel—and that it wasn't the loss of money that worried you either. Well, the dinner will be a sort of celebration. Good-bye."

"Good-bye." There was a faint accent of surprise in Gregory's voice. Ida smiled and returned to her interrupted toilette.

"Just let me get a good chance at him once more," she thought. "I'll be eating copper before I get through, but I don't know him or his sex if he won't be nibbling off the same chunk."

VII

THE next week was the busiest she had ever known. All the people that had called on her called again on Ora. Her cook collapsed when told to prepare a dinner for twenty-eight people, and Ida, who would not hearken to a public caterer and his too familiar idiosyncrasies, telegraphed to St. Paul for a chef. What moments she had to spare after consultations with this autocrat, with a temperamental designer of menu cards, and with two high-handed young women whom she had been persuaded by the charitable Mrs. Cameron to engage to decorate her rooms, were spent with certain works on copper and mining that she had procured from the public library.

She looked forward to the evening of her dinner party with a secret excitement that seemed to fork its lightning into every recess of her brain, and electrify it with a sense of the fulness of life—that hinted intoxicatingly of life's perfections. Not only was she to live the wildest dream of Ida Hook, but she had made up her mind to bring the most important man in Montana to her feet on that triumphant night. That the man was her husband, won the first time without an effort, lost through her own indifference and ignorance, added tenfold to the zest of the game. She knew the impression he must retain of her: crude, obvious in her sex allurement, cheaply dressed, a sort of respectable mining camp siren; all her fascinations second-rate, and her best points in the eyes of an absent-minded husband her good-natured mothering and admirable cooking.

If she had returned to find him as she had left him, a mere brilliant hard-working student, and automatically attentive to his home partner, no doubt she would have slipped into her original rôle at once, for she was normally amiable, and she had strict ideas of wifely duties, which her insistent vanity and deliberate flirtations never for a moment endangered. They also filled the practical wants of a nature not derived from artistic ancestors. She had had her "flyer", and, allowing for social triumphs, returned to Butte to settle down; although it had been with a certain complacency that she had reflected during the homeward journey upon the altered circumstances which would enable her to live like a civilised being in her own apartments and see far less of her husband than formerly.

Her complacency had been treated to a succession of shocks since her return; it had, in fact, finally gasped out its life; although it had left self-confidence behind to sit at the feet of her shrewd clear mind. She found a zest entirely new in bringing to his knees a man who had been her husband when she was too raw and conceited to appreciate him, who had developed into a personage, and who had conquered his mere maleness and put women out of his life: she had consulted a detective agency and convinced herself that her only rival was the mine. Ida was nothing if not practical. Before preparing for her siege she chose to know exactly where she stood. A rival of her sex would have demanded one sort of tactics; a mere mine and the quickened business instinct of a dreaming but outclassing brain, although she did not underrate their peculiar dead walls and buffers, exacted a different and more impersonal assault—at first.

Much that she had failed to understand in her young husband was clear to her now. His silences, his formidable powers of concentration, his habit of thinking out his purposes unto the smallest detail before verbal expression, his tendency to dream, combined with lightning processes of thought, were the indispensable allies of his peculiar gifts: she had talked with too many brilliant and active men during the past year, to say nothing of her daily association with Ora, for whose inherited and progressive intellect she had the highest respect, and her own development had been too positive, rapid, and normal, not to be fully aware that men born with the genius to conquer life were equipped with powerful imaginations that necessarily made them silent thinkers.

She had become intensely proud of her husband since her return, and his neglect, coupled with his scrupulous generosity, had stung her pride and aroused both desire and determination to recapture what she had lost. She had no great faith in her capacity for love; but not only was she fascinated by Gregory for the first time but she found him more worthy of her accomplished coquetry than any man she had met in Europe. She was firm in her resolve to repossess her husband, but not merely to satisfy that pride which was the evolution of a more primitive vanity; she felt a certain joyousness, a lilt of the spirit, at the thought of spending her life with him, of being the complete helpmate of such a man; even a disposition to dream, which was so new in her experience that she banished it with a frown. "If I let go like other fool women, I'll make a grand mess of it," was her characteristic reflection.

She was dressing for the dinner when she heard him enter the house. The parlourmaid for once remembered her instructions, and led him up to his room, which was on the opposite side of the hall from his wife's and at the extreme end. Her door was ajar, she heard his voice —whose depth and richness were decimated by the telephone—his light foot ascending the stair. For the moment she lost her breath, then with an angry jerk of the shoulders regained her poise, and, in tones careless enough to reassure any husband suddenly overwhelmed with the awkwardness of his position, called out:

"Good evening, Gregory. Hope you'll find everything you want in your room. Ring if you don't. See you downstairs."

"Oh—thanks!" Gregory swallowed an immense sigh of relief. "I'll be on time."

Ida, assisted by the "upstairs girl"—she had not yet found a ladies' maid willing to come to Butte—continued her toilette. Her gown was as nearly Renaissance as she thought her native Northwest would stand at this stage of her social progress. It was "built"—a word more appropriate to woman's dress A.D. 1600 than today — of heavy turquoise-blue brocade, the design outlined here and there with gold thread. The long wrinkled sleeves almost covered her hands, and, like the deep square of the neck, were tipped with fur. Her mass of blue-black hair was closely twisted around her head from brow to the nape of her neck, held above the low forehead by a jewelled stiletto Ora had given her in Genoa, "to remind her of her midnight diversions in the Renaissance palace over which her dim ancestral memories brooded." This she had dismissed as damn nonsense, but she liked the stiletto with its rudely set stones, and had promised to wear it the first time she got inside one of her near-Renaissance gowns.

The pale subtle blue of the dress made her eyes look light and altogether blue, the thick black underlashes and full white underlids giving them an expression when in repose of cold voluptuousness. Her skin against the dark edge of fur was as white as warm new milk. Her costume and her regal air would have made her noticeable in the proudest assemblage. She was well aware that not only was she a very beautiful woman tonight but a dangerous one. And she might have stepped from one of the tarnished frames in the Palazzo Valdobia.

After the maid had been dismissed, she examined herself even more critically. The coral of lip and cheek, while still eloquent of youth and health, was more delicate than of old; all suggestion of buxomness had disappeared. She looked older than when she had left Butte; the casual observer would have given her thirty years; her cheeks were less full, her mouth had firmer lines; the cold grey-blue eyes more depth, justified their classic setting. Even her profile, released by the finer contour of cheek and thrown into high relief by the severe arrangement of her hair, contributed to the antique harmonies of her head and form.

"You'll do," she said to her image, and went down stairs.

Several guests arrived at once and she was standing before her antique English chimney-piece carved in California, chatting with three of them when Gregory entered the room. She nodded amiably as if they had met too recently for formalities. He took the cue and paused to exchange a few words with two men that stood near the door. But Ida had seen the startled opening of his narrow eyes which meant so much in him. She also noted that, as other guests came in, he looked at her again and again. In truth Gregory was startled almost out of his trained stolidity. He had known a certain side of Ida's cleverness, and believed when he sent her abroad that she would make much of her opportunities, the greatest of which was her constant association with Ora Blake; but that she would return in less than a year looking the great lady, and the handsomest woman he had ever seen, even his energetic imagination had failed to consider. Magnetism, as of old, surrounded her like an aura, but to this he was insensible, his own magnetism having been caught and entangled with that of another. He felt very proud of his wife, however, and, with a sudden impulse of loyalty, he crossed the room and stood at her side. He also was prompted to say in a tone pitched to reach other ears:

"By George, you are simply stunning. I haven't seen this—a—frock—dress—before."

"Gown, my dear, gown. It only arrived a few days ago. I shall take you to Europe with me next time——"

"Take him soon!" said Mrs. Cameron. "Don't give him time to wear out before he has begun to live. Our tired business men!"

"Next year!" said Ida, gayly. "He has half-promised and I'll not let him off." As she looked into his eyes with bright friendliness, his face relaxed with the smile which, she suddenly remembered, always had won her from anger or indifference. He was openly delighted with her, the more completely as he was both puzzled and relieved to see that those splendid eyes held neither cold anger nor feminine reproach. Moreover, although they softened for an instant before she was obliged to turn away, it was with an expression that made her look merely sweet and womanly, not in the least coquette or siren. Other guests claimed her attention. He heard her give a little hiss, and saw her eyes flash. Then he forgot her. Ora had entered the room.

Her gown, of some soft imponderable fabric that gave the impression of depth in colour, was the peculiar flaming blue of the night sky of Montana. Gregory was reminded instantly of the night they had sat on the steps of the School of Mines, with the pulsing sky so close above them. The upper part of the gown was cut in points that curved above her slight bust, the spaces between filled with snow-white chiffon which appeared to be folded softly about the body. She wore her pearls, but at the base of her slender throat was a closely fitting string of Montana sapphires, of the same hot almost angry blue. Her little head with its masses of soft ashen hair seemed to sway on the long stem-like neck, her stellar eyes blazed. Her costume extinguished every other blue in the room.

"Really!" said Mrs. Cameron, whose black eyes under

her coronet of iron grey hair were snapping, "these two dear friends should have had a consultation over their costumes for tonight." She had never liked Ora, and although, as the leader of Butte society, she made a point of speaking well of all whom she did not feel obliged to ignore, she had taken a deep liking to Ida; moreover, always a handsome woman herself, she felt both sympathetic and indignant. This was Ida's night, and she scented treachery.

She had addressed her remark to Gregory, but although he looked at her politely he would not have heard thunder crashing on the roof. He wondered if he were standing erect; he had a confused impression that that wonderful blue gown was burning alcohol whose fumes were in his head and whose flames swirled through all his senses. And the woman within those curling blue flames was so much more beautiful than his memory of her that he forgot not only his recent tribute to Ida, but her bare existence until she tapped him sharply on the arm.

"Dinner has been announced," she said. "You are to take in Mrs. Cameron." Ida was smiling again; she had dismissed anger and annoyance; nothing was to dim the radiance of her spirits tonight. She and Ora would be at opposite ends of the table, and she could keep the length of the drawing-room between them when they returned.

Gregory's face never betrayed him, particularly when he kept his eyelids down, and, as he shook hands with Ora in the dining-room he told her he was glad to see her again as casually as if his hand had not tingled to crush hers. He talked with Mrs. Cameron, however, as long as possible, but when her attention was claimed by the man on her right, he was obliged to turn to Ora. By this time his blood was still. Eating is commonplace work, and talking the inevitable platitudes of a dinner's earlier courses will steady the most riotous pulses.

Ora smiled impersonally; her eyes might have beheld the husband of her friend for the first time.

"I am so glad to be able to ask you something about my mine," she said. "Ida tells me that you have reopened it."

"Yes, they are already through the fault and driving for the vein. There happened to be a good man here looking for a job when I got Mark's telegram, a young engineer from the East, named Raymond. The miners are good capable men, too, and as Osborne and Douglas installed a compressor, the work should be pretty quick. I fancy you'll recover the vein in a week or two."

"I wonder if I shall? Mark thinks you infallible, but it seems too good to be true."

"The vein is there, about a hundred feet down, but how rich it is I do not venture to predict."

"Well, never mind," Ora smiled happily. "I shall have the fun of looking for it, and I want to be with the men when they find it."

"Oh—Ah—It really would be better for you to give up that idea of going out there to stay——"

"I thought I would give to you the opportunity to say that at once! Do go on and relieve your mind."

"It is neither safe nor desirable," he said sulkily. "I may have a row on my hands any minute. Your men and my men are a decent lot, but the Apex have employed a lot of scum so ignorant that there is no knowing what they may do in a crisis—in the hope of currying favour with their superiors. They would merely be made scapegoats or —canned—I beg pardon, fired—but they don't know that, and they're as hard a lot as Europe ever kicked on to our dump heap. Better stay here for the present."

"I've sent out all the furniture for the bungalow, and Custer and a Chinaman to put it in order. I suppose my engineer can camp in the other cottage until it is finished. That is quite close to mine, I understand."

"Oh, of course—but why not stay at my ranch house——"

"That is too far from the scene of operations. Please don't bother about me. I should hate to think I was on your mind—you have enough! I shall be well protected, and I've even bought an automatic. I suppose being a born Westerner I should call it a gun. But it's such a little one. I shall carry it always——"

"Yes, promise that."

"I've even had a little bag made, like those they wore years ago, to fasten to my belt, and I shall keep it in that."

"Very well." He dismissed the subject. "I—ah— there's something I heard today, but perhaps I should not speak of it. Only Mark is such an old friend of mine——"

"I suppose you saw Mr. Luning and he told you that we are to separate."

"Yes, that is it."

"I intend to live in Europe: I suppose you think that a callous reason."

"It's as good as most reasons for divorce in this country. When is Mark coming back?"

"Not for two months. Nothing will be done until then. I want to have my mining experience first and I shall leave Montana as soon as the papers are served."

"Ah!"

Her partner claimed her at the moment and, his own still being occupied, he observed her furtively. He thought that she too looked older, but not because advantages had improved her; rather—he groped for the words that would give definiteness to his impression—as if some experience had saddened her. She had a softer expression. The blood rushed to his head and he almost choked with jealousy, his intuitions carrying him straight to the truth. "By God! She has loved some man," he thought. Then he set his teeth. So much the better.

But when she turned to him again, he said impulsively, although his tones were light:

"You never did fit this Western life of ours. Of course you have found a more civilised mate in Europe?"

"You are all wrong," she said gaily. "My only love at present is my mine. My mine! You should understand if anybody can."

"Oh, yes, I understand that magnet. But I naturally thought——"

"What everybody else will think when the news is out. But I am astonished that you should jump at anything so commonplace." Her heart was hammering under the concentrated intensity of his gaze; and as if he realised suddenly that he might be betraying himself he said sarcastically:

"As there are—I was told today—no less than six divorces pending in this set which my wife has the honour to entertain tonight, and as all are to intermarry, so to speak, when liberated, my conclusion in your case was probably due to the force of suggestion."

"Well, I forgive you if you promise to believe none of the absurd stories you are sure to hear. I am in love with freedom. Now tell me what you think of Ida? Isn't she wonderful?''

Gregory looked down the table at his wife sitting between the two most important men in Butte and entertaining both with animated dignity. She met his eyes and smiled brilliantly. She knew that he was proud of her; she had accomplished the second manœuvre in her flank attack; her first had been to put him at his ease.

"Yes," he said to Ora. "She is. It is almost beyond belief. And she is your handiwork!" The two might have been life-long intimates, and Ida a mere kinswoman of both, so little did the oddity of this discussion occur to Gregory at least.

"And in a way my present to you." Ora spoke with a charming graciousness. "Mark had given me a tremendous idea of your abilities. The day I met Ida I saw her possibilities, and I made up my mind then and there that when the world claimed you your wife should be not only an inspiration but equipped to render you the practical and social help that every rising man needs. Isn't it splendid to think that she will always sit at the head of your table?"

Gregory was staring hard at her again. "You did that deliberately?" he asked.

"Yes. Deliberately. Ida is so clever that she was bound to develop with your rising fortunes, particularly if you sent her to Europe. But it would have taken longer. I couldn't wait. My father inspired me with the deepest admiration and respect for our Western men. I had made up my mind that you were born into the front rank, and I wanted, as a Western woman, and my father's daughter, to do something to help you. Tell me that you are satisfied and that you are as proud of Ida as she is of you—that—that—you simply adore her." She did not flinch, and looked him straight in the eyes, her own full of young, almost gushing, enthusiasm. Her heart had almost stopped beating.

"I certainly am proud of her, and grateful to you. No doubt she will be very helpful if I am forced into politics to conserve my interests." His tones were flat. He had come to his senses, and he was too loyal to hint that he no longer loved his wife; but Ora's face was suddenly flooded with a lovely colour, and her eyes looked like grey mist through which the sun was bursting. She asked him,

"Aren't you going to stay with us for a few days? We'd love to have you?"

"I take the 6.10 for Pony in the morning. If I disappear before the others it will be to snatch a few hours' sleep in that gorgeous four-poster in my room. After living in two rooms for so long I am oppressed with all this magnificence——"

"Two rooms!" Ora's voice rang out like an excited child's. Gregory, marvelling at the quick transitions of her sex, thought he had never seen anyone look so happy. The gentle melancholy that had roused his jealousy was obliterated. "Two rooms!"

"There is another shack just beyond where my Chinaman cooks for me, and bunks, but I have only a bedroom and office—and a bathroom of sorts. Even my secretary sleeps at the ranch house."

"You dear innocent millionaire. No doubt the proletariat, reading of your sudden wealth, and cursing you, pictures you wallowing in luxury. Well, you shall come and sit sometimes in my comfortable living-room. It is time you relearned the a, b, c, of comfort—before you relapse into the pioneer."

"Your bungalow looks as if it could be made very homelike." He spoke with unconscious wistfulness, and she raised friendly and impersonal eyes to his.

"You shall see. I have what the French call the gift of installation, and I have sent out nice things. I shall make tea for you when you come to the surface at the end of the afternoon shift, and you shall sit in the deepest of my chairs."

"It sounds like heaven," said Gregory, who despised tea.

Professor Becke, who had taken her in, and Mrs. Cameron simultaneously addressed their temporary partners, and Gregory was now to listen to an account, both spirited and kindly, of the admiration his wife had excited in her native town. Mrs. Cameron suspected the breach, in spite of the clever acting of both, and made up her mind to do what she could to bridge it. She had not an inkling of the cause, for, like Ida, she knew nothing of that fateful hour on the steps of the School of Mines; but as there was no gossip abroad about either Gregory or his wife, she inferred that it was one of those misunderstandings that so often separate young couples, always prone to take themselves too seriously. She knew that Gregory would value her praise; he not only had been fond of her as a schoolboy, when he spent an occasional Saturday with her son, but he knew that her experience of the world was very wide. She was a woman whom long years of wealth had enabled to travel extensively, she visited intimately at some of the greatest country homes in Europe, and she had her own position in New York. She subtly made Gregory feel prouder still of Ida, and then said teasingly:

"It is well that you have her devotion. I know of three men that are quite off their heads about her——"

"Ah? Who are they?" A sultan may weary of his sultana, but his sultana she is all the same.

"That I'll not tell you. Even your wife could not, I fancy. I've never seen a woman treat men with a more careless impartiality. What a relief—with all these divorces pending. Merely a shuffling of cards, too, I understand. It is disgusting. I asked your wife as a personal favour to me to invite none of them tonight. Butte either has long orgies of respectability or goes quite off her head."

"My wife is singularly indifferent to men for a beautiful woman," replied Gregory, comfortably ignorant of his beautiful wife's depredations abroad. "Nor is she likely to countenance divorce. She has a good deal of her old New England mother in her." He had a haughty contempt for explanations as a rule, but his quick instinct had caught the significance of his companion's remarks; knowing that Ida must wish to stand well with this amiable but rigid arbiter of Butte's court of last resort, he added:

"I am sorry not to be in Butte oftener, and give her what little assistance a man may, but it is all I can do to leave the mine for a few hours every week or two."

"That is the fate of too many of our American women married to our too busy American men. But—well—Gregory—I have married sons and daughters, and I am an old friend of yours. Young wives must not be neglected, and resentment eats like a cancer until women are old enough to be philosophical. Just think that over." And before he could answer Ida gave the signal and the men were left alone.

VIII

A S the women dispersed about the long drawing-room
Ora laid her arm lightly round the waist of Ida, who
was standing for the moment apart.

"Your dinner is a tremendous success, my dear," she
said, "and so are you. That gown! It makes mine look
so crude. I wish I had worn white as I intended until
the last minute. How splendidly everything went off. Not
a detail to criticise, and every woman has worn something
new from New York or Paris. But you—well, Ida, you
are always beautiful, of course, but tonight you are something more than lovely."

"Oh, am I?" Ida gave a little gasp, forgetting her passing astonishment at so much tribute from Ora at once.
"Well, I ought to be. I never felt quite like this in all my
life. Geewhil—no, I'm too happy even for slang. I wish
I could sing."

Ora sighed. "I've always known you would get everything you wanted, and I can guess just how you feel tonight. You are a complete success. How many people
ever are able to say that?"

"Yes, I feel as if I owned the earth!" But her brows
met in a puzzled frown. "I never felt, though, as if even
the conquest of Butte would all but send me off my head.
I never feel very much excited about any old thing; it's
not my make; but I've got a sort of shiver inside of me,
and a watery feeling in the heart region. If that chef had
spoilt the dinner I'd have gone out and wrung his neck."

"Well, nothing can go wrong now. The worst is over,
and no dinner was ever more delicious. Why don't you
let them dance? I know that Mrs. O'Hara plays."

"Good idea! I'll ring this minute for a few of those
extra near-waiters to take out the rugs and move the furniture."

Two of the younger women, who had returned not long
since from San Francisco, were showing their scandalised

friends the turkey-trot when the men came down the hall from the dining-room. Ida drew Gregory aside.

"Tell me," she asked, with an eager almost childish note in her voice new to him. "Did it go off well? Am I all I ought to be after all the money you have spent on me? Do I look nice in my fine clothes?"

Gregory patted her on the shoulder. "I know little about such things," he said kindly, "but it outclassed all the banquets I've been obliged to attend in the last six or eight months. I felt quite proud that it was in my own house—yours, to be literal—and Mrs. Blake assured me that she had never seen anything better done."

"Ora is an angel, and without her—but you know all that. Tell me—well, Gregory, I want a good old-fashioned compliment!"

His voice lost its bantering tone and became formal with gallantry: "You are, as ever, the handsomest woman in Montana. I shouldn't wonder a bit if those New York reporters were right and that you are the handsomest woman in America."

Ida looked for a long moment into his eyes. Again her brows met in a puzzled frown, this time because her singular lightness of spirit had fled abruptly. She was too proud, too far developed beyond the old Ida, to put forth the arts of the siren until they were alone; but she asked softly, and again with that almost childish naïveté:

"Do you really admire me?"

"You are all right," he said with a heartiness that masked a sudden misgiving. "I must come in and take you to the theatre the next time a good show comes to town. Let me know. I'll gratify my vanity by sitting beside you in a box——"

"There's a play tomorrow night. Stay over!"

"I'm sorry. I don't dare. Apex is sinking for all she's worth. We may have a set-to any minute. It was a risk even to come away for a night."

"Oh, do let me go out, and down into the mine——"

"I should think not. And do your best to keep Mrs. Blake in Butte for at least a week."

"Well, let me go out when the danger is over. I long to see chalcopyrite in the vein. I saw some beautiful specimens at the School of Mines the other day. It looks like pure gold."

He looked at her in amazement. "What on earth do you know about ores? Did you include Freiberg in your itinerary?"

"This is Butte, remember. I no sooner returned than I realised how interesting she was."

"Ah, well, when this affair is settled, come out and stay with Mrs. Blake and I'll take you down. I've no place to put you up. Even the ranch house is full. Mrs. Blake's manager and foreman are boarding there at present, and Oakley also puts up my secretary——"

"And those crops Oakley put in with such enthusiasm?" cried Ida with a sudden inspiration, and racking her memory. "Did they turn out as he expected? Was there a drought—in—in—those states?"

"What a memory you have! Yes, Oakley is doing wonders, and the drought arrived as per schedule. He would scorn to put the ranch under the ditch, although that is my long suit at present."

"I suppose Circle G Ranch looks like Holland by this time."

"Not quite yet! But the work is progressing splendidly, all except——" He paused. It had never been his habit to talk to her, and the complicated details of business he regarded as beyond the intelligent apprehension of any woman. But as Ida moved closer to him with wide-open eyes she looked intelligent enough to understand anything, and a letter received that morning had been on his mind ever since. "There is some trouble about the railroad," he said. "The Land Company was to build it, but either doesn't want the bother or really has lost a lot of money, as it claims. I placed a deed in escrow which pledges me to build it if the Land Company failed to keep its agreement; and the seed houses, which bought several large blocks of land, and a number of private settlers are demanding that the railroad be begun—it was to be finished at the end of a year——"

Ida saw her opportunity and grasped it. "We both must do our duty, and not monopolise each other," she said hurriedly. "But tell me all about it after they have gone. Now, go and dance with Kitty Collier. She's the best-looking woman in Butte. I can't dance in this harness, but I'll talk English politics with my portlier guests."

As he smiled and moved toward the music, she laid her

hand lightly on his arm. "I want to thank you for coming tonight, Gregory," she said. "It means a great deal to me socially. Besides, it is good to see you again." And this time she looked very sweet; but there was a slight aloofness in her manner, as if to admonish him that, although he was forgiven, there was still a breach which it was for him to close. Then she added lightly: "Well, we'll talk it all over later. Go, now, and dance."

Gregory stood by the front door talking to two of the men, whose wives had walked on; their homes were but a door or two away. Ida ran up the stairs to Ora's room, where they unhooked each other.

"You look tired," said Ida, sympathetically.

"Oh, I am tired," replied Ora, her arms hanging. "Tired. Tired."

"It's a long while since you danced like that. Just drop into bed. Lend me a scarf, will you?"

She covered her opened gown with the lace and walked slowly over to her room. Then she suddenly turned back to the head of the stairs. The three men were still talking below.

"Gregory," she called, and her voice was very sweet.

"Yes?"

"Lock up, will you? The servants have gone to bed."

"I will."

"Don't forget," and omitting to add a good-night, she went swiftly to her room, changed her formal evening gown for a soft combination of yellow silk and lace that made her look like a tulip in a primrose bed, let down the black masses of her hair, and threw herself into a deep chair. But there was no repose in her attitude. More than once her body stiffened and she raised her head. Pride and shrewdness forbade her to leave her door open, and it would be impossible to hear that light panther-like tread on the heavy carpet of the stair. The front door might have closed while she was changing in the dressing-room.

Suddenly she heard it slam. Nervous as she was she smiled reminiscently. Gregory might be soft of foot, but otherwise he was as noisy as most men. Then the smile froze until her lips were distended in a grin. Another door had slammed. Gregory was in his own room.

After a few moments she became aware that her body was rigid and that she was grasping the arms of her chair. She rose with an exclamation of impatience, but stood with her head bent, listening intently. Suddenly she swayed a little, once more flooded with that sense of excited gladness with which guests and chefs had had naught to do: she thought she heard a door open softly, a light footfall. But her straining ear-drums had deceived her. The house was as still as a mausoleum. She pressed her hands against her breast in the gesture the stage has borrowed from life; her heart felt as if swimming against an undertow.

Then she began pacing up and down. After her habit she tried to arrange her thoughts by putting them into words, and, as people still do off the stage, muttered them aloud.

"My God! Do I care as much as that? Do I really *care?* No! No! No! Any woman of pride, let alone vanity, would make up her mind to bring her husband back—especially if she could make him as proud of her as I made him of me tonight. And when he still thinks me beautiful. What woman wouldn't? Even if she didn't have an ounce of any kind of feeling for him? Men are only interesting when they forget about us in that purely masculine world where women are warned off the grass. To lure them back—that is the spice of life in this country. And if one doesn't succeed the first time—he may be so tired and sleepy that he's forgotten about me—or shy, afraid I'd laugh at him—the world does not come to an end tonight—What an idiot I am! I made him admire me more than ever, astonished him—why am I not satisfied for the present?—It can't be that I care—that I long for him to come—Good God! I'd rather be dead than *that!*"

But she went to the door and, laying her ear against it, listened until she became aware that her lungs were bursting with imprisoned breath. Then she sank into a chair trembling, her eyes filled with fear. A moment more and she flung her arms over the table and dropped her face upon them and broke into heavy weeping.

IX

ORA looked round the large living-room of her bungalow with a deep sense of content. The walls were covered with a material coarse in weave and of a red warm but not too bright. The colour was repeated in the divan and chairs, melting softly into browns that harmonised with the heavy beams of the ceiling. A few Navajo rugs covered the floor. Above the divan of many cushions was a bookshelf crowded with the new fiction of two continents. Several shelves, built like a bookcase, occupied a corner and were furnished more ponderously. In the middle of the room a large table was half covered with the best periodicals of the day, although there was room for a large lamp with a red shade and a vase filled with wild flowers. Down at the far end of the room, which was about thirty feet long, and opposite the kitchen, were the dining-table and a small sideboard. The main door opened upon a verandah, and one beside the fireplace into a narrow hall, giving privacy to the bedrooms. Ora had no atavistic yearnings for the life of the pioneer; she might feel as much at home in a bungalow as in a palace, but elementals, save when pictorially valuable, like overhead beams, were rigidly excluded.

Her hands clasped behind her, she drifted up and down the long room, her mode of ambulation expressing the state of her mind. Quick and final as she could be in decision, if necessity spurred, the deeper sensuousness in her nature impelled her to drift whenever circumstances would permit. For two months she intended to drift—or gamble! She had not come out here further to alienate the affections of her friend's husband, and those old tumultuous dreams were still crowded in some remote brain cell with seals on the door. She had even told herself in so many words that she had no desire for anything so terrific as their complete materialisation. She had plumbed the depth and intensity of life in her imagination. Let that suffice. And reality was not so much to be feared because of the wreck it might make of her life as because it was reasonably sure to leave a corpse in her memory, instead of that ever burning soul of past delights.

But she had come out to her mine to enjoy the constant companionship of Gregory Compton before she left her country for ever and married a European. That much she owed to the extraordinary imaginative experience in which they had been one. If she could spend long hours with him, make him as eager for her companionship as she was for his, forget his mine now and then, feel that mysterious and satisfying bond of the spirit, she would ask no more, not even an admission of love when they parted.

When a woman goes on a still hunt for a man's soul she is far more dangerous than the obvious siren, for her self-delusion is complete, her guards are down, her wiles disarming. Ora had had too little practical experience of men to be prepared to admit, in spite of her abstract knowledge of life, that there has been but one foundation of love since the world began, and never will be another till life on this planet ends, whatever may be the starry mysteries of the spheres. But while she was (spasmodically) too honest to deny even her own sex encumbrance, she believed, like many other, particularly American women of narrow experience, that it had been politely emasculated by the higher civilisation, was merely synonymous with poetry, romance, and sentiment. This convention was imported to the New World by England's middle-class and became a convenient national superstition. It is on the wane.

That Gregory, granted she were successful in capturing his soul, might desire to contribute the rest of himself to the spoils, now that she no longer was the wife of his friend, let loose those subversive passions she had divined the night of their meeting and dared to recognise in the realm of imagination, she would have refused to admit had the possibility occurred to her. She was out for the ideal, and not yet had she learned to take her imagination in hand like a refractory child. Moreover, she had an imperious will, gracefully as she concealed it. This last year of freedom and wealth and feminine triumphs had tempered that will into a pliable and dangerous weapon. What she wanted she would have. As she planned a thing so should it work out. But the details—ah, they were veiled in the future, and from their mysteries came this reflex vibration, this pleasant sense of drifting, of wondering how it would all begin and what would happen next.

In a sense it had begun. Gregory had called two days before to ask if she were comfortable. He was in his overalls (purposely), and had refused at first to sit down, but finally had succumbed to the deepest of the chairs before the log fire. He had finished by remaining for supper, and again had occupied the chair until eleven o'clock. Neither had suspected the other's secret passion, for love before union, being nine parts imagination, needs solitude for indulgence, and is capable, moreover, of long and satisfying quietudes if fed with externals. There was sheer delight in sitting together by that warm intimate fire, at the dining-table at the end of the long shadowy room, in feeling cut off from the world on the edge of that rough mountain camp, in listening to the soughing of the pines during the silences. That both were on their guard lest the other take fright and the experience be impossible of repetition but exaggerated the atmosphere of friendliness, of almost sexless comradeship. Gregory betrayed one only of his reflections: he admitted to himself what Ora subtly compelled him to admit, and had no difficulty in divining, that the companionship of woman was a blessed thing, and that he had been the loneliest of men.

Their talk was mainly of ores! She was permitted to learn how little else interested him in comparison with the enthralling inside of Montana. But he told her also the legends of the great copper mines on Lake Superior, so old that copper was found pure, looking much like the smelted product from the copper ores of the later geological formations of the Rocky Mountains. These vast mines, particularly that on Isle Royal, bore unmistakable signs of having been worked systematically by a prehistoric people experienced in mining; presumably by the Atlantans, who, after their own mines were worked out and they still demanded "orichalcum" for their monuments and bronze for their implements, went annually in ships for the metal. That there had been a self-supporting mining colony on Isle Royal was indicated by certain agricultural remains.

Gregory and Ora had amused themselves reconstructing that old time when the metal island was as lively as today, and considerably more picturesque—owing to the alternative of skins for muck-spattered overalls; an underground chapter of the Niebelungenlied, its gnomes toiling down in those two miles of workings, stoping out less in a hundred years than the methods of today force a mine to yield in one. How they must have swarmed to the surface, regardless of discipline, at the first signal of the approaching ships, their one link with a world that was not all water and forest and underground cavern. By what tortuous way did those archaic ships travel from the Atlantic to the northwest corner of that vast inland sheet; unless, indeed, which is likely, subsequent upheavals have destroyed a waterway which may have connected sea and lake prior to 10000 B. C.* How many of those old ships lie in the bed of Lake Superior, laden with rude nuggets of copper, pounded from the gangue, or, who knows? smelted by a lost art into sheets and blocks? Archaic ships rode high, and no doubt those from Atlantis were overladen; for what has kept Atlantis in the realm of myth so long save the unscientific legend that she perished of greed and its vicious offspring? What archaic mysteries may not the terrible storms of that great north lake yet uncover? What strange variety of copper, washed and bitten by the waters of twelve thousand years, for which the enraptured geologist must find a new name? Who knows?—the bed of Lake Superior may be one unbroken floor of malachite; and the North American Indian of that region the descendant of those ancient miners, abandoned and forgotten when Atlantis plunged to the bottom of the sea.

It was Ora who advanced these last frivolous theories, and—the clock striking eleven—Gregory sprang to his feet.

"Likely as any," he said. "All theories change about as often as it is time to get out a new edition of an encyclo-

* Plato dates the submergence of the last of Atlantis (the island of Poseidonis) about 9,000 years before the priests of Sais told its story to Solon, who lived 600 B.C. The Troano MSS. in the British Museum, written by the Mayas of Yucatan about 3500 B.C., assert that it took place 11560 B.C. The archaic records of India give the date of the fourth and final catastrophe that overwhelmed the remnant of the once vast continent (which Darwin and other naturalists claim must have extended from the American to the European continent to account for the migration of plants found in Miocene strata) as 9564 B.C.

pædia, or develop a 'new school' which makes its reputation by the short cut of upsetting the solemn conclusions of its predecessors. I'm going down into the mine." He bolted out with no further ceremony, but Ora was long since accustomed to the manners of Western men. She went to bed feeling that sadness had gone out of the world.

She had not seen him since. Nor had anything new and interesting happened. Her manager, Raymond, refused to take her down in the mine, alleging that when Apex broke into the workings of Perch of the Devil, there was sure to be a fight, and the bohunks would retreat, not up their own shaft but through the tunnels of the Primo mine. The young man was manifestly distressed to refuse any boon to so charming a woman, and he and his foreman had moved at once into the half-finished cottage, but he heartily wished her back in Butte, nevertheless. The best of miners love a fight, and it would be impossible to protect her from flying bullets if the row was continued above ground. Ora merely had laughed when he begged her to return or to remain within doors, but had promised to be prudent and flourished her automatic .25.

X

SHE glanced at the clock. It was half past three. She knew that Gregory frequently went below in the morning, and had half expected that he would cross over to her hill for a moment when he came up at three o'clock. The drifting mood vanished. She decided that two days were enough for feminine passivity and went to her bedroom and changed her pretty house frock for a stout out-of-doors' costume of forest green tweed: as she had no mind to look either the outworn Western heroine of romance, or a fright, she had omitted khaki from her mountain wardrobe. She tied a light green veil round her head, put on a pair of loose chamois gloves, selected a green parasol lined with pink, and went out to give the fates a gentle shove.

Hitherto she had so far yielded to the solicitude of her manager as to take her walks through the pine woods above her bungalow, but today she marched deliberately through her grove and stood for several moments on the edge of the little bluff above the tableland on which her claim was located. It was her first prolonged look at the three mining camps, for she had arrived at night. She had driven out occasionally to mining camps with her father, once or twice with Mark; the scene was both typical and picturesquely ugly. In or near the centre of each claim was the shaft house; fifty feet beyond—the distance prescribed by law to prevent overhead fires from communicating with underground timbers—were the buildings containing the hoisting machinery and the compressed air plant. Scattered about were the shacks of the miners, the long bunk- and mess-houses, blacksmith and carpenter shops. Just below the Apex claim, and on Government land, an enterprising publican had established himself. On all sides were other claims of recent location, for there had been the inevitable rush.

The rude buildings were grey and weather beaten, and all traces of the gentle spring verdure had disappeared.

About the collar of each shaft was an immense dump heap, waste rock brought up from the depths, and the highest of these was on Perch of the Devil. Near each were the ore bins, but these for the most part were empty, and, save on the De Smet hill, there was a notable absence of "double-sixes." The Primo vein had not been recovered, Apex had not yet touched bottom; Gregory Compton, for reasons best known to himself, had changed his original plan and was merely uncovering his new vein, taking out as little of its ore as possible. His bins were furnished with ore from the second level of his mine, where work had proceeded steadily on the original vein.

The men off shift were standing about in groups as they did in Butte, or passing in and out of the saloon. And the racket was deafening: the roar of the machinery in the hoisting and compressor houses, the crash of rock dumped from the buckets or skips, the ringing of hammer on anvil. The scene was not beautiful but it was alive! One could fancy the thrill of the hidden metals, knowing that their hour, after vast geological ages of waiting, was come; that, like mortals, they were to agonise in the crucible of life and achieve their ultimate destiny.

Ora walked through the grove until she was beyond the long mess-house at the back of her claim, climbed over the abrupt rise of Apex—which, combined with the hardness of the rock, had made its task so long—and, ascertaining that the larger buildings hid her, crawled under the De Smet fence, and drew a long breath as she set her feet squarely on the famous Perch of the Devil. Here the buildings, large and small, were scattered up to the brow of the hill and over on the other side. It had, in fact, something of the appearance of a growing village with irregular streets; and before several of the cabins children were playing, or women took their Monday washing from the line. The fronts of some of these cottages were painted white, and here and there flowers grew in boxes. There were even a reading-room and a large "general store." Altogether Perch of the Devil looked as if it might grow larger, and more solid and permanent of aspect, with the years.

Ora walked through the crooked streets on the steep hillside until she reached the deep chamber into which had leached the acids of the centuries to enrich the ores, and incidentally Gregory Compton. Thousands of tons of dump made a hill in itself and shut off the view to the south, but below were the acres of waving wheat, the alfalfa with its purple flower, the sprouting flax, the winding creek that was often dry but sometimes wet, the brush sheds for the cattle, the substantial farm buildings. The broad peaceful expanse looked as if even a winter wind had never shaken it, so entirely did it seem dissociated from the frantic energies of its northeast corner. And still beyond was perfect beauty: the massive pine-covered mountains, rising tier above tier, ridges of the great Rockies, far away and up to the sky-cutting line, glittering with eternal snows. For a few moments Ora forgot the raucous noises about her, Nature delivering herself of her precious children with loud protesting pains. Then she turned suddenly and looked upward.

Gregory had just stepped from his cabin. For a moment he did not see her, but stood staring, his hands in his pockets, at the distant mountains. He wore his favourite overalls and a battered cap on the back of his head; but he looked so remote in spirit from that materialising costume that Ora watched him with a sensation of helpless jealousy. Not for a moment could she delude herself that he was thinking of her. He looked like a seer.

"Can you see right into the heart of those mountains?" she asked lightly, as she walked up the hill toward him. "You looked as if your imágination were 'blocking out' thousands of tons of gold quartz."

He started and coloured, but smiled with a sudden pleasure at the charming picture in the foreground. "Something like that. This mine is all right, and now that I've got over my disappointment, I have a feeling for it that I guess I'll never have for another mine— something like the affection for one's first born! But all the same I intend to have a gold mine one of these days. Have you been admiring my view?"

He had walked down and joined her.

"Yes, but that is not what I came over here for. Nor is it what I came out to the mines for. I brought a small library, but I find I am not in the humour for books. I want to be doing something myself. Mr. Raymond won't take me down into my mine. I want to go down into yours—now."

He hesitated a moment. "Well—why not? Apex is not working this afternoon—something the matter with their compressor. They sounded pretty close to our workings this morning, but the men quit about one o'clock, and as they didn't blast it was probably because the holes weren't deep enough. I've just been told that they can't get to work again before tomorrow. But you look much too fine!"

"Everything cleans; and I'll leave my veil and parasol in the shaft house."

"All right," he said abruptly. "Come along."

When they were in the shaft house he asked, "Will you go down in the skip or by the ladder?"

"Oh, I couldn't possibly do anything so ignominious as to go down in a bucket, and I'm very agile. How far is it?"

"A hundred feet. I shall only take you to the first level."

Ora peered down into the black and slanting and apparently bottomless well. A ladder was built flat against one side. A skip full of ore was banging against the sides of the other compartment on its way up. She looked again at the ladder, shuddered, and set her teeth.

Gregory put two candles in his pocket, inserted his long limber body into the narrow aperture and ran down sideways.

"Oh!" gasped Ora. "I can't do that. Please wait. I—I think I'd better go down backward."

"By all means. Sit down and turn round. I'll catch hold of one of your feet and put it on a rung. The rest will be easy."

Ora followed these instructions gingerly, concluding that the skip would have been more dignified. Then she forgot dignity and only wondered if her bones had gone out of her: she had rolled over on her equatorial zone and was kicking helplessly in the void. But as Gregory caught her feet and planted them safely she set her teeth once more and summoned her pride.

"Glad you have on stout boots," he said, practically. "We've not enough water in the mine for pumps, but it's a little damp underfoot. Wait a minute while I light a candle." He struck a match and performed this feat; how, Ora could not even guess; but she glanced down sideways and saw that he was holding the lighted candle up at arm's length.

"Come on," he said. "You mustn't be frightened."

"I'm not a bit frightened, but don't go too fast."

Gregory, who was running down the ladder, moderated his pace, and sent up an occasional word of cheer. Suddenly Ora heard a horrid noise below like the crash and roar of an express train. "Has the mine fallen in?" she gasped.

"Hope not. That's the tram with ore and rock for the skip. By and by we'll use the waste rock to fill up the stopes with, but we're only blocking out at present."

"How frightfully interesting mining is—in all its details!" Ora's hands were smarting, and every part of her, not excluding her imagination, felt as if on the rack. "That noise is over!"

"Did I hear you say 'Thank heaven'?"

"Of course not. How much farther is it? Haven't we passed the first level?"

"If we had I should be carrying you. Only about twenty feet more."

And a few moments later, with the deepest sigh of relief she had ever drawn, she was standing in the small station beside the shaft.

"It's hard work the first time," he said sympathetically. "But you'll soon get used to it."

"How dark it is!"

"I'll put in electricity when my troubles with Amalgamated are over." He lit another candle and handed it to her. "Be careful of your frock."

The ore car was rumbling away in the distance. Gregory followed the sound down the tunnel and Ora kept close at his heels. "I suppose we'll see something after a while?" she ventured. "I can't see even you now, only your candle."

"We'll soon be out of this," he said cheerfully. "You see, we've had to walk under the chamber from which I took that great deposit of carbonates, and then some——" He paused a moment, but not before he had turned acutely to the left. "This is where I lost the vein. We are in the fault now. How would you like to be in an earthquake that broke a vein in two and hurled one end——" His voice was lost in the rattling roar of the compressed air drills, although there was nothing to be seen until they reached another little station and faced a wider drift on the right, some twelve feet long. Candles were flaring from the miners' candlesticks, whose long points were thrust into stulls or the softer part of the rock, and four men were manipulating two of the cumbersome air drills which stood on tripods. Gregory made a sign to the shift boss, who shut off a valve, and the din stopped abruptly.

"Now," said Gregory. "This is what you have come for." He moved his candle along the brassy glitter of chalcopyrite in the vein, steadying her with his arm, for the floor was uneven and littered.

Ora trembled. She forgot the arm about her; it felt like mere steel for that matter; she was in one of the magic caverns of her dreams and she thrilled to the magnet of the ores. "It looks like pure gold," she whispered.

"So it is in a sense, and far more beautiful to look at in the vein." They had been standing near the opening of the drift. He guided her down toward the farther end; the miners made way for them and went out to the station nothing loath; owing their lives to what has cost many a man his life and more, the caprice of a woman.

"I want to show you how the holes look before we put the sticks of powder in," Gregory began, as he waved his candle once more aloft, this time over a less dazzling surface. He stopped abruptly. She felt his body stiffen. Then, as he whirled her about, he screamed to the men: "Get out! Run!"

Ora had the sensation of being swept along by a bar of steel burrowing into the flesh of her waist. But in another instant she had lost all sense of her body. There was a shock as if something had hit the hill at its foundations, a dull roar, and then the crash of falling rock behind them.

The men were all ahead. Ora dimly could see them running like rabbits up the fault drift. Then she became conscious of the stifling sickening smell of powder and a bursting sensation in her head. No one paused for a second, nor drew breath until all had turned the corner and were in the main level. For a space nothing was heard but the hoarse effort to refill tormented lungs. The men leaned against the walls of the tunnel. Ora leaned against Gregory. All sense of fear had departed out of her. She had had her baptism of fire and doubted if she ever should be capable of the sensation of fear again.

The silence lasted but a moment. Out of the intense darkness flew oaths like red-hot rocks from boiling craters.

"Shut up!" said Gregory sharply. "There's a lady here. And light up if you have any extra candles. I've dropped mine. We must find out if anybody is missing."

"I held on to mine," said Ora proudly. Gregory lit it, and the shift boss counted his men. "All here, sir; but by jink, it was a narrow squeak. The—the—the——"

"Never mind—who's this?" A man was running toward them from the direction of the shaft.

"It's me, sir." Gregory recognised Mann's voice. "I've just got on to what they were up to. There wasn't a blamed thing the matter with the compressor. They just meant to catch us off guard—anybody hurt?"

"All right. How did you find out?"

"I suspicioned something crooked, so I got one of those damned bohunks drunk and bribed him. They'd put in the sticks before they quit, pretending the compressor had gone wrong and they couldn't finish drilling. I suppose they sneaked back while I was getting the story, and lit the fuses."

"You'll let us get back at 'em, boss?" demanded the men.

"Oh, yes," said Gregory, in a voice of deadly irony. "We'll get back at them."

He was holding the candle. Ora saw him bend his head forward in the attitude so characteristic of him. But he raised it in a moment.

"Go up, every one of you," he said, "and down to the saloon. Talk about what happened, but assume that it was an accident. Any fighting above ground and you'll be canned. Say that there's a big cave-in and we're obliged to quit work on this level for the present. See that that spreads all over Apex camp. Say that I've given you the rest of the shift off. Come down as soon as you've had your drink and said your say. Jerry"—to the shift boss—"you watch the Apex shaft house. I don't figure that they'll go down under an hour, on account of the smoke, but if they do just drop below. I'll wait for you here. And before you come," he added grimly, "go over to the compressor house and tell them to turn the steam on the air line.''

"Hooray!" The shouting of the men made almost as much noise in the tunnel as the recent explosion. "That's the ticket, boss. Oh, we won't do a thing to them!"

"Get out of this," said the shift boss. "Don't take more than one drink; and hold on to your tempers, or there'll be no fun below.''

A moment later Gregory and Ora were alone in the tunnel.

XI

"**H**OW did you guess?" asked Ora.

"I didn't guess. I saw a drill hole just beyond where my men were working. I also did a little quick deduction. Miners blast just before they go off shift. The afternoon change of shift is at three o'clock. As I told you I had seen the Apex men come up about one o'clock when their compressor stopped. That hole not only told me that they were closer than we had thought, but that they were up to devilment. I guessed that they had timed to blast just before we were ready to drill at that point. Were you very much frightened?"

"I didn't like it." Ora knew that bravery in woman makes no appeal to the lordly male. "But I hardly had time to think; and after all you left me nothing to do."

"Well, you were game and didn't scream or cry," he conceded handsomely. "Let's light up."

They had walked as far as the station at the foot of the shaft. Gregory unlocked the door of a small cupboard, found two candles and inserted them in miners' candlesticks that were stabbed into the walls. They flickered in the draft as a skip rattled up from the second level, but relieved the oppressive darkness.

"Why, your hair is down!" exclaimed Gregory.

Ora put up a hand. "So it is! Well—I am sure I never should know if my hair fell down at a good play, and ours was live drama. I'll braid it and put on my veil up above."

He watched her for a moment as she sat on a box braiding her long fair hair, vaguely recalling the legend of the Lorelei. He noticed that her eyes as she peered up at him looked green in that uncertain light. But in a moment his thoughts wandered from her. He folded his arms and stared downward.

Ora leaned back against the wall. She saw that he had forgotten her, but had made up her mind to accept him as he was; she had no more desire to dictate his moods than to read in advance the book of the next two months. There was the same pleasurably painful vibration in her nerves as on the night when she had piled stake upon stake at Monte Carlo. From that scene her thoughts travelled naturally to Valdobia and she suddenly laughed aloud.

"What are you laughing at?" demanded Gregory suspiciously.

"I was trying to imagine that we were imprisoned in the underground dungeon of an Italian palace in the middle ages."

"Hard work, I should think. Although if we had a cave-in I guess the results would be about the same."

"And you? Were you seeing your minerals winking three thousand feet below?"

He laughed then, and sat beside her. "At all events the mystery down there is more romantic than your mediæval dungeons—and so will the great underground caverns be when the ores have been taken out."

"Pity the caverns—stopes!—have to be filled up with débris to prevent the mine caving in," said Ora flippantly. "I went underground in Butte last week—to the eighteenth level of the Leonard. Nothing but endless streets and cross-alleys, all numbered——"

"And you didn't find that interesting?" he asked indignantly. "To be a third of a mile below the surface of the earth and find it laid out like a city, with streets and rooms, and stations ten times as large as this, and lighted with electricity?"

"Yes, but the knowledge that you have a third of a mile of those streets and rooms—seventeen levels of them—on top of you, supported only by waste rock in the stopes, and timbers that are always snapping in two from the terrific pressure—timbermen working at every turn—'Save YOURSELF' the first thing you see when you leave that cage—Oh, well, I felt there was quite enough romance on top of the earth."

"I am deeply disappointed in you. You told me once—why, even lately——"

"Oh, I haven't changed the least little bit. Nothing in life," and she looked at him with laughing eyes, "interests me as much at present as these two mines. But I am thankful that we are still within a reasonable distance of the surface. I am quite content to screw up my eyes and wander in fancy among the primary deposits close to the central fires. If I had a mine like yours, full of the beautiful copper ores instead of that hideous pyroxenite of mine, I should leave a glittering layer in every stope, support the roof with polished stone columns, light with hidden electric bulbs, and wander from one to the other imagining myself in Aladdin's palace.''

''A fine practical miner you would make. It's lucky that your mine is pyroxenite, not quartz. That is if you want to live in Europe.—Do you?''

''Of course. What have I in this part of the world? A mine cannot satisfy a woman for ever. I suppose you wouldn't care if you never saw a woman again!''

''Oh!'' He was looking hard at her.

''What else were you thinking of just now?'' asked Ora, with that perverse desire to be superficial which so often possesses American women in decisive moments.

He sighed impatiently. ''I've got a big job on my hands, one that will take me away from here more or less. Did Mark tell you of a land deal I put through?''

''I should think so!''

''Well, I've got to build that railroad. Apex will close down when it finds I won't let its men work underground. Amalgamated's next move will be to bring suit for apex rights, and get out an injunction to enjoin me from working on that vein until the case is decided. As soon as I have driven them out now, however, I must get to work on the railroad—find my engineers—Oh, there are too many details to bother you with. But it means that I must spend a good deal of time in Butte until the thing is started——''

''How delighted Ida will be!'' interrupted Ora softly. ''And that house will be so comfortable after your cabin.''

For a moment he did not speak. Nor did his face betray him; but she fancied that his muscles stiffened. He replied suavely: ''I should have gone on to say that it is more likely I shall have to attend to the matter in Helena. That is the centre of the land interest. It is doubtful if I could find the sort of men I want in Butte.''

''Have you any other land schemes on hand?''

''Not at present.''

''What does that mean?''

''Well—when I have taken a couple more millions out

of this hill I shall begin to buy land, put it under the ditch, build the short railroads that may be necessary, and sell to small farmers—in other words push along the colonisation of this state. I believe you gave me that idea —the night we talked Butte—the first time, I mean.''

''I thought you had forgotten that night altogether.''

''Forgotten it!'' Ora's heart stood still at the explicit vibration in his well-ordered voice. She leaned back and closed her eyes. He had loved her all these months, dreamed of her as she had dreamed of him. Her first sensation of wonder and delight was succeeded by a faint disappointment.

She had the instinct of the born huntress, although she was far too highly civilised to have recognised it before. She wondered if his capitulation meant her own deliverance, too ignorant in the ways of love to guess that whether this were a passing or a permanent phase depended on the man.

While Gregory hurried on to tell her of all he should be able to do for Montana with the millions at present locked in the vaults of his hill, she had a full moment of honesty, and confessed that she had come out here to make Gregory Compton love her. And he did! It was a mighty personality to conquer; and the victory had been won long since! But the disappointment passed in a cynical smile. That he had no intention of declaring himself her lover was as patent as his inhuman power of self-control. Here were barricades to storm if barricades she wanted? What difference? And did she?

He sprang to his feet and stood at the foot of the shaft, looking up.

''They're coming down,'' he said.

Joshua Mann emerged a moment later.

''Apex bunch being rounded up to go below,'' he said. ''Our men are on the way.''

''Steam on the air line?''

''You bet!''

''Let's get to work.'' He turned to Ora. ''Stay here till I come back,'' he said peremptorily. ''I can't take you up in the skip now.''

''I am quite comfortable,'' said Ora, coolly. ''How many men will come down?''

''Five.'' And he and Mann disappeared into the tunnel.

Ora waited until the other men had descended one by one and run into the blackness. Then she dislodged one of the candlesticks from the wall and ran after them. When she reached the fault drift she thrust the long point of the candlestick into a stull before turning the corner. Then she crept toward the station, from which she could witness the punishment about to be inflicted upon the Apex men, whatever it might be.

There was a glimmer of light in the new drift. Ora saw the men binding a piece of hose to the same length of pipe. They attached the hose to the air line and held it just inside the ragged hole some twelve feet above.

There was a distant murmur of voices overhead and to the right. The solitary candle was extinguished. The murmur of voices in the drift which led from Apex shaft along the continuation of the Primo vein grew louder. Men were laughing. One man was giving orders. It appeared that they were to let themselves down and go systematically to work on the Perch vein, which was now driving under the Apex claim.

Ora heard a sharp whispered word: "Now!" and barely recognised Gregory's voice. A second later and she was deafened by the roar and hiss of escaping steam, mingled with shrieks of agony above, and fiendish cat-calls and jeers below, all expressed in the spectacular profanity of the mining camp. The episode was over in a moment. The Apex men tumbled over one another in their anxiety to leave the scene, and those manifestly disabled—Ora could hear them gasping horribly as the steam was turned off abruptly—were dragged away. She felt her own way rapidly along the fault drift, snatched her candlestick from the wall as she turned the corner, and scampered back to the shaft station. When the men arrived she was sitting demurely on the box. Gregory evidently had telephoned from the other station, for the skip came rattling down just before his appearance at the head of his laughing, cursing column.

"Did it go off well?" asked Ora.

"Did it?" cried Mann, tossing his cap in the air.

"They're settled for the moment," said Gregory. "They'll come back at us later with steam on their own air line, and slacked lime; but we'll be ready for them. They stand no show."

Two of the men had been left on watch. Gregory lifted Ora into the skip. He and Mann stood on the edge. A second more and Ora was holding her breath as they were hurtled upward at express speed, the metal car banging from side to side of the shaft. In something under three-quarters of a minute Gregory helped her to alight in the shaft house, while the skip descended for the miners.

"Well," he said, smiling, as she lifted her braid to the top of her head and wound the veil about it, "have you supped full of sensations for one day?"

"The last was the worst! And I do mean the skip. Now that we are where you cannot beat me I will confess that I followed you and saw your neat little mediæval revenge from the station——"

"Hush!" Gregory glanced about apprehensively, and drew her outside. "You mustn't tell anyone else that. You don't want to be summoned to the witness stand, I suppose?"

Ora gasped. "I never thought of that."

"When will women let men do their thinking?" Gregory looked the primeval male as he scowled down at her. Nor did he mitigate her alarms with the information that underground battles seldom were continued in the courts. "Now, I am going to take you to your cottage, and I want you to stay there until the trouble is over. The men are bound to get drunk and fight. Better go to Butte——"

"I won't."

"Very well, then, stay in your house."

"And be bored to death? Besides, I need exercise. I'll roam all over the place unless you promise to come to supper every night and then take me for a walk in the woods."

His eyes flickered. "Perhaps your engineer——"

"He's a mere child. I hate boys. And I must have exercise."

He looked at her with apparent stolidity for another moment, but she knew that he was investigating her expressive orbs. They expressed nothing that could be construed as flirtation, coquetry, or personal interest in himself. He saw himself mirrored there merely as the friend of her husband and the husband of her friend. "Very well," he said curtly and swung on his heel. "I suppose I must look out for you. Come along."

XII

GREGORY had worn a clean suit of overalls into the mine. He was now spattered from head to foot, including his face and hands, but he swung along beside Ora with an unconsciousness of his disreputable appearance that was quite superb. All the miners of the three camps off shift were gathered about the saloon. As Gregory appeared the greater number of these men cheered wildly, but the "dark men," who stood apart, maintained an ominous silence.

"Aren't you afraid they'll take a shot at you some night?" asked Ora. "How they must hate you!"

"You don't go into any business nowadays and put it over without running the risk of being shot by some sort of down-and-outer. What's the sense in worrying? Unless I'm much mistaken we'll be rid of that scum inside of twenty-four hours."

And he was right. There was another battle underground, in which more of the Apex men were scalded, and the Perch men unhurt. Then the Apex men refused to work, and the mine closed. Gregory was shot at on the following night, and Joshua Mann was slightly wounded. Both the Perch and Primo men tumbled out of bed, hunted down the offenders, and chased them into Pony, riddling the air with shot and rending it with bloodthirsty yells. It would be some time before Apex would be able to hire miners of any nationality willing to trust themselves between the two belligerent camps. But bohunks—more recent importations—would return in the future, if any. These ignorant and friendless South Europeans can be killed for about two hundred dollars apiece, whereas it costs several thousands to kill an American, Cornishman, or Irishman, as he leaves behind him an equally intelligent family or friends. It was unlikely, in any case, that high class miners would "take a job" in the predatory Apex. They not only liked Gregory Compton because he was his own manager and worshipped by his miners, but because he possessed in overflowing measure the two qualities that the American in his heart of hearts respects most, luck and bluff.

Amalgamated immediately brought suit against Gregory Compton, charging not only that the faulted vein apexed in their claim, but that his original patent was agricultural and gave him no lateral rights in mining; furthermore, that a patented claim could not be repatented. This was a fine legal point and could impoverish several generations before it was decided.

Gregory paid no attention to this suit beyond issuing an invitation through the press to eight of the leading geologists of the United States and Canada to come to Montana at his expense and make a personal inspection of the two veins. If they did not agree that the vein on which he had been working, containing a shoot of chalcopyrite six feet wide, and of the highest grade, was the original vein, and the Primo-Apex a mere stringer, or at most a fork from his, he would let the suit go by default. The geologists promptly accepted, and it was agreed that they should all arrive in Butte on the second of June.

Once more Gregory Compton had scored. Scientific men are normally honest, although the great fees offered to geologists frequently infuse their judgment with that malleable quality peculiar to the lawyer under the subtle influence of his brief. But these men, all of high repute, would be too afraid of one another, and of the merciless newspaper men that would accompany them, to deliver aught but a just verdict. Gregory knew that Amalgamated was profoundly disconcerted, and that in the face of public opinion it was improbable that the suit ever would be brought into court. But they could devil him meanwhile, and he was enjoined from working on the recovered vein until the case should be decided. He accepted the injunction without protest and transferred the miners, whom he had kept hard at work blocking out until the last minute, down to the second level of the mine.

"They'll get a jolt from that quarter, too," said Gregory to Ora, and he was not referring to the miners. "They'll go on fighting me for years, no doubt, but I'll spring some sort of a facer on them every time. They may have more money, but I have enough."

"You never feel afraid they may beat you in the end?"

"Beat me?" Gregory's eyes glittered. "Not unless they bore a hole in my skull and introduce a microbe that will devour my brains. I can get ahead of them in more ways than one. Long before all the ore on the second level is stoped out I shall be in a position to put up my own reduction works if they freeze me out of Anaconda or Great Falls. If I ever go into politics it will be to fight for a state smelter."

Ora looked at him speculatively. He was walking up and down her living-room with a swift gliding motion peculiar to him in certain moods; his head was a little bent as if his narrow concentrated gaze were following a trail.

"I believe you love the fight as much as any part of it," she said.

"I do. And as soon as I've taken out money enough I'm going to buy a big tract of land, irrigate it, plant it in beets, put up a sugar refinery and fight the Havemeyer trust."

"Why don't you form a company, buy your beet land, and put up the factory now? You could raise all the money you wanted."

"No companies or partners for me," he said curtly. "What I'll do I'll do alone. I want no man's help and no man's money. And I certainly want no other man's ideas interfering with mine."

Ora sighed. He had been away for a week on his railroad and land business, and during this, their first meeting since his return, he had talked of nothing save his mine and the new possibilities of Circle G Ranch. Investigation of the soil and timber values of the 35,000 acres which he had originally hypothecated as a guarantee that the railroad should be built, but which perforce had reverted to him when the Land Selling Company had failed to keep this part of their contract, would be worth, after proper transportation facilities were insured, not less than twenty-five dollars an acre. A member of the Land Selling Company whom he had taken with him had been convinced of this, and that the soil was peculiarly adapted to the raising of apples by intensive culture. As soon as the railroad was built there would be no difficulty in selling the timber and the rest of the land, and the Company had agreed to buy it. His profits would be $875,000, and the railroad would cost but $300,000.

No wonder, thought Ora, that a man with a business brain of that calibre had little place in it for woman. True, he had called her up once from Helena, evidently seized with a sudden desire to hear her voice, but he had been interrupted; and the only tangible result had been to keep her in such a fever of expectancy that she barely had left the house lest he call her up again and she miss him. He did not, and her nerves had become so ragged that she almost had hated him and obeyed the impulse to pack her trunks and flee to Europe. He had come to see her within an hour of his return, but, beyond his rare delightful smile and a hard pressure of the hand, he had manifestly been too absorbed to feel any personal appeal beyond her always welcome companionship.

And the next morning he telephoned that he was leaving for Butte. Ida had reminded him of his promise to appear in public with her. Mary Garden was to sing that night and she had taken a box. He had grumbled but finally agreed to go, as he had business in Butte which might as well be transacted that afternoon. Ida thanked him politely and promised him an interesting party at dinner. Then she called up Ora and invited her, but Ora declined on the plea of good taste; the story of her impending divorce was common property, and it was hardly decent for her to appear in public.

XIII

REACTION, after the emotional recognition of the subtle but certain change that had been wrought in her unsuspected depths, had filled Ida for many hours with a sullen rage against Gregory Compton and herself. But in a day or two the buoyancy of youth and the common sense, of which she possessed an uncommon store, asserted themselves, and, while devoting her time to the small daily distractions of society, her determination to win back her husband never waned for a moment. She knew that she must play the waiting game, keep a sharp eye out for the blessed opportunity and pounce upon it, but make no attempt to "rush things."

The day after the Apex mine closed down, she rang him up and offered her congratulations, told him something of the excitement in Butte, then rang off before he began to feel detained. As he passed through Butte later, on his way to Helena, he could do no less than call on her, and, to his relief and her secret rage, he found several pleasant people taking tea in the library. But she showed her pride in him so frankly that he could not but be flattered, and talked so intelligently of the undoubted sequel of the battle underground that he forgot her guests and addressed his conversation to her. She drew him on to describe that grim but picturesque episode underground, and he would have been less than man had he failed to be sensible of the rise of his chest while surrounded by a breathless circle of charming women. When they were about to withdraw tactfully and leave him alone with his wife, he glanced at his watch, bade them all a hasty goodbye and bolted out to catch his train. Ida once more had been able to exhibit to her little world an evidence of the pleasant understanding between herself and her busy husband, and got what consolation out of this fact that she could.

"I can wait," she thought grimly. "I can wait! I

guess patience is my one all-wool-and-a-yard-wide virtue. I'll wait!''

She gave several small dinners and a dancing party, devoted to the new excitement of ''ragging,'' in which no one became more proficient than herself. She ''went'' harder than ever, and even joined the more extreme younger set (elegantly known as ''The Bunch'') one night in a progress among the road houses of The Flat, and danced in the ballroom of the Five Mile House until dawn. But she had no real taste for this side of life; and did penance by visiting the Poor Farm and several other charities under the wing of Mrs. Cameron. Her popularity on all sides was unchallenged, and not only was she firmly established in the city of her heart, but Mrs. Cameron had offered to take a house with her in New York for the following winter if she cared to mount still higher. She was gratified and grateful, but she was filled with that desperate loneliness that only a man can banish.

On the night of the opera she wore black velvet unrelieved and never had looked handsomer. The neck of the apparently inseverable gown was cut square, and her beautiful arms were exposed as far to the top as fashion permitted; she wore her hair banded closely about her head, and, at the base of her throat, a barbaric necklace of dull red and blue stones that she had picked up in an antiquity shop in Munich. As she sat in her box between Mrs. Cameron and Mrs. Collier, one of the handsomest and best dressed of the younger women of Butte, Gregory, who sat behind and facing the house, saw that during the first entr'acte the audience levelled its glasses at her constantly, and that, indisputably, she divided the honours of the night with the prima donna.

He looked at her more than once himself, her classic beauty, or the classic effect she made it produce, appealing to his æsthetic sense as beauty in any form always did. He wondered a little that it should so have lost its once irresistible appeal to his senses, wondered again if he could not still have loved her well enough to live with had Ora never entered his life. Certainly he was very proud of her, and her conversation as well as her personality interested him. He respected her profoundly for what she had achieved, giving her full credit for the revolution in appearance, manners, and speech, in spite of her exceptional opportunities. Then he forgot her as his thoughts wandered to Ora, whom he saw sitting alone in her warm shadowy room, in which he had come to feel so much at home. As he always went to her when he was tired after a day filled with excitement or hard physical labour, he experienced only peace and content in her nearness; but when away, as tonight, and with the music of Thaïs singing into his keen responsive nerves, he was filled with an inexpressible longing.

He was roused by a faint exclamation from Ida. She was leaning forward. A moment later a man, whom he had never seen before and who looked like an Englishman of distinction, silently entered the box. Ida left her chair, and gave him both her hands in greeting, then went with him out into the passageway where their conversation would not interfere with her guests' enjoyment of the music.

Gregory felt very much like any other husband at that moment. He was conscious of no sting of jealousy, or stab of doubt, but he did not like it. He also received a distinct impression that his rights of proprietorship were menaced. Moreover, he was so invaded by mere curiosity that it was with difficulty he refrained from gratifying it at once. But, although he belonged to the type of Western man who would shoot the filcher of his woman without an instant's consideration, he was the last man in the world to make a fool of himself.

Ida tried his patience but a few moments. As soon as the curtain fell she re-entered the box and presented the stranger as Lord John Mowbray, who had arrived by the evening train and sought the opera house as a relief from the hotel. She did not add that he had telephoned at once to her house and followed her as quickly as he could change his clothes.

The husband was the last to be made known to the distinguished stranger, and in spite of Mowbray's ability to look vacuous, and Gregory's to look like a graven image, neither could repress a spark under his lowered lids. Mowbray reared his haughty crest at once and turned away. Like many young Englishman he blushed easily, and he was by no means the first man to feel uncomfortable under the eyes of Gregory Compton. He felt the colour rising to his white forehead, and was not sorry to present his splendid back and length of limb to that search-ing gaze.

He sat close to Ida during the last act, and then the party went to her house to supper, there being no res-taurant worthy the name in Butte. Gregory detained Ida at the door after the other had entered.

"Good night," he said. "Luning promised to wait for me at his office. I shall talk to him until it is time to catch the train for Pony."

"Oh, I am so sorry," said Ida politely, and smiling charmingly. "So will the others be. And I wanted you to talk to Lord John. His brother has a ranch in Wy-oming, and he has come here on some mining business. I am so glad to see him again. The men here are—well, they are all right, but quite absorbed in one thing only—what-ever their profession or business happens to be. Lord John knows a little about everything. I am sure you would like him. Do ask me to take him out to the mine. He is a friend of Ora's, too. She will ask us if you don't."

"Come whenever you like. If I'm not there my fore-man will show you round. Good night." And he was off. Ida, feeling that Mowbray's arrival had been timed by Providence, went in to her guests.

XIV

"WHO is this Mowbray?" Gregory asked Ora abruptly on the following evening. He was in Ora's living-room, his long legs stretched out to the fire.

Ora, who was working on a small piece of embroidery in a frame, superlatively feminine, enveloped in a tea gown imponderable and white, looked up in surprise. They had been sitting together for an hour or more and their conversation had been wholly of his plans to entertain his party of geologists, and the attention this sensational flank attack had attracted throughout the country.

"Is Lord John here?"

"Yes. Came into the box last night. Handsome chap."

"Mowbray is a dear. We saw a great deal of him, and he bought our tickets and helped us off generally, when we were so upset over your cable."

"Ah! Tame cat? General utility man?"

"Hardly! He's full of life and a charming companion."

"Hm."

There was another silence and then he asked abruptly: "Is he in love with Ida?"

This time Ora dropped her work and sat up rigidly; her hands turned cold. There was a peculiar alteration of pitch in Gregory's voice that might register jealousy in a hypersensitive ear. And when his face looked most like a bronze reproduction of itself, his friends deduced that he was masking emotion.

Ora's brain always worked swiftly. Was it possible that by subtle manipulation she could reunite this man and her friend? That he loved herself she no longer doubted, but it was equally doubtful if he would ever confess it; on the cards that if he did he never would see her again. If she left the country after adroitly re-awakening his interest in Ida and playing on his vanity and jealousy, would not reaction, the desire for consolation and companionship, carry him straight to the wife whose beauty and magnetism had once, and not so long ago, aroused all the ardours of his manhood? Ida was far more beautiful now, and quite capable of holding any man. Ora did not for a moment believe that Ida loved her husband, or never would she herself have returned to Butte; but she had divined her mortification, her wounded pride; and as a young and beautiful woman Ida needed and was entitled to the protection of her husband.

Was this her moment? Her great opportunity? Her bosom heaved, her breath came short. Almost she experienced the subtle delights of renunciation, of sacrifice, of the martyrdom of woman. It would be a great rôle to play, a great memory. And after all she had Valdobia. It was this last irresistible reflection that gave her soaring spirit a sharp tumble and she laughed aloud.

Gregory turned his head and smiled as he met the cynical amusement in her eyes. "What is it?"

"I was merely commiserating poor Mowbray. Of course he is more or less *épris;* but Ida—she hasn't it in her to love any man."

"That is the conclusion I arrived at long ago. But it looked as if he had followed her here, and I don't care for that sort of talk."

"He had planned to visit his brother in Wyoming before we met him in Genoa. Don't worry. Ida never will let any man compromise her. She'll parade her son of a duke for the benefit of Butte, but if he shows signs of getting out of hand she'll pack him off."

"Yes, Ida is too ambitious to compromise herself."

And then another little arrow flew into Ora's brain. Her hands trembled, but she clenched them in her lap. "Gregory," she said steadily, "as you and Ida no longer love each other, why don't you suggest a divorce? She could marry Mowbray and have a big position in London —his brother is almost sure not to marry—is a wreck— Ida would be quite in her element as a duchess—and you— you—would be free—if you ever wanted to marry again."

When nature has given a man a dark skin and he has permitted it to accumulate yearly coats of tan, it is difficult for him to turn white under the stress of emotion; but Gregory achieved this phenomenon as he realised abruptly what freedom might mean to him. He stood up and leaned his back against the high chimneypiece, thrusting his hands into his pockets; he had long nervous fingers which sometimes betrayed him when his face was set.

"Ida would never consent to a divorce," he said heavily. "She's got all sorts of old-fashioned American ideals. The West has the reputation for being lawless, and it's got more Puritans to the square inch than are left in New England. Ida's one of them."

"She may have acquired more liberal ideas in Europe."

"She told me that she didn't care if she never saw Europe again. Last night I had quite a long talk with her before the others came in for dinner. She said she thought it the duty of Western women—particularly the women of the newer Northwest—to live in their native state and only go away occasionally in order to bring something back to it. She intimated that you put that idea into her head when you two first met."

"Oh, yes, I believe that to be right, whatever I may do, myself."

"What is your idea in going to Europe to live? You are just the sort of woman the West needs." He bit out his words in the effort to be calm and casual.

"I don't feel that I have any place here."

Gregory started on a restless walk up and down the room.

"Look at here," he shot out finally, "are you—I haven't said anything about it—but—of course I've wanted to—are you determined to leave Mark? He's one of the best fellows in the world. I hate to see him thrown down. You—you—I think you should reconsider."

"I had done all my considering before I spoke to Mark. I am doing him the greatest possible kindness. He needs another sort of woman altogether to make him happy. And I? Have I not my right to happiness? Do you think I could find it with Mark?"

"No!" The word exploded. "And you—shall you marry again?"

"I don't know." Ora spoke in a strangled voice. New possibilities were shaking her to her foundations. For a moment the perverse imp in the purely feminine section of her brain counselled her to run away as ever from the serious mood in man, to play with great issues and then dodge them. But she brushed the prompting aside with frantic haste and summoned her courage. If this was happiness coming to her grasp she would seize it.

Gregory came swiftly back from the farther end of the room and stood before her. He had set the muscles of the lower part of his face so tightly that he could hardly open his mouth, but his narrow eyes were blazing. "If Ida would give me my freedom," he said, "I should want to marry you. Do you understand?"

Ora stood up. Her white face was so radiant that Gregory fell back. "You love me?" he asked.

"Yes.—Oh, yes——"

"You would marry me?"

"Yes!"

Gregory stared at her, wondering if she really were suffused with white fire. Her hands fluttered toward him, and his own face was suddenly relaxed, unmasked. Ora's lips parted and she bent forward. She knew then why men and women sacrificed the world when they found their predestined mates. Here was the one man who could give her primal joy, suffocate her intellect. And the knowledge that she was capable of such passion and of the sacrifices it might involve gave her far more satisfaction than her former brief mood of renunciation.

She made another step forward, but Gregory was at the door. "Talk to Ida!" he said harshly. "I leave it to you. Go to see her tomorrow. You can do anything with her. You must!"

And he was out of the house. He left the door open and Ora could hear his light running footsteps.

XV

ON the following morning Gregory, who had spent the night in the mine and had just come up to the cabin, heard his telephone ring as he was about to take his bath and go to bed. His first impulse was to ignore the summons, but, his business instinct prevailing, he went into the office and unhooked the receiver.

"Well?" he asked, in a voice both flat and uninviting.

"It is Ida. How tired your voice sounds. I won't keep you a minute. I have a plan to suggest. Why not let me put up those geologists? Mrs. Cameron has asked me to stay with her and will come over and help me entertain them at meals. It will not only save you a fearful hotel bill but keep them from wandering into the wrong fold."

"Good idea!" Gregory's voice was more animated.

"I'll get Professor Becke to take them down into one of the big mines here, take them out myself to yours, amuse them between times with the prettiest women in town—in short stick to them closer than a brother."

"Good! You are the right sort. I'll meet them at the train—on the night of the second, it is—and take them right up to your house. It's putting you to a lot——"

"Not a bit. It will be immense fun. Good-bye."

On that same morning Ora went to Butte. She had telephoned to Ida, and Mowbray met her at the train with the limousine.

"Mrs. Compton had to go to some charity meeting or other," he said, as they shook hands warmly. "I am to drive you about for an hour."

This was better fortune than Ora, who possessed little of Ida's patience and talent for the waiting game, had dared to anticipate.

"How jolly!" Her face lost its traces of a sleepless night as it flashed with hope and enthusiasm. "And after that dreadful train! Drive to the Gardens," she said to the chauffeur.

She pointed out Anaconda Hill as they passed under that famous portal, and the shaft houses of other mines, suggesting that he go down with the geologists when they made the inevitable descent. "But you will find your visit to Mr. Compton's mine more satisfactory," she added lightly. "You will see more ore in the vein. How do you like him?"

Mowbray growled something in his thick inarticulate English voice, and Ora grasped her opportunity. She turned to him with the uncompromising directness her sinuous mind knew so well how to assume.

"Take me into your confidence," she said peremptorily. "I can help you. At all events keep you from making any mistakes with Ida. She is what is called a difficult proposition. Are you in love with her?"

Mowbray turned a deep brick-red and frowned, but he answered intelligibly: "You know jolly well I am."

"Then let me tell you that there is only one way you can get her. Ida is moral to the marrow of her bones. You might make her love you, for she and her husband are practically separated, but you can get her only by persuading her to divorce Mr. Compton."

"I've thought of that. Of course I'd rather marry her. I'm a decent sort myself—hate skulking—and lying—she's the last woman I'd want to compromise. But I'm so beastly poor. I've only twelve hundred pounds a year."

"And she has forty thousand pounds now of her own. You need not hesitate to spend the capital, for Mr. Compton is most generous, and is sure to give her much more. He is bound to be a multimillionaire—it is only a question of a few years."

"Does he want his own freedom?"

"I am not in his confidence. But as they no longer care for each other and have agreed to live apart—merely showing themselves together in public occasionally to avoid gossip—it is natural to suppose that he would be indifferent, at least. He cannot be more than thirty, and will be sure to want his freedom sooner or later."

"This is splendid of you!" cried the Englishman gratefully. "She's not happy. I know that, and now I shall know just what to do."

"Sympathise with her. Make yourself necessary—make her feel the neglected wife, and what a devoted husband would mean. You have the game in your own hands, and I will help you."

XVI

ORA discerned certain changes in Ida as the three re-
united friends, with so many pleasant memories in
common, talked gaily at luncheon. It was not only that
she was a trifle thinner but there were shadows in her
eyes that gave them troubled depths. The curves of her
mouth also were less assured, and her strong, rather large,
but beautiful hands had a restless movement. Ora, whose
imagination was always ready to spring from the leash
and visualise a desired conclusion, pictured Ida, if not
already in love with this good-looking and delightful Englishman, as circling close; neglected and mortified, she
longed for the opportunity to live her life with him; in
short was champing the bit.

Ora led the conversation—no great adroitness was necessary—to the many divorces pending in Butte at the moment. Ida sniffed. Ora asserted gaily that they were
merely a casual result of an era of universal progress and
individualism; one of the commonplaces of modern life
that hardly called for comment. "You are so up to date
in everything else, my dear," she concluded, "that I wonder you cling to such old middle-class prejudices."

"I guess there are a few conservatives and brakes left
in this country," said Ida, drily. "I may look back with
horror at the time when I chewed gum and walked out of
a restaurant with a toothpick in my mouth, but Ma hammered most of my good old-fashioned prejudices into my
back with the broom-handle, and I'm no more likely to
forget her opinion of divorce—the poor get it sometimes
as well as the rich—than the bastings I got if I played
hookey from school, or sneaked out after dark alone with
a beau."

"My mother was exactly the same," said Ora, with that
charming spontaneity which so often robbed her words
of the subtle insult of condescension, or the more cryptic
of irony. "If I hadn't happened to be a book-worm and

312

had indulged in clandestine love affairs I should have been shut up on bread and water. And she had all a Southern woman's horror of divorce. But, dear Ida! That was in the dark ages. We live in the most enlightened and individualistic era of the world's history. I have kept my eyes and ears open ever since. Nor do I believe for a moment that we are getting any worse—we merely have achieved a more well-bred indifference toward other people's affairs. One can hear a scandal a minute in large towns and small, if one has nothing better to do than listen; but whereas in our mothers' time a woman was dropped if she was 'talked about,' today we don't turn a hair at anything short of a quite superlative divorce court scandal—not even about girls; always provided that they continue to dress well, and keep on being charming and spending money."

"That is about the most cynical thing I ever heard you say."

"The truth always sounds cynical. You laugh at me for dreaming and being an idealist, but I never have shut my mind to facts as you do."

"I don't even blink the old facts. I don't like them, that's all. I don't say, of course, that if I were married to a brute who came home drunk and beat me—but this swapping husbands like horses—well, I'm content to be a brake as long as there's any wheel to freeze to. You know I'm not hitting at you," she added hastily. "I'd give you the moon if you wanted it; but I put you in a class by yourself, that's all."

"Oh," cried Ora, laughing. "Let us change the subject before you prove that your logic turns feminine at the crucial test. Heavens! How hideous Butte is. We drove——"

"Hideous? Butte?" demanded Ida indignantly.

"Oh, you see it through the glamour of a triumphal progress. Wait until the novelty has worn off. How do you find it?" she asked Mowbray, who had relished his excellent luncheon and admired his ally's tactics.

"Rippin' air. Nearly took a header out of the window this mornin' thinkin' I had wings. But as for looks—those mountains in the distance are not half-bad, but the foreground is — er — a little ragged — and — new — you know." He smiled into Ida's warning eyes. "Really, dear lady, I can understand that you were keen on gettin' home again, because home is home, don't you know. But beauty—tell me just where you do find it."

Ida tossed her head. "Beauty is in the eye of the beholder, and mine beholds it. That is enough for me. Now, run along to the Club. I haven't seen Ora for ages. You may come back for tea."

She led the way up to her bedroom and they made themselves comfortable and lit their cigarettes.

"Odd as it would seem," said Ida, "to those east and west of us who have an idea that Butte has been on one prolonged spree since she was really a camp, I have to enjoy my occasional cigarette on the sly. A few of the younger women smoke, when they have locked the doors and pulled the blinds down—and of course The Bunch does; but the majority—and those that never bat an eyelash at cocktails and champagne—think it indecent for a woman to smoke. Funny world."

"Butte is a provincial hole. As there are no strangers present you needn't bother to defend it. I've just had a brilliant idea. Why don't you divorce Mr. Compton and marry Mowbray?"

"Aw!" Ida dropped her cigarette and burned a hole in her skirt. "Are you raving crazy?"

"I thought I was advancing a peculiarly level-headed suggestion——"

"None of it in mine!"

"But, my dear Ida, you will tire inevitably of this old camp. The glamour of all this return in a gilded chariot drawn by the cheering populace will wear off in about six months. So will your own novelty for them. It is all indescribably cheap, anyhow. If you send Mowbray away now, he will try to forget you, and forgetting is man's peculiar accomplishment. You will have missed a great opportunity. You and Mr. Compton are manifestly indifferent to each other. Seize your chance, dear—not only for happiness, but for a splendid social position, before——"

Ora paused. Ida was glaring ahead of her with her heavy black brows pushed low over her flaming eyes. Her lips were drawn back over her sharp little teeth. Her nostrils were distended. She looked like some magnificent beast of the jungle stalking her prey.

"By God!" she whispered, her whole body heaving, "I'll have him back. I was a fool before I left, and maybe I shouldn't have left him at all. It's never safe to leave a man. But when I do get him back he'll be glad of all I've learned. He's like a lunatic with a fixed idea just now—but wait."

Ora felt cold and numb. She tried to rise, and wondered if the shock had paralysed her. She managed to articulate: "You love him then?"

But not even to Ora could Ida make any such admission; she who always had flouted both sentiment and passion! She recovered herself and tossed her head.

"Love! Who cares about love? Do you think I'm the sort of woman a man can throw down for a mine? I wouldn't stand it even it were another woman—but ore! It makes me sick. I won't be thrown down. And I'll get him back!"

Ora too had recovered herself. She lit another cigarette. "I'm so glad you don't care, dear. No man is worth agonising over, as you so often have said yourself. Forgive the doubt. I should have remembered that you were far too clever and worldly-wise for that sort of thing. That is the main reason that I am willing to marry Valdobia: I can be fond of him, like him always, be grateful for his companionship, but he can't tear my heart out."

"I thought you told me when you came back that you were mad about him?"

"Oh, I fancy I was strung up that day. When I am excited I always exaggerate. But do think over what I have said about Mowbray. And it would be heavenly to have you in Europe."

"My mind's made up. I guess I'm American to my core and marrow. Titles will never seem natural to me, and I guess we'll both live to see them so tangled up with democracy that those that are left will look like old labels on new cans. No has-beens in mine. Oh, chuck it! What's this I hear about little Whalen—that he's resigned from the High and been out in the mountains prospecting since the beginning of Spring? I've only seen him once since I came back and then he looked like a viper that had been stepped on."

"I met him the other day when I was out walking. He bought a claim of one of the prospectors that swarmed out there as soon as they heard of the Primo and the Perch strikes. He wore overalls and a beard. I scarcely knew him. He talked rather wildly about the hill he has located on being another Perch of the Devil.''

"I guess Gregory is responsible for that and a good many other wild dreams. I hear that a lot of young men are coming out from the East this Summer to prospect in those hills. Well, they'll succeed or fail according to their luck mostly. Let's go out. You've got two hours before your train goes—but if you've got a list a yard long——''

And the two sallied forth in perfect peace to shop.

XVII

ORA had more than one cause for uneasiness when she returned to her little home in the pine woods, but paramount was the fear that she should not see Gregory Compton again unless by accident. She rose early after another almost sleepless night and spent a distracted day wandering over the hills, returning at intervals to inquire if her telephone bell had rung. Once more she felt a disposition to run away, anathematising the slavery of love. Only the hope that Mowbray would wear down Ida's resistance kept her from yielding to the impatient, imaginative, too highly organised woman's impulse to flee when love seems hopeless and a nervous explosion imminent. She still refused to feel traitorous to Ida, but she did wonder once or twice if she ever should dare to face her as Mrs. Gregory Compton. Ida was the reverse of a fool. She might be blind now, for obvious reasons—but Ora shrugged her shoulders at the vision of Ida's horror and wrath. What did she care for Ida or any other woman if she got her man?

She made one of her sudden dashes into the house as the telephone bell was ringing. For the moment she thought she was about to faint; then, both appalled and angry at the lawless behaviour of her nerves, she stamped her foot, shook herself, marched over to the telephone, took down the receiver, and asked in a bored voice: "Well?"

"I shall come to supper tonight if you will have me?" Gregory's tones were those he employed when "canning" a miner.

"Delighted." Ora's nerves fell into place like good little soldiers. "Will you be here at seven?"

"About. I prefer to have you tell me here what she had to say."

"Constitutionally opposed at present, but that was to be expected. Seeds always sprout if well planted and judiciously watered. Our friend from England will do his part."

317

"Good. We'll say no more about it. But I shall go to see you as usual."

"Why not? We are not fools or children. Any new developments at the mine?"

"Shaft has reached third level. Vein seems to be about the same richness as on the second. Mann is here. Good-bye."

As Ora, her body no longer braced and rigid, but so filled with the languor of happiness that she wanted to throw herself down on the divan and sleep, crossed the room, she became aware that some one was standing in the outer doorway. His hat was in his hand, and as she focussed her absent gaze she managed to recognise Professor Whalen. Her impulse was to turn her back and run into her bed-room; but Ora was always a great lady. She could be extremely rude to a member of her own class, but she had never permitted herself to wound the morbid sensitiveness of those to whom fortune had been less kind. So, secretly wondering if the little man really stood there, or if any-thing so insignificant mattered, she went forward smiling and offered him her hand.

"So good of you to come and have a cup of tea with me." She rang a bell and ordered tea of her Chinaman. "But why did you dress up? I am accustomed to overalls and flannel shirts, and quite like the idea of living in a mining camp."

Whalen sat on the edge of his chair and stared into the fire, twirling his hat in his hands. "I guess I've got to be a gentleman again," he said with a short laugh. "There's nothing else left for me to be."

"Oh! I hope——"

"My find—and I paid a thousand dollars for the claim —was nothing but a gash vein. Nothing in that but low grade carbonates."

"But are you so sure? Often veins appears to pinch out a hundred feet or more above a really rich lode."

"I've poured into that hole all my savings; all I had saved from my salary during four years, and every cent of my reward in the field of letters. I even—and against my secret resolutions—consumed a legacy left me by an uncle."

"Perhaps if you would ask Mr. Compton to look at your claim—he is a sort of ore wizard——"

"I'll ask no favours of Gregory Compton!" Whalen burst out, violently. "Were it not for him I never would have been enticed into this foolish venture. I cannot realise it—I, who was brought up in the most conservative corner of this conservative country—I, a pedagogue, a man of letters, that I should have so far descended as to become a prospector—live in a hut, cook my own bacon, dig with a pick——" He paused choking.

"Doubtless you remembered that some of the greatest millionaires in the country began that way. Or possibly the Northwest kindled your sense of adventure—that is inherent in every real man. But why blame Mr. Compton?"

Whalen had recovered his breath. He spat out his words. "Why should a man like that have all the luck? And such colossal luck! Who is he? What is he? In what way does he compare with me—a man of no family, of no culture, of no intellect——"

"Mr. Compton has given evidence that he has one of the best brains this country has produced." Ora spoke evenly but with a glint in her eye.

"Oh, yes, *brains!* I make a fine distinction between mere brains and intellect. He has the sort of mental composition those men always seem to have in order that they may make use of their luck and roll up millions. But intellect? Not a cell. He has never read anything. I journeyed with him from Pony to Butte not long since and endeavoured to engage him in conversation. I might as well have tried to talk to a mummy—and an ill-mannered one at that. The moment I left the subject of mines he merely looked out of the window."

Ora laughed merrily, and poured out the tea the Chinaman had brought in. "Perhaps it is just that lack of overdevelopment that we call intellect which permits these men to concentrate upon their genius for making money."

"But that has nothing to do with their luck in the beginning. Luck! Blind luck! Fool's luck! And why not to me? Why to this Gregory Compton? I never believed in luck before, but since this rush, and my own personal experience——" He swallowed a mouthful of tea too hastily, scalded himself, and, while he was gasping, Ora said soothingly:

"You cannot help believing in luck if you study the

early history of any mining state. There are hundreds of stories of prospectors—you have told of many yourself; the majority had little or no education, less science. Out of a hundred evenly equipped with grit, common sense, some practical knowledge of ores, perhaps two would find a rich pocket or placer. Four or five possibly made a strike that would insure them a competence if they neither gambled nor drank. The rest nothing—not after forty years of prospecting in these mountains. I fancy there is something in that old phrase about the lucky star; in astronomical parlance the position of the planets at the moment of one's birth.''

"But why not I?" wailed the professor. "Why—why this—well, he is a friend of yours—Gregory Compton?"

"*Why not?*"

"I am infinitely his superior in every way!" cried Whalen in perfect good faith. "It is I who should have discovered those millions and taken them to Beacon Street, not this obscure young Westerner, son of an illiterate old ranchman——"

"But you didn't," said Ora, patiently. "Besides, the fates are not unjust. They made you a member of the New England aristocracy, and gave you intellect. Do not be unreasonable and demand the mere prospector's luck as well."

Whalen looked at her suspiciously, but her eyes were teasing, not satiric. He had admired her always more than any woman he had met in the West, and had come to her blindly to be consoled. Suddenly he saw an indefinable change steal over her face, although her mouth remained curled with the stereotyped smile she kept for the Whalens. It was as if something deep in her brilliant eyes came to life, and her slight bust rose under the stiff shirt-waist. Whalen's ears were not acute and he did not hear the light footstep that preceded a peremptory knock. Ora crossed the room swiftly and opened the door. Whalen was no fool, and he had written fiction for four years. He had guessed at once that his beautiful hostess loved the man who demanded admittance, and when he heard Gregory Compton's voice he almost whistled. But he merely arose and frowned.

"Knocked off and thought I would run in early," Gregory was beginning, when he saw Whalen. "How are you?"

he asked with more cordiality than he usually wasted upon the little man. His spirits always flew to his head when he met Ora, stolid as he might look. "How's your mine getting on?" he added, as he selected the longest of the chairs before the fire. "Heard it had petered out."

"It has!"

"I'll go over and have a look at it tomorrow if you like. I fancy you're located too close to one of the faults. The trouble with you amateur prospectors—or buyers of prospectors' claims—is that you don't take a geologist out with you. You lose your heads over an assay report on exceptional specimens. But I'd like to see for myself."

"It's no use," said Whalen gloomily. 'I have used up all my money in that——" He had learned to swear in mining camp society, but he pulled himself up hastily, "that hole."

"If I think there is anything there I'll grub-stake you. Nobody would buy your claim, but somebody might jump it if you let it lapse, and I want to know who my neighbours are. Have you patented it?"

"Not yet."

"Spent five hundred dollars on it?"

"*Have* I!"

"Well, I'll look at it tomorrow, and if I think it's good for anything I'll help you out. I am going to Helena in a day or two. Come along and apply for your patent."

"You are very kind." Whalen felt repentant, and more grateful than he had ever condescended to feel before. "I'll expect you tomorrow." He inferred that he could best show his gratitude by taking himself off, and rose. "Good afternoon, Mrs. Blake. This hour has been refreshing and inspiring after my long absence from civilisation."

"You must come soon again," said Ora sweetly, as she marshalled him out. "The best of luck."

She went to her bedroom for a few moments, and when she returned wore a soft tea gown made of several shades of woodland greens. She seated herself in her favourite chair, straight, with a high carved back, and took up her neglected embroidery. "Dinner will not be ready for half an hour," she said. "How long that little man did stay. I am glad you made a friend of him, for I have always imagined that he could be venomous, and before you came in he was by way of hating you. Now tell me the surprise you have for the geologists and newspaper men on the second level.''

And for the next three hours they talked of ores.

XVIII

"GIVE me your hand, Gregory. I am no coward, but this is the first time I have ever been underground. My father would never permit it, nor my mother after him."

Gregory extended his long arm behind him and Ida's warm firm fingers clung to his hand. They had just left the skip at the second level of his mine. The geologists and the newspaper men, together with herself, Lord John, Gregory, and Mann, had entered the mine by way of the Primo shaft, inspected the insignificant vein of copper which had merely been blocked out, awaiting the possible erection of a concentrating plant—for it was not worth the expense of freight to Anaconda—thence down the ladder from the hole blasted by Apex, and into the drift where the magnificent vein of Perch of the Devil also merely had been blocked out; but for a more subtle reason. The case in Gregory's favour was so flagrant that the great men had laughed, although gracefully submitting to interviews on the spot and expressing themselves with as few technicalities as possible. That the Primo copper upon which Apex had also sunk was a mere attenuated fork of the great vein which indisputably had faulted from the original vein in Gregory Compton's property the reporters could see for themselves. Under the Apex law Gregory was within his lateral rights in sinking under the adjoining claim and thence under the Primo mine; and as far beyond as the vein persisted.

Against a man less determined and resourceful than Gregory Compton a wealthy corporation could obtain any verdict it demanded; but to persist in a suit for Apex rights after this public exposition would make any trust the laughing-stock of a continent. Even to persist in the claim that he was mining under an agricultural patent, and therefore outside his rights, would be mere petty persecution; and inevitably both suits would steal noiselessly to limbo. Amalgamated knew when it was beaten and would take its medicine with a grimace and watch for its next opportunity.

Ida, although she disliked the sensation of being underground, the chill of the tunnels and the drip of candlegrease on her smart linen skirt, had been deeply impressed by the scene in the excavation on the Perch vein: the men with their keen upturned faces, their peering eyes so close to the moving candles, the little yellow flames travelling along the beautiful yellow metal, the eager nervous hands of the newspaper men, the intense blackness beyond the radius of the candles. But her eyes returned constantly to her husband's face. His eyes gleamed with copper fires. His profile against the dark background of the cavern looked as if carved in the rock by some prehistoric race.

The blood scorched her face and her heart leapt with pride as she heard these distinguished men defer to him, express their admiration without reserve. A year ago he had been as little known as when she married him. To-day his extraordinary abilities were recognised by the entire country, and tomorrow he would be one of its colossi.

She was the only woman that had gone down. Mrs. Cameron and Mrs. Collier had preferred to remain comfortably with Ora in the bungalow, or to help her spread the tables under the pines, where luncheon was to be served. Therefore was she privileged to keep close to the host, and when they descended into the blackness of the second level she embraced further her feminine prerogatives. Mann had gone down first, the guests had followed, and Gregory, after a vain protest, had taken her down in the skip when it returned for himself.

The rest of the party had pushed forward, for they had been promised a surprise. Ida would have lingered, but Gregory pulled her on. He wanted to hear the comments. The racket of the drills had stopped. Ida saw the last of the guests disappear up a short ladder.

"Am I to go up into a stope?" she asked.

"If you want to see what we've come for." He ran up the ladder, and she followed, insinuated herself into the hole and stood upright in the large excavation on the vein.

"Is it gold?" she gasped.

"No, but it's a streak—a shoot—of chalcopyrite ten feet wide and of the highest value. And it may go down eight or nine hundred feet before it loses its richness and degenerates into a lower grade of ore. But there may be millions of tons of that. This is one of the few great shoots of chalcopyrite known."

"Gregory!" said Ida ecstatically, "do you remember I always had such faith in you that I urged you so often to prospect on the ranch that you got quite cross?"

"Yes, I remember."

"Never say I doubted you. I may be enchanted at all this success and recognition of your abilities, but I have never had the least sensation of surprise."

Gregory smiled down into the eager beautiful face so close to his shoulder. She had manipulated him down the ladder into the tunnel and for the moment they were alone. "I hope you are half as proud of me as I am of you," he said gallantly, although he was a trifle uneasy; not because she looked as if she might kiss him there in the semi-dark, but because he felt an impulse to kiss her. For the moment he regretted the wild romance upon which he was embarked, the torments of its present, the tragic possibilities of its future. Ida now would make an ideal wife, demanding far less of his jealously guarded inner self, to say nothing of his time, than Ora, who had that most terrible of all gifts, a passionate soul. But this disloyalty was brief, and he frowned and disengaged his hand, although he was far from suspecting that Ida had yielded to the temptation to pay him deliberate court.

"I shall be able to give you a string of pearls before long," he said lightly, "or a million or two to play with. I want to hear what these men have to say. Suppose you go back with Lord John, and tell them that we are coming up soon for lunch. Ring the bell in the station twice for the skip and three times for hoist."

Ida shrank back against the wall as if she had been struck, but when Lord John, who had made several futile attempts to separate her from her husband, came eagerly forward, she left Gregory to the chorus of enthusiasm and congratulation, and obeyed his directions.

XIX

IDA was in such high spirits during the luncheon that she managed to be brilliant and amusing within the limits of her expurgated vocabulary. Only Ora, who knew her so well, saw the sombre fire in the depths of her eyes, the sudden twist of her mouth at the corners, noted that her cheeks were crimson instead of their usual delicate coral, the occasional clenching of her hands. But she had little time to speculate upon the cause, for the large party were her guests, and, like any other Rocky Mountain hostess in the liquid month of June, she feared the sudden drenching of her tables.

But the day remained fine, and the geologists, who ever since their arrival in Butte had evinced a remarkable indifference to geology as a topic for conversation, were as lively as the newspaper men, and deeply appreciative of the good looks and animated conversation of the four women who ate almost nothing in their efforts at mental subdivision. Ora had invited also her engineer and Professor Whalen, placing the latter as far from Ida as possible; but she saw that he was covertly watching the woman he must hate. Ida had thrown him a careless nod when they met by the tables in the grove; and he had returned it with a bow of surpassing dignity.

Gregory, now that the men of science and of the press had served his purpose, was eager to be rid of them, and excused himself when the luncheon was half over, on the plea that he was his own manager and needed at the mine. He disappeared into the Primo shaft house, as he often took that short cut to his own shaft, and Mowbray, who had been silent, for Gregory affected his buoyant spirits unaccountably, moved his chair up beside Ida and endeavoured to divert her mind from the general to the specific. But she snubbed him and he relapsed into gloom. On the train, however, when she saw that Whalen, who was on his way to Helena to apply for his patent, was

326

watching her, she flirted pointedly with the handsome Englishman.

The guests were to leave Butte on the seven o'clock train, which, fortunately for the strain that all were beginning to feel, was only half an hour late. When it had pulled out and Ida had waved her last farewell, she walked in silence to her car, and intimated with a curt nod that Mowbray might take the seat beside her. "But tell Ben where you want to go," she said, "for I can't ask you to dine with me tonight."

Mowbray told the chauffeur to drop him at the Club and then asked his lady, whose animation had dropped to zero, if anything had happened to annoy her, or if she were merely worn out.

"Don't ask me any questions," said Ida sharply. "I'm sorry to seem inhospitable but I've got something to think out. You can go to the dance at the Country Club."

"I shall more likely go to my rooms and write letters. Don't worry about me. Shall we have a ride tomorrow morning?"

"I don't know."

Mowbray was always philosophical about women, having been brought up with many sisters. "You are tired out," he said without too much sympathy. "Just call me up if you feel like doing anything in the morning."

"All right. Good night."

She left him at the Silver Bow Club. Her own house was only a few blocks distant. She told the maid who admitted her that she wanted no dinner and should go to bed at once and without assistance. When she reached the seclusion of her bedroom she locked the door, flung her hat on the floor and stamped on it, broke several valuable objects, and then paced up and down, gritting her teeth to keep from screaming.

There was but one person on earth that she hated more than she hated Gregory Compton and that was herself. She had meant to play a waiting game of many interviews, in which her fine calculation had mapped out the insidious approach, the adroit pushing aside of barrier after barrier, until Gregory returned almost inadvertently to his allegiance. She had no desire for romantic scenes; they would have embarrassed herself, and, with her instinctive knowledge of man, she knew that Gregory would shrink back from any situation that might involve explanations. Nor did she wish to let a man so absorbed as Gregory feel that he was loved too much, lest he chafe at the thought of feminine exactions, and his mind continue to dwell upon the delights of freedom. He might be capable of moments when the woman alone existed, but there would be long intervals when he would hate a woman's clinging arms if they made him ten minutes late for his work, particularly if he was headed for his beloved mine. Ida, shrewd, self-controlled, watchful, knew herself, now that her powers were developed, to be the natural mate for such a man. He would drive a temperamental woman mad.

And she had seemed to make a steady progress. The geologists had remained for three days in Butte before visiting Perch of the Devil. On the second evening they had been entertained by the professors of the School of Mines, but on the other two evenings she had given them elaborate dinners, and Gregory had attended each. She had seen that he was increasingly proud of her, and grateful. Upon both occasions they not only had had a little talk apart but he had drifted back to her more than once.

And today she had spoiled everything! In the darkness of that mine she had weakened and made open love to him. She had practically offered herself—she ground her teeth as she thought of her clinging fingers, her appealing eyes, her cheek almost brushing his—and he had rejected her—with consideration, but finality!

If he had knocked her down she would have cherished hope. But in this hour she had none. His indifference was colossal. The busiest men in America had their women; she no longer could comfort herself with the delusion that the mine was a controlling and exclusive passion; she merely had ceased completely to attract him—and she remembered how thorough he was; she no more could relight those old fires than she could blow life into the dead ashes of Big Butte. He would turn to another woman one of these days; it was not within human possibility that he would go through life without love; but not to her! not to her! She would do to entertain his friends, to flaunt his wealth and advertise his success; in time no doubt he would treat her as a confidential friend; but sexually she was an old story. It was apparent that the mere thought bored him; it was only when Gregory was bored that he was really polite.

If she could but have accepted this, resigned all hope, instead of subjecting herself to humiliation; she, who had never failed to send the blood to a man's head with a glance! She didn't want to hate him. She didn't want to hate herself. Why could she not have been content to accept the inevitable with philosophy and grace?

The answer that, owing to some mysterious law of her being, she loved him, made her want to smash everything else in the room; but she would have some difficulty concealing the present wreckage from her servants, so she bit her handkerchief to shreds instead.

When the furies had tired her body she fell into a chair and although her brain was still hot with the blood sent there by excitement and lack of food, she admitted frankly that the peculiar nature of her agitation was due to wounded pride and intense mortification; had she arrived at a point where she no longer could hope, but without self-betrayal, she might have wept bitter tears, but there still would have been a secret sweetness in loving him. Now, she growled out her hatred. She longed to do something to hurt him. If she only were another sort of woman! She would go to Mowbray's rooms, go to Helena with him for a week. And simultaneously she yearned to be consoled, not only in her heart but in her wounded pride.

Should she ask her husband for a divorce; revenge herself by becoming an English duchess? Ora, in the moment or two they had found together at the station, had told her that Mowbray's older brother was at Davos, unmistakably dying of tuberculosis, and that his engagement, insisted upon by his father, had been broken. Valdobia had given her this news in his last letter, adding the hope that his friend would bring Ida back with him that they might all be together once more.

Was this the solution of her problem? A marriage that would demonstrate to Gregory Compton that her moment of seeming weakness was mere coquetry; a marriage that would raise her an immeasurable social distance above him; a permanent dissociation from everything that could remind her of him and this terrible obsession that had disorganised her being, reduced her to the grovelling level of the women whose dependence on the favour of man she had always despised?

When she reflected that her revenge would fall flat, Gregory's not being the order of mind to appreciate the social pre-eminence of a titled race, she ground her teeth again. There was nothing left but to consider herself. Should she choose the part that not only would exalt her station and fill her life with the multifarious interests of a British peeress, but banish this man in time from her memory; or stay on and alternate torments with moments of indescribable sweetness when he smiled upon her? And might she not yet manipulate him into her net if she continued to play the waiting game? Or would she go wholly to pieces the first time they were alone together?

Her pride strangled at this possibility and brought her to her feet. The blood was still boiling in her head, she knew what nerves were for the first time in her life. She made up her mind to go out and walk. In this part of the town she was not likely to meet anyone.

She found another hat, put on a warm coat, and let herself out of the house. It was ten o'clock. All the West Side, no doubt, was at the Country Club.

For a time she walked rapidly and aimlessly, trying to focus her mind on other things. But when a woman is in love and the path is stony, she is obsessed much as people are that suffer from shock and reiterate ceaselessly the circumstances of its cause. Her brain seethed with hate, longed for revenge. Nothing would have gratified her more than to take the secret revenge of infidelity. Many a woman has taken a lover for the satisfaction of laughing to herself at her husband's dishonour; to dishonour being the most satisfactory of all vengeance, whether open or concealed.

She realised abruptly that her thoughts had led her unconsciously to the door of John Mowbray's lodgings. The flat had been lent him by a banker to whom he had brought a letter from his brother, and who had gone East immediately after his arrival; the banker's wife lived in Southern California. It occupied the second story of a house in West Broadway and had its own entrance on a side street. Mowbray had given a tea there a day or two before, and Ida had presided.

She did not delude herself for a moment that she could

take her full revenge upon the unconscious Gregory, but at least she could do something quite shocking, something that would infuriate a husband. Ida was not afraid of any man, least of all one that wished to make a duchess of her, but it would be an additional satisfaction to torment him, and an adventure with a spice of danger in it no doubt would restore her equilibrium. If Mowbray made violent love to her she felt, by some obscure process of feminine logic, that she would forgive Gregory Compton.

She glanced hastily up and down the street, then more sharply, wondering if she had dreamed that once or twice she had looked over her shoulder with the sense of being followed. It was a bright moonlight night. No one was in sight. She rang the bell of Mowbray's flat. The door was opened from above. At the head of the stairs stood the Jap who served as housekeeper and valet.

She hesitated a moment, taken aback. She had forgotten the servant. Then she closed the door behind her. "Is Lord John in?" she asked negligently.

The Jap spread out his hands deprecatingly. "His lordship not at home," he announced.

Ida hesitated another moment, then ascended the stair and entered the living-room. "Turn on the lights," she said, "I shall wait for him."

The Jap obeyed orders, bowed, and withdrew. For a moment Ida was tempted to telephone to the Silver Bow Club, but Mowbray was sure to return soon to write his letters, and she liked the idea of giving him a surprise. She lit a cigarette, selected a novel from the bookcase, and sank into the most comfortable of the chairs. The room was warm; both body and brain were very weary. The cool night air had driven the blood from her head. She yawned, dropped the book, fell sound asleep.

She awoke as the clock was striking half-past one. She was still alone. For a moment she stared about her, bewildered, then rose and laughed aloud.

"This is about the flattest——" She went swiftly out into the hall and awoke the slumbering Jap, "You little yellow devil," she cried, "why didn't you tell me that his lordship had gone to the party at the Country Club?"

Once more the Jap was deprecating. "Madam did not ask."

Ida produced a gold piece. "Well, you are not to tell

him that I came, nor anyone else. If you do I'll wring your neck."

The Jap's eyes, fixed upon the gold, glistened. "Why should I tell?" he asked philosophically; and having pocketed the coin ran downstairs and bowed the lady out.

When Ida was about to turn the corner she whirled about, this time with a definite sensation of being followed. But the street was empty save for a man slouching down the hill with an unsteady gait, his head nodding toward his chest. It was a familiar sight in any mining town; nevertheless she quickened her steps, and in a moment was safe within her own house.

XX

ON the morning following the departure of the geologists Gregory took the bit between his teeth and went in to Butte to see his wife. In his first moment of shock and confusion it had seemed to him best that Ora, whose subtlety he recognised, was the one to manipulate Ida's still too formalistic mind toward the divorce court; but he was unaccustomed to relegate any part of his affairs to others, least of all to a woman. Nor did he think it necessary to inform Ora of his sudden decision. He might work almost double shift to keep her out of his thoughts and diminish temptation, and he might marry her and continue to love her passionately; but she would obtain little ascendency over him. He knew what he wanted; he had trained his will until at times it appeared formidable even to himself, and he was as nearly the complete male that regards woman, however wonderful, as the supplementary female as still survives.

He had few illusions about himself, and it had crossed his mind more than once, since the hope of divorce had dazzled both of them, that for a year or two or least there must be a certain amount of friction between a nature like his and a complex, super-civilised, overgrown feminine ego like Ora Blake. While he had sat with his legs stretched out to the fire and his eyes half closed, his body weary, but mentally alert, he had received certain definite impressions of an independent almost anarchical mind, contemptuous of the world and its midges save as they might be of use to herself; of a mind too well bred ever to be managing and exacting in any vulgar sense, but inexorable in its desires and as unscrupulous in their pursuit as her father had been; of a superlative refinement coupled with a power of intense and reckless passion found only in women possessing that quality of imagination that exalts and idealises the common mortal attributes. Moreover, it was a mind that, the first joy of submission and surrender diminished, would think for itself.

Until that night when both had dropped the mask for a moment he had never thought of her as a complicated ego, merely as one from whom he felt temporarily separated after a union of centuries; and it had been the reluctant admission that he knew her very little, save as a gracious woman and his own companion, that had enabled him to school himself to spend long hours with her alone as before. He had tumbled blindly into matrimony once, and no matter how much he might love this woman, to whom he had seemed from the first to be united by a secret and ancient bond, he was determined none the less to marry the second time with his eyes wide open.

But although his glimpses of Ora's winding depths gave him moments of uneasiness he always fell back upon the complacent reflection that he was a man, a man, moreover, with a cast-iron will, and that the woman did not live who would not have to adapt herself to him did he take her to wife.

Until the day before the party at the mines he had been content to drift, but a certain moment down in his own mine had given a new and abrupt turn to both thoughts and purpose. Ida might have spared herself her agonies of shame: she had not betrayed her love, but she had given him a distinct impression that she was employing her redoubtable feminine weapons to reduce him to his old allegiance. He had remembered for a poignant moment that he once had loved this woman to distraction, and during that moment he saw her again as the most beautiful and distracting of her sex. His brief surrender had filled him with fury. He had no intention of despising himself. From boyhood up he had had nothing but contempt for the man that did not know his own mind. If it had not been for this serene confidence in himself, he, who was constitutionally wary in spite of the secret and wistful springs of romance in his nature and the apparent suddenness of his bold plunges, never would have married Ida Hook, nor any woman, until he had sounded her thoroughly. But he had behaved like any hot-headed and conceited young fool, and, much as he now admired Ida, it both infuriated him and appalled him to feel even for a moment toward her as he had in his raw inexperienced youth.

He therefore made up his mind to go to her like a rational being and ask her to give him his freedom. They had made a mistake. They were reasonable members of an advanced civilisation, where mistakes were recognised and rectified whenever possible. He did not doubt for a moment that reason and logic must appeal as forcibly to a woman as to himself.

The door of his wife's house was opened after the usual delay, and the maid told him that Mrs. Compton was upstairs in the billiard room "or somewheres." He took the stairs three steps at a time lest his courage evaporate; but drew a long breath of relief when he entered the large square hall and saw nothing of Ida. He would have rung for the maid, but reflected that no doubt he had already provided enough gossip for the republic below stairs without admitting that he did not know his way round his wife's house. He was about to knock on each door in turn when he noticed that one in a corner at the end of the hall was open and that it led into a narrow passageway. Beyond there was light, possibly in one of those boudoirs of which he had heard. Mrs. Murphy would have been sure to have a boudoir, and no doubt Ida, little disposed as she was to indolence, spent some part of her mornings in it.

He adventured down the passageway that terminated in a large room full of sunlight. He saw his wife standing in the middle of this room looking about her with a curious expression of wistfulness. The little hall was carpeted, but she heard him almost as soon as he saw her; she would have known those light swift footsteps in a marching army. He was inside the room before she could reach the doorway and close it behind her and astonished to see a deep blush suffuse her face. His quick darting glance took in his surroundings as he shook hands with her. The room was a nursery.

"I had two beds put in here and have just seen that they were taken out," stammered Ida.

Her embarrassment was communicable, but he said gruffly as he walked to the window, "Didn't know the Murphys had children."

"Oh, yes, they had two little ones. Seven in all. I think it odd they should have left the toys here even if they are rich enough to buy toys every day. There is something sacred about a child's toys."

Ida was merely talking against time, but she hardly could have said anything better calculated to arrest his attention.

He turned and looked at her in astonishment.

"Do you mean to intimate—that you wish you had children? You?"

Ida's brain as well as her body was very weary, but it sprang to action at once. "Oh, yes," she said intensely. "Oh, yes! And I might have had two! They would be wonderful in this house."

"But——" He cast about desperately. "With two children you could not have gone to Europe."

"That wouldn't have mattered."

"But—don't you realise that it is this last year of unusual advantages that has developed you so—so—remarkably? You hated children——"

"And do you suppose it was Europe that made me want children?"

"Oh, of course, nothing is as simple as that. You were taken out of yourself, out of your narrow self-sufficient little life; all your fine latent powers were developed——"

"But not altogether by Europe! Still, I don't deny that it woke me up, gave me not one new point of view but many, developed me, if you like that better. Would you like lunch earlier? You get up at such unearthly hours——"

"I'm not hungry. I want to talk to you. That is what I came for. Won't you sit down—no, not here! Let us go where there are comfortable chairs. I—I am tired."

"Very well. Let us go down to the library." As she walked before him he noted that her superb body, which usually looked as if set with fine steel springs, was heavy and listless.

The masculine looking room below restored his balance.

"You don't look as well as usual," he remarked, as he threw himself into the deepest of the chairs. "Yesterday was a hard day, and you had had those men on your hands for——"

"I am tired," said Ida briefly, "but it doesn't matter. What do you want to talk to me about?"

He did not answer for a few moments, then he stood up and thrust his hands into his pockets and scowled at the carpet. Involuntarily Ida also rose to her feet and braced herself, crossing her arms over her breast.

"It is impossible for this to go on," said Gregory rapidly. "It is unnatural. People don't submit to broken lives in these days. I think you had better get a divorce and be happy. Mowbray seems to be a fine fellow. Of course no one doubts that he has followed you here. He could make you happy, and as soon as I am able—in a year or two—I shall give you a million; in time more."

"Oh! Oh!"

"You surely cannot want to live for ever like—like—this!"

"I have no desire to marry again. Have you?" She shot the question at him, every nerve on edge with suspicion.

But the last thing in his mind was to betray Ora, and he answered promptly. "No. But I am absorbed in my mine, and my life will be more crowded every year with accumulating interests. You are a woman. You are young —and—and—you wish for children."

Ida believed that after her revelation of yesterday he had come to let her down gently. She determined to throw her all on one heavy stake. If she lost, at least she would have had the satisfaction of telling him that she loved him; she had already sacrificed her pride, and there was a reckless sweetness in the thought of revealing herself absolutely to this man. When a woman loves a man not quite hopelessly she experiences almost as much satisfaction in listening to her own confession as to his.

She drew herself up, her arms still across her breast, and Gregory thought he had never seen a woman look so dignified and so noble.

"Listen, Gregory," she said, with no tremor in her voice but deepening sadness in her eyes, "I regret that I have no children because they would be yours. I am willing to live and die alone because I have lost your love. I know how I lost it, but, as I look back over my crudity and ignorance, I do not see how I could have kept it. You were immeasurably above and beyond me. Nature, or some mental inheritance, gave you sensitiveness, refinement, distinction, to say nothing of brains. I had to achieve all that I am now. I was a raw conceited fool like thousands of American girls of any class, who think they are just a little too good for this world. I had ceased to love you in my inordinate love of myself, and the natural consequence was, that as I made no attempt to improve myself, I lost you as soon as my halo of novelty had disappeared. I took for granted, however, that I was returning from Europe to the old conditions. When I discovered that you had no such intention I was piqued, astonished, angry. But when I thought it all out I understood. You were within your rights, and you have behaved with decency and self-respect. I have nothing but unmitigated contempt for two people that continue to live together as a mere matter of habit and convenience. They are the real immoralists of the world, and the girls that 'go wrong' know it and laugh at the reformers. Of course I never had ceased to love you down deep, but it took just the course of conduct you pursued to make me known to myself. I realise that it is hopeless—too late. I never intended to betray myself, but I did so in an unguarded moment yesterday. Otherwise I never should have told you all this. I have realised since then that I have lost you irrevocably, but at least if I cannot be your wife I will be no man's, and I shall continue to bear your name—and see you sometimes.''

Gregory, feeling as if he were being flayed, had dropped upon the edge of a chair and buried his face in his hands. When she finished he said hoarsely: ''I never dreamed— I never imagined—I thought you incapable of real feeling——''

''I think I was then. And since—Well, you are only a man, after all, and I made you think what I chose until yesterday—Do you mean——'' she added sharply, ''that you did not guess—did not *know* yesterday?''

''It never occurred to me. I thought you merely were flirting a little——''

''Hi!'' cried Ida. Then she got back into her rôle. ''It doesn't matter,'' she said with sad triumph. ''I am glad I have told you. As for the future? You have convinced Butte that we are the best of friends. Stay away if you wish unless I give an entertainment where your absence would cause too much comment. You don't want to marry again, but you may feel yourself as free as air. And one day—when you are worn out, tired of the everlasting struggle in which you moneymakers work harder than the day labourer, with his eight-hour laws and freedom from the terrific responsibilities of money; when you begin to break and want a home, I will make one for you. There is the doorbell. Lord John is coming for lunch. I shall give him his dismissal—once for all.''

Gregory stood up and took her hand. He had a vague masculine sense of unfairness somewhere but he could not begin to define it, and he was as deeply impressed as discouraged. ''You are a grand woman, Ida,'' he said. ''This is not an hour that any man forgets. I wish that you might be happy.''

''Nature never intended that people on this planet should be happy—only in spots, anyhow. And don't worry about me. You have put me in the way of getting a great deal out of this old game we call life, and I am grateful to you. Good-bye.''

They shook hands and Gregory went out into the hall as the maid was admitting Lord John. This time the men made no pretence at politeness. They merely glared and passed.

XXI

THE Primo vein had been recovered some time since and Ora had traversed the fault drift twice and watched the drilling from the station; not only to assert her rights as mistress of the mine but to experience the sensations she had anticipated. She soon discovered that when a woman is in love, and the issue doubtful, other interests fail to provide sensations. But she went down into the mine every day and roamed through the older workings. She was tormented and restless, but by no means without hope; and this being the case she sometimes wondered why she continued to write to Valdobia as if nothing had occurred to interfere with their tacit engagement. It was her duty to tell him the truth, at once, but she switched off all other currents every Saturday morning and wrote her Roman long gay tantalising letters; being gifted as a scribe, like so many women, she made them notable with amusing and enlightening incidents of mining-camp life.

She had not seen Gregory since Monday evening. He had gone suddenly to Butte on the morning following the visit of the geologists, and had telephoned her that he should take the afternoon train to the Capital and no doubt be detained for several days. She had expected that he would telephone or telegraph from Helena; that he would write was too much to expect; she had never seen his handwriting. But he had not recognised her existence.

Four days after his departure she went down into her mine and walked as far as the ragged opening blasted by the Apex men, thinking of Ida. How much longer would it be before Mowbray overcame her prejudices, and her own independent and proud spirit revolted under her husband's complete indifference? Few women were given such an opportunity for revenge both subtle and open as Mowbray was offering to Ida Compton.

It was at this point in her reflections that Ora heard a light footfall coming down the fault drift of Perch of the

Devil. Without an instant's hesitation she descended the short ladder that had been placed between the two drifts for the benefit of the geologists, and relit her candle. She met Gregory in the little station. He also held a candle, but he was so startled at the apparition that he dropped it. She thrust the point of her candlestick into a wooden post.

"I was going over to see you," he said unsteadily as he picked up his candle, relighted it, and mechanically followed her example. He turned abruptly and walked half way up the drift and back, while she stood still, shivering with anxiety. Something had put his determined serenity out of joint. A crisis impended. She felt her unsteadiness and sat down suddenly on the edge of an ore car, fancying this dimly lighted room and the black passage leading to it looked as a death-house cell must look on the eve of execution.

Finally she stammered: "What is it? Please tell me?"

He leaned against the wall in front of her. "I am afraid it's all up," he said lifelessly. "I went in on Tuesday to ask Ida to obtain a divorce. She refused to listen. She has no wish to remarry and will have none of divorce. Nothing could have been more definite than our interview."

"But—but surely in time—if we have patience——"

"There is no hope. Mowbray entered as I left. She intended to dismiss him at once."

Ora, without reasoning, of which she was incapable at the moment, felt that he had been convinced by more than argument and mere words. She flung her arms over her lap and dropping her head upon them burst into a wild transport of tears and sobs; she was so unused to all expression of emotion that she neither knew nor cared how to control it, and the tears swept out the floodgates that had held her passion in check.

She looked up suddenly and saw Gregory standing over her with twitching face and clenched hands; and exulting in the complete abandonment of all the controls that civilisation has bred, she sprang to her feet, flung herself into his arms and her own arms about his neck. She had her immediate reward, for he nearly crushed her, and he kissed her until they both were breathless and reeling.

This was the passion she had read and dreamed of; for once the realities were commensurate; instinct warned her to postpone argument and prolong the moment to its utmost. There was room in her brain for the doubt if such a moment ever could come again, so little of lovemaking is wholly unpremeditated. So she clung to him and kissed him, and in that dim cavern his dark face, so reminiscent of those great prehistoric races that interested him, looked as he felt, primeval man that had found his mate.

But, whatever his ancient inheritance, he was the immediate product of a highly practical civilisation. His keen calculating brain sent a lightning flash across his passion. He lifted her off her feet and sat her down on the ore car. Then he took a candlestick in either hand.

"Come to the other station," he said peremptorily, and led the way to a less dangerous seclusion.

He was half way up the fault drift before Ora, subdued but rebellious, stooped mechanically and found the veil that she wore in place of a hat when in the mines. She followed him slowly. She felt rather than reasoned that she had missed her opportunity and wished angrily that she had had lovers and knew better how to manage men. By the time she reached the shaft station the confusion in her mind had lifted somewhat and she had arrived at the conclusion that she could not overcome him in the same way again, but must use her brains. She sat down on the box and smoothed her hair with apparent unconcern.

Gregory had disposed of the two candlesticks and said, his voice still unsteady: "There isn't much to say, but I want to have my last interview with you in my mine. I cannot get away from here for two or three days. Will you leave at once?"

"Will you listen to me? I have my right to be heard?"

"What is there to say?"

She clasped her hands in her lap and looked up at him. Gregory sighed and set his teeth. She looked surpassingly lovely and rather helpless—women, at their best, always seemed to him pathetic.

"Gregory," she said, "you don't doubt that I love you?"

"No. But what is the use? Do you suppose I am going to make you my mistress—all Montana would know it in

less than no time. I'm no saint, but it wouldn't work—
not for us!''

"But you want me?"

"Oh!" He turned away, then swung round upon her.
She had stood up. Her head was bent forward. "You
should help me out!" he cried angrily. "Can't you see—
it's you I'm thinking of. Do you suppose I want all the
sporting women in Butte making horrible jokes about you
—all your friends cutting you? What's a man good for
if he doesn't protect a woman?"

"Love affairs have lasted for years without being found
out."

"Precious seldom. And we are not buried in a big
city. I must live out here and you would either have to
live out here too, or I should be sneaking into your house
in Butte. A business-like intrigue! Remember I lived
somewhat before I married. Sentiment and romance soon
evaporate——"

"Oh, yes, that is always what I have thought when I
have read the American novelists' attempts to portray
what they call a 'guilty love'.'' The only word that ex-
presses it delicately is *liaison*, and the setting should be
foreign as well. There is no background here. We are
still under the drab shadow of Puritanism. I have heard
it estimated that twenty-five thousand American women
go abroad every year to indulge in a fleeting *liaison* that
gives them courage to endure the desperately material and
commonplace life of this country for another year. You
don't understand that because you never have been in
Europe. But Egypt—Italy—in Southern Europe anywhere—with its unbridled beauties of nature and its far
more poetic beauties that centuries of art have given it—
and a thousand years of love behind us—Oh, cannot you
imagine how wonderful love would be? Do you think *I*
should ever want to come back?"

Gregory was staring at her. "Do you mean," he stammered, "that you would sacrifice your reputation openly
—your future—do you care enough for that?"

"I mean I love you so exclusively that I wish I had a
thousand times more to sacrifice."

"But—but—there are always Americans travelling—
and you know many Europeans——"

"They are always easy to avoid. There are villas with

walls, and pink flowers on top of the walls. And we could travel and see the wonders of art when the tourist season was over. Nor would I monopolise you. You could have the society of men of brains and achievement everywhere."

He continued to stare at her radiant wistful face. He had known that she loved him, but it had never occurred to him that she would be willing to give up the world for his sake. She was a proud woman, an aristocrat, she had an exceptional position everywhere; the great world when they parted stood ready to offer its consolations.

She had unrolled a heavenly vision! His mind had revolted from debasing her to the status of what is euphemistically known in the West as "sporting women"; he also remembered the immediate disillusionments of his younger manhood and wondered if the hideousness of Butte had been responsible. The Mediterranean with its ancient civilisations flourishing and forgotten before the historic period, Egypt, full-grown offspring of a still more ancient but vanished civilisation—both called to that archaeological instinct so closely allied to the geological, made him fancy he heard faint ancestral voices. Ora's eyes were holding his, and her gaze was as powerful as his own. For the moment he no longer was a son of the newest section of the newest world. The turquoise waters of the Mediterranean spread before him, but he saw it alive with galleys——

He jerked his eyes away, folded his arms and stared downward. He must think rationally, not with vapours in his brain. It might be that he would be more than fool to sacrifice to any consideration the one chance for happiness in perfect union that life would offer him.

Suddenly he became aware that he was staring at the rocky floor of his mine, of its first level; the flickering candle flames revealed bits of bright yellow metal. And below was the second level with its superb shoot of copper ore ten feet wide. And below, on the third level, still was the vein far more beautiful than virgin gold. And down—down—in those vast unlocked caverns—what mysteries—what wonder-ores might not the earth harbour for him alone to find and name——

"What are you thinking of?" cried Ora sharply. Then she threw out her arms wildly. "I know! I know! It is those accursed ores! Oh, God! What have I in me,

I, a mere woman, to compensate for the loss of a mine? I was a fool—Of course! Of course!''

But Gregory, although his blood had frozen in his veins at the horrid vision of a permanent divorce from his mine, would make no such admission.

''Ora,'' he said quietly, ''it would be very wonderful—for about three months. You would despise me if I were content to dawdle away my life in an olive grove, or throw away my best years and these great energies nature has given me, doing nothing in that old civilisation in which I could find no place. And in time you would resent the weakness that had stranded you with no recourse in life but myself. That sort of thing has never been a success and never will be, because nature did not make man to live on love alone, and it is much the same with the intellectual woman. It wouldn't work. Not with us. I have known from the beginning that it must be marriage or nothing. And Ida would not divorce me if I ran away with you. She would be entitled to her revenge and she would take it.'' He leaned forward and signalled the station call. ''Please take the skip when it comes. I am going below.'' And he ran down the ladder.

XXII

ORA got into the skip and was whisked to the surface. She drew the veil over her head and face, wishing dimly that she had gone home through the mines; but a moment later the veil fell to her shoulders unnoticed. As she crossed the Apex claim she was vaguely aware that some one, almost in her path, lifted his hat. She bowed automatically, feeling like those poor wound-up royalties who must smile graciously upon their loyal people even though a cancer devour the body or the brain reel with sorrow.

Whalen, abnormal in vanity and conceit though he was, took no offence; not only was this in his estimation the one great lady of the Western annex, but he was startled by the expression in her fixed eyes of anguish, terror, and surprise. He had seen Gregory Compton go down into his mine not a half an hour ago, and it was easy for his fictionised if unimaginative mind to conjure up a hazy picture of the scene underground. He turned very red, partly from gratification at being so close to human passion and pain, but more from the knowledge that he shortly could offer all the elements for another and a still more dramatic crisis. At the same time he could do the one woman he admired in this wilderness a good turn and heal his cankerous ache for vengeance.

Ora went on to her little house and sank into a chair before the burnt-out logs. Her body felt as if it were a vessel into which had been poured all the waters of woman's bitterness and despair. Nevertheless, her predominant sensation was astonishment. For a year she had lived in a fool's paradise, indissolubly mated with Gregory Compton. It was only in the moment when the idea of his own divorce flashed into her mind that she realised she had meant to have him for ever, that her imagination had been a mere playground on which she had romped, and

346

abruptly abandoned when she saw reality standing at the gate.

Since that day, interrupted only by the fevers and doubts of love, she had accepted with joy her predestined fate as the visible mate of Gregory Compton. Else what did it all mean? She had counted on marriage, but that respectable solution had faded into utter insignificance as soon as the shock of Ida's refusal had passed. To fling the world aside, to regard it as a mere whirling speck in the void, followed as a matter of course. She and this man would fill all space.

And she had lost. It was over. *Over. Over.* For a time the astonishment consequent upon the mental reiteration of this fact held her. Her mind, quick, alert, sinuous as she had always found it, was unable to readjust itself. How could anything be over that manifestly had been created to go on for ever? What, then, did it all mean: that mutual recognition when they had sat together that night in Butte, that long mental obsession, this later perfect understanding, this indubitable power to find in each other complete happiness? Over. And by the man's decree. How odd. How odd. And what a tragic waste.

She knew that the mine had pulled him, but she was too much the woman to take a mine seriously. There had been some other reason. He loved her; she never doubted that. He had resisted—why? She groped back through her limited experience, wondering if the trouble were that she had had so little. Life had not begun with her until a year ago. She had been a mere student, deliberately living in the unreal, often deluding, world of books, the worst of all preparations for life.

Some women were independent of experience, knew men by instinct. She felt that Ida, in a similar situation, would have had her way. She had not managed cleverly; no doubt with all her charm and her natural allurement for men, even a certain acquired coquetry, she was one of those women that could theorise brilliantly, but failed utterly to manage their own affairs at critical moments.

She was well aware that she had not been developing along ideal lines of late, particularly since she had come out here with the unadmitted intention of stealing her friend's husband. By all the laws of tradition she should be wicked all through. Pride, diffidence, fastidiousness—

one or all, she was in no condition to decide—had prevented her from playing the deliberate rôle of siren. She sighed and wished that life could be played upon the formula adopted by so many brilliant novelists: a steady unrelenting development of character upon strictly logical lines and by means of cunningly created situations, that was as much like life as a mother's formula would be for the thoughts and deeds of her children at a given hour a year hence.

Ora did not know that most people in their rare moments of honest introspection find themselves singularly imperfect. She had looked for greater consistency in her complex recesses; assuming that if she made up her mind to take the husband of any woman, and that woman her best friend, she would be wholly hard and wicked, and, for the sake of the result, quite willing to achieve this consistent imperfection. And such hardness would be the surest of all solaces in the event of failure. She felt neither hard nor nearly as wicked as she should, but she did recognise the fact that if she had one more chance she would win by hook or crook.

Her thoughts swung to Ida. What had she said to Gregory in that last decisive interview? Ida was as clever as the devil. She would watch her chance and make just the right appeal at the right moment. Gregory could be ruthless to the woman of whom he had wearied or to the woman he loved, but if his wife played upon his honour, his Western chivalry, his sense of fair play, and reiterated her own rights—to her would he lower his flag if it struck the life out of his own heart, and left himself nothing to feed the deep passion and romance of his nature for the rest of his life.

In any case Ida had won.

Once more Ora wished that she had gone to work when she found herself penniless after her father's death. She would have developed normally, and it was unthinkable that in the little world of Butte she would not have met Gregory Compton while he was free. Then not only would she be happy today but know nothing of those abysmal depths in her soul which she execrated while yielding to them and lamenting that for the time being they were no worse. Love may be divine when all goes well, or one is born into the cult of the martyr, but when it comes too late to passionate natures associated with virile and accomplished minds, it can be the very spawn of hell. Ora's regret that she was not of the breed of those finished wantons of history that rose to fame on the shattered hearts of men was born of expediency. Could she have been given her choice and Gregory Compton she would have elected to be fine and noble, consummating the lofty dictates of her superior intellectual endowment. Not yet had she realised that lacking a ruthless centralised ideal, rarely allied to brilliant intellects, the souls of women even more than those of men (who have less time and more poise) are the playthings of Circumstance.

She became aware that her Chinaman was crossing the room, and before she could refocus her wandering mental vision and intercept him, he had opened the front door and admitted Professor Whalen.

XXIII

IDA had broken a dinner engagement and sat alone in her library. She knew that Gregory had passed through Butte that day on his way from Helena to Pony; she had seen him leave the Block where his lawyers had their offices and jump into a waiting taxi. He was not the man to take a cab for anything but an imminent train. She had rushed home, but he had neither called nor telephoned. She reasoned that he would be more than man if he were not reluctant to see her again after their last embarrassing interview, that there was no cause for fresh doubts, and that there was literally nothing for her to do at present but continue to play her waiting game. But she felt both sad and nervous, and wondered if it were in her to despair, to "cut and run" like other women; or whether it might not be wise to absent herself for a time. Gregory was the sort of man to appreciate delicacy, and after an absence of two months they would meet quite naturally. She could visit Yellowstone and Glacier Park, and send him pleasant impersonal postcards.

But although she hesitated to acknowledge it, she was tired of her waiting game, she wished that "fate would get a move on", and she had left her husband once with unforeseen results. She leaned her elbows on her knees and pressed her hands against her face. She had always cherished a high opinion of her cleverness in regard to men, but she was nonplussed. For a woman of her resource there should be some alternative to waiting. She knew that she had made a deep impression on her husband in that momentous interview, but who could say that he had not deliberately put the memory of it out of his mind? Certainly there was no sign that it had softened him or paved the way for her reinstatement into his life.

She was alarmed at her waning self-control. During these last few days she barely had been able to play her part in society; the people at the various functions she had attended had seemed to her confused and absent mind like marionettes that she could sweep off the stage with her arm, and she had retreated into her shell lest she insult them irreparably.

She brought her heavy brows together. Could there be another woman after all? Gregory was cleverer than any detective. Why should it occur to him to suggest divorce, he a man so absorbed in a mine that he had forgotten how to live—merely out of consideration for a discarded wife whose existence he generally managed to forget? It was certainly odd, and its idiosyncrasies grew and swelled as she brooded. She wondered if she had been a fool. But who in heaven's name could the woman be? Of course it was only a passing fancy, but could she wait, *could she wait?*

She was aroused by a slight cough, discreet but full of subtle insolence. She sprang to her feet, and Whalen smiled as he saw her drawn face and bloodshot eyes. He stood just within the door, and held a cap in his hand. He wore a light automobile coat; a pair of goggles only half covered his bulging brow. His upper teeth were clamped down over his lower lip, a habit when steadying his nerves. Ida thought she had never seen him look so hideous, so like a mongrel cur.

"What do you want?" she asked.

"How gracious you are! How like Mrs. Blake, who would not forget her manners if she——"

"I've got no manners for your sort. Get out."

"Oh, not yet. I've something to say. I've waited for over a year, but my time has come——"

"You'll go out the way you went last time if you don't say what you've got to say pretty quick and get out by yourself."

Whalen looked over his shoulder nervously, and measured the distance to the front door. He had asked leave of the maid to announce himself, and, when she had disappeared, reopened the door and left it ajar.

"It won't take me long," he said grimly. "It took me a little longer to tell Mrs. Blake, for she was hard to convince; but she *was* convinced before I left. It is merely this: I saw you go into Lord John Mowbray's rooms on Monday night shortly after ten o'clock and come out at half-past one."

"Oh, you did, did you? I had a feeling all the time there was a sneak in the neighbourhood. Well, much good your spying will do you. Lord John was at the Country Club until three in the morning and everybody knows it."

She spoke calmly, but she was profoundly disturbed. She continued, however, in the same tones of cutting contempt, for she saw that he was taken aback, "I merely misunderstood an invitation of Lord John's for a bridge party. I thought it was for that night, and although I was surprised to find myself the first and Lord John not there, I sat down to wait and fell asleep. I had had a hard day. I only condescend to explain," she continued witheringly, "because you are as venomous as a mad dog and it is as well to muzzle you at once."

'I don't believe a word of that yarn, and neither will anyone else. I certainly managed to convince Mrs. Blake——"

"Not she. She must have laughed in your face——"

"Oh no! Not Mrs. Blake! But I will admit that it was not easy to make her believe ill of you. Perhaps I should not have succeeded, but when a woman is eager to believe——" He laughed and shrugged his shoulders; but once more he cast a quick glance at the line of retreat. The heavy library table was between them.

"What the devil do you mean?" Ida spoke roughly, but her heart began to hammer. She felt a sudden impulse to run away, but she stood rigidly and glared at him. "Here!" she continued, "come to the point. Spit out your poison. What particular object had you in trying to set my best friend against me? It would have been more like you to run to a newspaper."

"That later. I wanted to do Mrs. Blake a good turn and at the same time let her be the one to tell your husband that he could secure his freedom without further delay——"

"What do you mean? What do you mean?" Ida's eyes were staring as if they saw a vision of herself at the stake; she tossed off her pride as she would a hampering cloak. "Ora! Ora! Oh, not Ora! You liar!" she screamed. "Prove what you said quick——" But he saw that she had caught the edge of the table and that her body was swaying.

"Oh, neither will deny it now," he replied in a tone of

deadly quiet. "She went out there to be near him, no doubt of that; and he's spent hours on end in that bungalow. I went to Helena and back with him and I guessed that something was up, for he was glummer and more disagreeable than usual; and this afternoon when I saw her come up out of his mine I guessed they had had a painful scene and parted. So I told her she had the game in her own hands, and that I'd go on the stand and swear to what I saw. No husband would believe anything but the truth, nor this town either. You might prove that your lord made a fool of you and amused himself elsewhere, but you're done for all the same; and I guess Mr. Compton would manage his divorce all right. Then two people that are madly in love will be happy——"

Ida's strength rushed back and the world turned scarlet. She picked up a heavy bronze from the table and hurled it at him. But Whalen was expecting a physical assault in some form. He ducked and fled. When she reached the open door he was not in sight.

XXIV

ORA watched the clock until twenty minutes after eleven. The miners changed shift promptly, and the last should have gone down the Primo shaft by a quarter past at the latest. The shaft house would be empty, as no hoisting was being done on the night shift.

She turned out the light in her living-room, wrapped herself in a dark lodenmantl, a long cape with a hood that she had worn while climbing in Bavaria, and let herself out. She walked through the grove to the edge of the bluff above her camp and stood for a few moments, listening intently. Some ten minutes since she had heard the warning shriek of an automobile horn, but the garage of her manager, who had motored Whalen into Butte, was on the flat, and he had had time either to go down into the mine or climb to his own cottage.

The moon was at the full and the scene as sharply outlined as by day, although less animated. Save for the usual raucous noises of a mining camp the only sign of life was in the saloon. Some one was playing a pianola, and through the open door she saw men standing at the bar. For a moment she was tempted to take the surface path across the camps; but the risk was too great. Some one was sure to be abroad, and although she had been willing to brave the scorn of the world when there was no apparent alternative, she shrank from the plain Saxon the miners would use if they saw her. From Gregory's shaft house she could reach his cabin by the path behind the abandoned cut.

A light was burning in her shaft house. She was not expert enough to descend the ladder candle in hand, and for a moment faltered above the darkness of the well; she had not been down before at night. Then she reflected that it was always night in the mines and descended without further hesitation.

At the foot of the shaft the usual station was one with

the chamber left after removing the first large deposit of ore. They had merely cut through the vein at this point without stoping, and the great excavation had a lofty roof. Ora struck a match and lit a candle near by. On the day of the geologists' visit a number of miner's candle-sticks had been thrust into what little wood there was in the chamber, and the candles were but half burnt out. Then she lit the one she had brought in her pocket. Ac-customed as she was by this time to the route underground by chamber and gallery to the Perch mine, she always picked her way carefully, particularly down the first drift; her lessees, impatient at the leanness of the connecting vein, and not wishing to spend either the time or the money to sink the shaft another hundred feet, had understoped, and the holes were ill-covered.

She crossed the large black cavern toward the first of these tunnels, or drifts, sweeping the candle about her head, and then holding it downward, for she always feared cave-ins. The room was almost untimbered, owing to the hardness of the rock.

She had almost reached the mouth of the drift, when she paused suddenly, listened intently, and then blew out her candle. Some one was on the ladder. It was one of the miners, no doubt. Something had detained him above ground, and not daring to summon the shaft house man, he was sneaking down the ladder. He would go on down to the second level of the mine. Ora stood motionless, her hood pulled over her white face. Her miners were good average men, but the saloon flourished, and was no doubt responsible for the present delinquency.

Then once more she listened intently. The upper part of her body stiffened like a startled animal's. Whoever was coming down was making his first descent by foot; not only was his progress slow, but he was breathing heavily, and hesitating between rungs, as if it were his first experi-ence of an inclined ladder. Miners hate the shaft ladder, and will resort to any subterfuge to avoid it, but they are experts in "negotiating" it nevertheless. No doubt this was some green hand, recently employed. Or possibly the man was drunk.

Then suddenly Ora turned cold with the chill of the mine itself, a mere physical attribute that her warm blood had never deigned to notice before. A form was slowly coming into view below the high roof of the cavern, and although it was little more than a blot on the general blackness, Ora's keen eyes, accustomed to the faint relief given by the candle near the shaft, noted as it descended further that it covered more of the ladder than it should. Miners are almost invariably thin and they wear overalls. This person wore a heavy cape like her own. But it was not alone the garment, which any miner would scorn, that betrayed the sex of the invader; it may have been the physical awkwardness, the shallow breathing, or some subtle psychical emanation—or all—that warned Ora of the approach not only of a woman but of a malignant force.

And this woman was following her. There was no doubt in her mind of that. She suffered a moment or two of furious unreasoning terror as she crouched against the wall and watched that shadow against a shadow slowly descend the final rungs of the ladder. Her first impulse had been to flee down the drift, but there was danger of falling into one of the gouge holes and disabling herself. She dared not relight her candle.

Shaking, terrified as she never had been in her life—for she was normally brave, and it was not a normal woman she feared but that aura of hate and lust for vengeance—undecided, putting up a frantic prayer that Gregory would come to her rescue, she pulled the hood over her face and almost sank to her knees. The woman, breathing heavily, reached the last rung and touched the ground as warily as a cat. For a moment she stood drawing in deep breaths like sighs, but which escaped, to tormented ears, like a hiss. Ora, her eyelids almost meeting over the intense concentration of her gaze, saw the woman fling back the mantle that covered her, throw out her arms as if to relax the muscles after the strain of the descent. Then she turned suddenly, snatched the candlestick from the wall and held it above her head.

For the moment Ora thought her heart had stopped. The woman was Ida. Her heavy lowered brows were like a heavy band across the white ghastliness of her face. Her eyes glittered horribly. Her lips were a mere tight line. Her black hair, loosened, fell over her face. Ora's hypnotised gaze tore itself from those slowly moving eyes and lowered itself instinctively to Ida's right hand. It held the stiletto she had given her in Genoa. The slanting rays of the candle fell on the jewels of the hilt. Then she knew that Ida had followed her down into the mine to kill her.

Her courage came back as quickly as it had fled. Ora's brain might be democratic but her soul was haughty. The friendship of the past eighteen months between herself and this woman suddenly shaped itself as forced and artificial, and she was filled with a cold surprise and anger. *Who* was Ida Hook that she should presume to question Ora Stratton? Similar reflections, no doubt, stiffened many a noble when on his way to the guillotine at the behest of the *canaille*.

Ora was beyond the ray of the candle at present but Ida was beginning to move forward, her eyes, almost blank in spite of their brilliancy, moving from side to side, striving to pierce the darkness, her head bent forward to catch the slightest sound. It was evident that she had seen Ora go into the shaft house, and knew that she could not be far off.

Ora took the automatic from the bag at her waist, pointed it at the roof of the cave and fired twice. The din was terrific in that confined space. Ida shrieked, dropped the stiletto and candle, and flung her arms about her head. Ora hastily lighted two other candles, and then retreated against the wall. She believed that the terrible inhibition in Ida's tormented mind was shattered, but she kept the automatic in her hand, nevertheless.

The reverberations died away and once more the mine was as silent as only a deserted level of a mine can be. Ida raised her head and saw Ora. She gave a strangled cry and moved forward a step. Then her arms fell heavily to her side. She did not even pick up the dagger. The inhuman tension of her mind relaxed, the body barely had force enough to hold itself together.

"I came here to kill you," she said. "But I can't do it. I've been mad for hours, and I wish I could have found you in bed as I thought I would. I could have killed you then. But I saw you come down here—Have you told him?"

"No. He was down in the mine until eleven. I was on my way to tell him—to break down his resistance to-night!"

"His resistance?" Ida raised her head. She had lost the pitch necessary for murder, but her mind began to recover its alertness and her drooping body to set its springs in motion. "What do you mean by that? I thought he was in love with you."

Ora laughed. She was filled with an utter despair, but the knife was still in Ida and she could turn it round. "Oh, yes, make no doubt of that. He loves me and will as long as he lives——"

"Not much he won't!" roared Ida. "If I've been too quick for you you'll never tell him now, and he practically gave me his word the other day that he'd never ask even me for a divorce again. That means you go and go quick, and if you think Gregory will have nothing to do but sit down and nurse your memory——"

The blood flew to Ora's head and she hastily dropped the automatic into her bag. "I'll not go!" she said. "And what is more I shall tell him. When Gregory knows that you spent three hours in Mowbray's rooms at night——"

"Mowbray was not there! He was at the Country Club——"

"*Was* he?"

"Yes, and it can be proved. Moreover, you know me well enough——"

"It doesn't matter what can be proved or what I believe. You waited for Mowbray—Do you suppose that Gregory —or any court of law——"

"My God!" cried Ida. "You! You! I think it was that drove me off my head more than the prospect of disgrace and losing Gregory. You! What in God's name is possessing you? I always knew that you would be the concentrated essence of all damn fool women that ever lived when you did fall in love, but I never believed it was in you to do anything dishonourable——"

"And would you have believed that you, the concentrated essence of all that is cool, deliberate, calculating, would ever be inspired to commit murder? And for a man? What's the use of talking? People possessed by love either are wholly themselves while it lasts, or are abnormal and should not be held accountable even to the law. I suppose this means that you too love Gregory Compton?"

"Yes it does!" cried Ida, the more vehemently because it shamed her to put this unwonted weakness into words. "I do, damn it all! I do. I thought I was immune, but I guess we are all born with the microbe and it bites when the soil is good and ready.'' Her anger had vanished, for in spite of Ora's defiance she knew that she was master of the situation. She kicked the stiletto contemptuously aside, clasped her hips with her large firm hands and threw back her shoulders. "Now!" she said, "admit right here that you know I didn't go to Mowbray's rooms for any old intrigue. That kind of thing isn't in me and you know it."

"I will confess I was surprised—I refused to believe it at first—Oh, I suppose I don't. But it doesn't matter——"

"Are you ready to come with me this minute to Gregory and tell him that yarn—knowing that I can prove Mowbray wasn't there—I say *go with me*—not by yourself."

Ora made no reply. She was beaten but she was not ready to admit it.

"You may bet your life on one thing," continued Ida. "You go with me or you don't go at all, for I'll stick to you like wet paint until this thing is settled once for all. Now just tell me what you meant a while back by Gregory's resistance? When you found I wouldn't consent to a divorce—of course you put him up to ask me, you traitorous little white devil—did you want him to elope with you?"

"Yes I did!"

"And he wouldn't?"

"He—he would not sacrifice me——"

"Shucks! Where did you want him to go? To Europe?"

"Yes."

"Good Lord! And what did you think you were going to do with him over there? Spoon in orange groves for forty years?"

"There are several thousand resources in Europe besides orange groves—but you would never understand——"

"Oh, don't I understand? It's I that does understand, not you, or you would never have made such an asinine proposition to Gregory Compton. Why on earth didn't you propose some place with *mines*—Mexico, Alaska, China—Then you might have stood some show—but Europe—Gregory—Do you remember those American business men that always looked as if they had left their minds in an office at the top of a thirty-story building, and their bodies were being led round by a string? The vision of Gregory astray in Europe for the rest of his life would be funny if it weren't so pathetic. Talk about the conceit of man. It isn't a patch on that of a woman when she gets the bug inside her head that she can be 'everything' to a man. I can manage Gregory till doomsday when I get him back, but you'd lose him inside of six months no matter which way you got him——"

"That couldn't be true! I recognised that he was mine —*mine*—the night we met before I left——"

"What's that?"

"Oh, yes, I met him once before I went abroad with you—we talked for an hour——"

"And he was the man you wrote those letters to in Europe——"

"Yes."

"And I your most intimate friend!"

"I never sent them, and you did not care for him then——"

"Oh, I don't see you apologising if you had turned heaven into hell. You made up your mind then to have him, I suppose?"

"No. And not even when I came out here. I only wanted to be with him—know him a little better—have that much—Oh, I couldn't make you understand any more than that I can suffer as much as if I were the best of women who had lost her husband by death. It was only after Mowbray came—there seemed a prospect——"

"Well, I don't know that I blame you so much, for I certainly bluffed it pretty well. I can forgive you for that but not for meaning to make me out a strumpet and send me to the muck heap, disgraced for the rest of my life. Well, come along. Let us go straight to Gregory and let him decide."

Ora did not move.

"It's either that or you go back to Butte with me tonight and start for Europe tomorrow morning."

"I know when I am beaten. I will leave. And don't imagine that you have won because you are in the right. We have emerged from the dark ages of superstition, and we know that the wicked are not punished if they are strong enough. Nor are the virtuous rewarded for mere virtue—not once in ten thousand times. You have won because you are stronger than I. That is all."

"It's enough for me."

Ora laughed. "Do you really believe that you can win him back? He'll not forget me, because I can always fire his imagination. He is as indifferent to you as only a man can be when the woman is an old story."

"That was a nasty one! But I'm not worrying. I have been at a disadvantage since I got back, thinking my only rival was a hole in the ground. But take this from me, Ora: when a woman knows where she stands, and has the inside track, and has her nerve with her, the man has no show whatever. Nor the other woman. I'll get him back all right. And he'll forget you. That's a man's long suit."

"We'll neither of us ever know, so it doesn't matter. I shall never see him again. That is all that matters to me."

"And Valdobia?"

"I shall marry him, I suppose—after a while."

"I don't mind saying that he is much too good for you."

"Possibly. And he'll love me the more."

"And shall you tell him of this little interlude?"

"Certainly not."

"Well, I always have maintained that the woman who confessed anything to a man was a fool, but it certainly is a queer mix up."

"I don't know that I should so much mind telling him, after all. Men are too practical to resent any but the literal infidelity. And he is the only person living that understands me. Gregory does not and never would care to. Why could not I have had this madness for the one man who is really fitted to be my mate—whose ideas of life are my own, who has so much the same order of mind? Why should I love Gregory Compton, a man I not only cannot marry, but with whom I never could find a real companionship. My God! Why? Why?"

"There are several ways of getting ahead of life," said Ida drily, "and one is not asking 'Why' too often. That's just one of her little traps to keep you discontented. You and Gregory Compton! It certainly is funny. What did you talk about anyway?"

Ora threw out her arms and laughed wildly. "Ores. Ores. Ores. I tried to interest him in many of the things that interested me. He didn't even try to understand what I was driving at. One night I offered to read to him—I had a lively new volume of memoirs in mind—he asked if I had any work on copper. I read to him for three hours from a book called 'The Copper Mines of the World,' technicalities and all. Of course he had read it before, but it seemed to delight him. We literally had no common meeting ground but ores, but we loved each other madly. Oh, don't tell me that it was mere passion!" she broke out as angrily as if Ida had interrupted her. "Valdobia is attractive in far more ways and better looking. Gregory has met many women.—If that were all we should have bored each other long since—we never could have held each other's imaginations while apart.— I tell you it is some deep primary bond—something that older races perhaps could explain. Why should we meet at all in this life——"

"I guess when we understand all the different brands of love we'll vaccinate and be immune. Shut your teeth, Ora, and take your medicine. And for heaven's sake let us get out of this damp hole. I'll help you and Custer pack and we'll go to Butte in the car I came out in. Have I got to go up that ladder?"

"No, we'll go over to the Perch mine and ring for the skip there. My engineer is not on duty during the 'graveyard shift.'"

XXV

ON the following morning Ida, having seen Ora on the
train bound for Chicago, went at once to a public
garage, rented the touring car she had used the night
before, and was driven out to the mines. She walked up
to the cabin on the crest of Perch of the Devil and, finding
it empty, summoned a miner who was lounging near and
bade him call Mr. Compton. The man asked to be allowed
to use the telephone in the office, obtained connection with
the second level of the mine, and announced in a few
moments that the boss was on his way up.

Ida, who had dropped wearily into a chair, merely
nodded as Gregory entered. He was as pale as a dark
man can be, and his voice when he spoke sounded as if
he had been running.

"What is it?" he demanded. "Has anything happened——"

"To Ora? Nothing, except that she is on her way East
and to Europe. Tired, no doubt, but quite well."

Gregory drew a short sigh of relief, and sat down before
his table, shading his eyes with his hand. "Well?" he
asked. "What is it?"

"I haven't come out here to make a scene, or even to
reproach you. I believe that I should have the self-
restraint to ignore the subject altogether if it were not
for that man, Whalen. Some one must put an extinguisher
on him at once and you are the one to do it. That is why
I am obliged to tell you that I found out yesterday about
you and Ora. I had begun to believe there must be some
woman in the case but I had not the least suspicion of
Ora. I not only believed her to be the soul of honour, but
I thought she was really in love with the Marchese Valdobia, a Roman who has everything to offer that a woman
of her type demands, and to marry whom she had demanded a divorce from Mark. She has been tacitly engaged to him ever since we left Europe."

Ida saw the muscles in Gregory's long body stiffen as if he were about to spring, and his eyes glitter through the lattice of his fingers. But he made no comment, and after giving him time to assimilate her information, she added more gently:

"Console yourself with the reflection that she would have thrown him over for you. But she knows now what a mistake she would have made. Ora is one of those atavistic Americans that are far more at home in Europe than in the new world. She has gone where she belongs and Valdobia is her man."

She paused again. He was still silent, and she continued less fluently: "Now I come to the unpleasant part for myself. To begin at the beginning: I made an enemy of little Whalen before I went abroad. He had the sublime impudence to kiss me one day, and I simply took him by the back of his neck and the seat of his pants and threw him out of the window. He has had it in for me ever since."

In spite of the various emotions raging within him, Gregory laughed aloud at the picture. The atmosphere felt clearer. Ida went on with more confidence:

"Of course you know that Lord John Mowbray followed me here. He wanted me to get a divorce and marry him, as Valdobia had planned with Ora. I liked him well enough, but even if I had been free it never would have occurred to me to marry him, and no one knew better than he that I didn't care a copper cent for him. His hope after he came here—a hope in which he was encouraged by Ora—was that, as you were so loudly indifferent, pride might drive me to leave you and make a brilliant marriage. Well, I was tempted for a moment. It was on the night of the day I had been down in the mine with you. I believed that I had given myself away absolutely, offered myself and been refused as casually as if I had been some woman of the streets; told you almost in so many words that I loved you and been invited with excruciating politeness to go to the devil.

"Well, that night I nearly went off my head. I had a whole mind, for a few moments, to ring up Mowbray and tell him that I would get my freedom and leave the country for ever. But that passed. I couldn't have done it, and I knew it, in spite of the blood pumping in my head.

I went out for a walk, for I had smashed a few things already. Then the mad impulse came to me to call on Mowbray. I knew that I'd treat him no better than I had treated Whalen if he so much as tried to kiss me. But I wasn't afraid. He was too keen on marrying me to take any risks. What I wanted was to do something real devilish—to be more elegant, something quite the antithesis of all that is *comme il faut*. So I went. Mowbray wasn't there. He had gone to the dance at the Country Club. I sat down to wait for him and fell asleep. When I awoke it was after one o'clock and I was still alone. I can tell you I got out pretty quick. I had slept the blood out of my head and I felt like a fool. I bribed the Jap not to tell Mowbray or anyone else.

"Well, the point of all this is—and the only reason I have told you—Whalen saw me go in and waited for me to come out. He believed that he had found his chance for revenge at last. No doubt he would have told you on the way to Helena, but he hasn't the spunk of a road agent at the wrong end of a gun. So he took his tale to Ora when he got back.—But before I go any further I want you to say that you believe I had no wrong motive in going to Mowbray's rooms. Of course a hundred people could testify that he did not leave the Country Club until three o'clock, but that is not the point with you."

"I believe you," said Gregory. He was intensely interested.

Ida drew a long sigh and the colour came back to her face. Her eyes, heavy with fatigue, sparkled. "Well! Whalen was all for drinking his cup of revenge down to the dregs. It wasn't enough to spring a mine under me, he must see what I looked like when it blew up the first time. After he told Ora he posted into Butte and managed to get into my house unannounced—that maid has been fired. I was in the library on the other side of the room. The doorway was good enough for him. He told me. Some time I'll tell you all I felt. After he had lit out with the Venus of Milo flying after him, I went stark mad. I made up what mind I had left to kill Ora and kill her quick."

"What?" Gregory sat up and stared at her, his eyes wide open. And, astounded as he was, the immortal vanity of man thrilled responsively to the reckless and destructive passions he had inspired in these two remarkable women.

"I got a touring car and arrived at the foot of her hill—a little after eleven it was, I guess. There was a light in her living-room, and I made up my mind to wait until I was sure she was alone and in her bedroom. Then I intended to get in somehow or other and kill her with that stiletto she gave me in Genoa. It was a notion of hers that I had been one of the wicked dames of the Renaissance, and I just naturally took the hint. While I was waiting the light went out and almost immediately I saw her hurry down the path that led to her claim and go into her shaft house. I knew on the instant that she was going to you, and that she took that route to avoid being seen. My mind could grasp that much in spite of the fixed idea in it—that she was on her way to tell you Whalen's story. This was true as I found out afterwards. She went that night, partly because she couldn't keep it any longer, partly because she wanted to tell you when you were alone in your cabin at night and she could also bind you hand and foot with that Lorelei hair of hers. It takes the hyper-civilised super-refined Oras to stick at nothing when their primitive instincts loosen up.

"Well—I went into the shaft house, and listened until I no longer could hear her on the ladder. Then I followed. Glory! Shall I ever forget going down that ladder? I felt as if every muscle in my body were being torn up by the roots; and I had to carry the stiletto between my teeth. And pitch dark. All my clothes in the way every step. It was enough to take the starch out of tragedy, and I guess it would have flattened me out if it hadn't been just the one thing that could make me madder still.

"I'll give you the details of that scene some other time. I'm too tired now. It is enough to say that she had a pistol and made such an infernal racket with it—shooting at the roof—that something busted in my head and I came to. Then we had it out. She agreed to leave because she knew me too well to believe I had gone to Mowbray's rooms for any horrid purpose, and he hadn't been there anyway. I told her that if she told you it would have to be before me, and she knew that she couldn't brazen it through. So I packed her and got her off this morning. That means that I had no sleep last night."

She stood up and Gregory rose also. "Now, there are two things more," she said with no lack of decision in her voice, whatever her fatigue of body. "You must settle Whalen, and you must move to Butte and live in my house, even if you are only there once or twice a week. Whalen, the moment he discovers that Ora has gone, will run about Butte defaming me, or carry the story to the papers. It wouldn't do me much good to prove that Mowbray wasn't there. People like to believe the worst, and in time would forget that Mowbray had been at the Club on that particular night. My set might be all right. But the rest— and my servants—and Ruby and Pearl! They always use the word 'bad,' and, as Ora says, an intrigue is only decent in a foreign language. It gives me the horrors to think of it. But if we are seen together twice a week, and you are known to be living in the house, however often you must be absent, nobody will listen to a story that is not headed toward the divorce court."

"I'll buy Whalen's claim and tell him to get out of Montana. He'll go! As for the rest of your programme— please be sure, Ida, that I stand ready to protect you now and always. You are not only my wife but an extraordinary woman, and I am very proud of you."

"Oh, the extraordinary woman hasn't been born yet, in spite of the big fight the sex is putting up," said Ida lightly, as they left the cabin and walked down the hill. "When women really are extraordinary they will be just as happy without men as they now want to be with them. They try with all their might to be hard, and they can ring outside like metal, but inside they are just one perpetual shriek for the right man to come along—that is all but a few hundred thousand tribadists. But they've made a beginning, and one day they'll really be able to take men as incidentally as men take women. Then we'll all be happy. Don't you fool yourself that that's what I'm aiming at, though. I'm the sort that hangs on to her man like grim death."

"You're all right!" said Gregory, who, man-like, was automatically readjusting himself to the inevitable.

He handed her into the tonneau of the car, and tucked the robe about her. She gave his hand a hearty friendly

shake, for she was much too wise and too tired for sentiment. "Don't you worry about Ora," she said. "Custer
is with her and she has the drawing-room, and is probably
sound asleep at this moment. It must be very restful to
get a tragic love affair off your chest."

And then the car rolled off and she fell asleep at once.

PART III

PART III

THEY stood together in the dawn, the blue dawn of
Montana. Silver stars were winking dimly in the
silver sky, clear save above the glittering peaks of the
distant range, which reflected the blue of a bank of clouds
above. And all the vast and snowy expanse was blue; and
the snow on the pine trees of the forest.

No one stirred in the two camps, not abroad at least;
and even the shacks and larger buildings built with as
little regard for beauty were transformed and glorified
by the white splendour of winter. On the crest of Perch
of the Devil was a long gracefully built bungalow, also
heavily laden with snow, and between the posts of its
verandah hung icicles, iridescent blue in the dawn.

A small lawn had been cultivated, and they leaned over
the gate of the fence that surrounded it, not wrapped in
one buffalo robe, but in heavy automobile coats, their
heads protected from the intense cold by fur caps. But
they stood close together, and even a passing stranger
would have known that there was harmony between them.
Both were looking at the cold loveliness of the dawn and
admiring it subconsciously, and both were thinking of
other things. Gregory was visualising a ranch he had
bought not long since near those mountains, and the wire
gold but a few feet below the surface, found a fortnight
ago while ditching. He had his gold mine at last, but it
merely would hasten his grooming for the millionaire
brotherhood, and had given him none of the exultant
ecstasy he had dreamed of in the days before he had
opened Perch of the Devil. The gold mine was not in his
hill! Only the sharp, cool, calculating business wing of
his brain appreciated it. The mine beneath his feet was
still the object of his deep affections.

And sometimes, down in the depths of that mine (never
above ground), he sat alone for a few moments and thought
of Ora. He had forced her out of his mind when she went

371

out of his life, but nothing could dislodge her from his ivory tower, although in time to come she might gather dust for years on end. For months after she married Valdobia she seemed to have taken his memory to Rome with her; but she brought it back in time.

In those rare moments when he peered through the windows of that inner temple, he, too, sometimes asked, "Why?" What had it all meant? It had been perfect love—yet so lamentably imperfect; not only because they were torn apart, but because they would not have found permanent happiness together. Between some subtle essence of their beings there was an indissoluble bond, but their minds were not in accord, and neither would have been adaptable save during that fluid period when even strong egos lose their bearings and float on that inevitable sea of many tides called Love; knowing that when it casts them on the shore whence they came, once more will they be as malleable as rock crystal. But what had it all meant?

And his wife made him very happy. He found her increasingly desirable as a life companion. She adapted herself to every angle of his character while losing none of her own picturesque individuality; made no impossible exactions either on his soul or his time; was always beautiful to look at; and the most level-headed of his friends.

Even men of less complicated egos have been able to love two women at once and survive.

And Ida? She at least had what she wanted, she was a philosopher, and therefore as happy as may be. By constant manœuvring she saw more of her busy husband than falls to the lot of most American wives married to too successful men. She had made herself so necessary to him that he returned from his many absences almost as eager to see her as his mine. On these hurried trips she never accompanied him, not only because it was wise to let him miss her, and to think of her always in the home setting, but because they gave her the opportunity to retain her hold on Butte; to enjoy her beautiful house there and her many friends.

Suddenly Gregory raised his head. Then he lifted the ear flap of his fur cap. High above there was a loud humming, as of the wind along telegraph wires, or the droning of many bees, or the strumming of an aerial harp. The month was March and the weather forty degrees below zero. The very sky, whose silver was growing dim, looked frosted, but a moment later Gregory felt a warm puff of air on his cheek.

"The Chinook!" he said softly.

Another puff touched them both lightly, then a long wave of warm air swept down and about them.

"It's chinooking, certainly," said Ida, opening her fur coat and pushing back her cap. "I hope that means we've had the last of winter."

Again there was a long diving wave, almost hot in its contrast to the cold air rising from the ground, and still accompanied by that humming orchestra above. But in a few moments the hum had deepened into a roar down in the tree tops and about the corners of the buildings on the hill. The icicles fell from the eaves and lay shattered and dissolving on the porch, the snow was blown up in frosty clouds and melted as it fell.

"It's the last of winter, I guess," said Gregory. "We're not likely to have another long spell of cold. Spring has come. And so has daylight. Let's go in, old girl."

THE END

—